Culture

Beacon of the Future

Culture

Beacon of the Future

D. Paul Schafer

Praeger Studies on the 21st Century

Westport, Connecticut

Published in the United States and Canada by Praeger Publishers,
88 Post Road West, Westport, CT 06881.
An imprint of Greenwood Publishing Group, Inc.

Printed in the United States of America

The paper used in this book complies with the
Permanent Paper Standard issued by the National
Information Standards Organization (Z39.48–1984).

10 9 8 7 6 5 4 3 2 1

English language edition, except the United States and Canada,
published by Adamantine Press Limited, Richmond Bridge House,
417–419 Richmond Road, Twickenham TW1 2EX, England.

First published in 1998

Library of Congress Cataloging-in-Publication Data

Schafer, D. Paul.
    Culture : beacon of the future / D. Paul Schafer.
        p.   cm.—(Praeger studies on the 21st century, ISSN
    1070–1850)
    Includes bibliographical references and index.
        ISBN 0–275–96499–X (alk. paper).—ISBN 0–275–96500–7 (pbk. :
    alk. paper)
        1. Culture.   2. Culture—Forecasting.   I. Title.   II. Series.
    HM101.S2819   1998
    306—dc21   98–37914

Library of Congress Catalog Card Number: 98–37914

ISBN: 0–275–96499–X Cloth
        0–275–96500-7 Paperback

Copyright © 1998 by Adamantine Press Limited

Contents

Preface

There is mounting evidence to suggest that culture will play a powerful role in the world of the future.

One evidence of this is the growing importance of culture in individual, institutional, community, national and international affairs, as confirmed recently by the creation of a World Commission on Culture and Development and a World Decade for Cultural Development by Unesco and the United Nations. Another is the increased use of terms like global culture, corporate culture, media culture, political culture, social culture, and environmental culture in public discourse. A third evidence is the commitment of many educational institutions to departments, courses and chairs in cultural studies. A final evidence is the predication of a number of scholars and statesmen that the world is entering a period of cultural conflict and confrontation, characterized by 'the clash of cultures and civilizations'.

Clearly much more will have to be known about culture in general and cultures in particular if culture and cultures are to play a constructive rather than destructive role in the world. On the one hand, this means dealing with culture and cultures as concepts, particularly as this manifests itself in theories, ideas, ideals and definitions. On the other hand, it means dealing with culture and cultures as realities, especially as this manifests itself in the development of cultures, a cultural interpretation of history, the cultural life of the individual, the community, the state and the world, and the art of cultural development and policy.

Dealing with culture and cultures as concepts and realities makes it possible to examine real and ideal situations, as well as to profit from the age-old adage that theory informs practice and practice informs theory. It is the author's hope that this highly interactive and exploratory approach to the problem will help to broaden and deepen collective knowledge and understanding of two of the most evocative but elusive terms imaginable. For if one overriding conclusion emerges from this intensive probe into culture and cultures, it is that culture and cultures have a crucial role to play in human affairs, environmental sustainability and global well-being in the future, particularly when they are dealt with in positive and holistic terms and the proper precautions and safeguards are taken.

A work of this type would not be possible without contributions from many different sources. First of all, there are the contributions of generations of cultural scholars. Without the legacy of ideas, insights, works and research findings they have created, a book of this type would not be possible. Next, there are the contributions of many friends and colleagues, such as John Fobes, Guy Métraux, Eleonora Barbieri Masini, Ervin Laszlo, Henri Janne, Paul Braisted, Magda Cordell McHale, Biserka Cvjetičanin, Robert Vachon, Andreas Wiesand, Erika Erdmann, Prem Kirpal, Augustin Girard, Richard Hoggart, Maurice Strong, Mochtar Lubis, Kurt Blaukopf, André Fortier, William McWhinney, Walter Pitman, John Meisel, Mavor Moore, Tom Symons, Paul Weinzweig, Greg Baeker, Bill Poole, Frank Pasquill, Sal Amenta, Arthur Witkin, Barry Witkin, Jill Humphries, Steven Thorne, and others. Without their support, encouragement and assistance over many years, this work would never have been completed. In addition, there are the contributions of several organizations and journals, including Unesco, Culturelink, Razvoj Development International, Cultures, Futures and World Futures which published articles or documents relevant to the subject matter of the book. Finally, there are the contributions of some very special people, especially my wife Nancy, daughters Charlene and Susan, parents Harold and Belle, brother and sister-in-law Murray and Jean, Joy MacFadyen who spent endless hours working on the manuscript, Jeremy Geelan at 21st Century Studies Limited and Lloyd Allen for the layout design and typesetting. While recognizing these contributions, I nevertheless assume responsibility for everything contained in the text.

D. Paul Schafer
Markham, Canada
1997

1. The Centrality of Culture

Culture, however we define it, is central to everything we do and think. It is what we do and the reason why we do it, what we wish and why we imagine it, what we perceive and how we express it, how we live and in what manner we approach death. It is our environment and the patterns of our adaptation to it. It is the world we have created and are still creating; it is the way we see that world and the motives that urge us to change it. It is the way we know ourselves and each other; it is our web of personal relationships, it is the images and abstractions that allow us to live together in communities and nations. It is the element in which we live.[1]

Bernard Ostry

Profound changes are taking place in the cultural complexion of the world. Not only is the world being transformed as a result of countless communications, political, economic, environmental, educational, technological, social and artistic changes, but also culture and cultures are rapidly becoming powerful forces in individual, institutional, community, national and international affairs.

Of all the changes that are taking place, none may be more significant than the shift that is occurring from a passive to an active approach to culture. Twenty years ago, culture was treated passively and largely ignored. Today, virtually every country in the world is involved in many measures to promote culture, from passing legislation to protect the heritage of history to executing plans, programmes and policies to guide cultural development and increase citizen participation in cultural life. Whereas culture has usually been viewed as a consequence of change, and hence an activity over which humanity could exercise little or no control, it is being viewed more and more as a cause of change, and hence an activity over which humanity must exercise a great deal of control. As this happens, there is a much greater awareness of the power culture possesses, as well as a far more deliberate, conscious and systematic approach to it.

If we are to be successful in understanding the role that culture and cultures appear destined to play in the world of the future, much will depend on our ability to size up the present situation and interpret it correctly. A misreading of the present situation could have adverse consequences for the future.

The Global Transformation

There can be little doubt that political developments are having a phenomenal impact on the current situation. Not only are the forces of liberalism, democracy, conservatism and independence blowing more and more freely throughout the world, but also they are having a profound effect on every country. There is hardly a country anywhere in the world which is not experiencing fundamental shifts in political ideologies, constitutional arrangements, bureaucratic practices, governmental structures or geographical borders as a result of these changes.

Closely connected with the political changes are the economic changes. The shift to conservatism, capitalism, democracy and free trade has brought with it greater emphasis on the private sector and the marketplace, and with it, increased emphasis on commercial ventures, concentrations of wealth and power in fewer hands, and the division of the world into larger trading blocks. While some countries have been more fortunate than others in coping with these changes, few have managed to escape the consequences of radically-changed methods of production, distribution and consumption, altered forms of employment, income and expenditure, rapid escalations in taxes and public debts, and increased inflation. Clearly a new economic reality is taking hold in the world—a reality which suggests that the days of continuous growth and expansion are over and the days of consolidation, frugality and thrift have set in. One needs only to look at the lists of welfare recipients, the proliferation of food banks, and the growing ranks of the unemployed and underemployed to confirm this.

These transformations in political and economic practices are being matched by countless environmental changes. While the environmental movement has been going on for some time, it is evident that a new ecological consciousness is gripping the world. Not only is it becoming increasingly clear that the world's natural resources are being consumed and contaminated at an alarming rate, but also there is a growing realization that a new set of environmental policies and practices is needed to protect the globe's fragile ecosystem.

New environmental policies and practices are mandatory in a world threatened by rapid population growth and standing room only. Even the most optimistic forecasts suggest that expanding numbers, particularly when they are etched against shrinkages in arable land and depletion of the world's renewable and non-renewable resources, may prove to be one of the most demanding challenges of all.

Although urbanization may offer a temporary reprieve in a purely spatial sense, largely by sanctioning vertical as opposed to horizontal expansion and by compressing more and more people into the same physical space, it does so at an exorbitant price by increasing the amount of noise, air, water and traffic pollution and making it more difficult to sustain the level of social, recreational, human and medical amenities necessary for a healthy and sustained existence.

It would be foolhardy to underestimate the impact that developments in communications and technology are having on this situation. The computer is transforming economic, industrial and commercial practices in all parts of the world, and the rapid growth of genetic engineering, biotechnology, the mass media, electronic highways, internets, web sites and the communications industries is revolutionizing the way people live everywhere in the world.

Technology is clearly a double-edged sword. On the one hand, it opens up enormous opportunities for the storage, retrieval and utilization of knowledge, information and ideas in every field of human endeavour. On the other hand, it makes it difficult to cope with the demands and dictates of a technologically-oriented and media-dominated world. While the cruelties of war, poverty, famine, human rights abuses, and corruption are never easy to accept, they are much more difficult to accept when they are transmitted around the world every second of every day. Obviously it is going to take a great deal of psychic stability and emotional fortitude on the part of people everywhere in the world to deal with the profundity and propinquity of these changes.

Alongside the political, economic, environmental and technological changes are all the social and demographic ones. The populations of most countries are becoming increasingly multicultural and pluralistic in character, while fundamental changes are taking place in gender relations and in the concept of equality between the sexes. While much more needs to be accomplished in these areas, fortunately old methods and techniques are giving way to new patterns and possibilities.

These changes are occurring at a time when many of the traditional safeguards and support mechanisms that were designed to cushion the shocks of unprecedented and unpredictable social and demographic change are undergoing profound transformation. Whereas it was once possible to look to the family, the church, the temple, the mosque, the synagogue, the community and the neighbourhood to cushion the shocks of pronounced economic, technological, political, demographic, environmental and social dislocations, today this seems less and less possible.

There is one final development which should be mentioned since it is having such a profound effect on the world situation. This is the reaction that people are having to globalization as perceived in the emergence of larger and larger trading blocks, the creation of economic and political superstates, and the increased concentration of financial, corporate and technological power into fewer hands. There can be little doubt that changes in this area are having a disorienting effect on people everywhere in the world as manifested in a number of countervailing movements aimed at increasing people's sense of empowerment and control over the decision-making processes affecting their lives. Whether it is the quest for sovereignty, independence and autonomy, or the resurfacing of interest in neighbourhoods, communities and regions, the consequences are everywhere much the same. The more pressure is exerted toward globalization, the more people draw into themselves and institute countervailing measures aimed at providing greater control over their destinies and their lives.

If changes and developments like these were limited to a few sectors of society or parts of the world, they could be dismissed more readily as forces to be reckoned with in the future. However, when all the multifarious changes occurring in politics, economics, the environment, communications, technology, social and demographic affairs, globalization and localization are placed side by side and added up, they produce the portrait of a world that is in a profound state of cultural transformation. Most distinctive about this world are the dynamic nature of its contemporary change, and its extreme fluidity, complexity and interdependence. Events are happening at lightning speed, and are inexorably interconnected.

Under these circumstances, it is easy to understand why more and more people in Africa, Asia, Latin America, North America and Europe are feeling confused and disoriented. It is not that all of the changes and developments taking place are negative. In fact, many of them, like the quest for ethnic and gender equality and the movement to save the environment, are exceedingly positive. It is just that they are accumulating at such an accelerated rate, are occurring at such lightning speed, and are so pervasive in scope, size and influence, that they are making it difficult for people in all parts of the world to cope with them.

What stands behind all this is a matrix of local, regional, national and international problems that appears to defy traditional solutions, systems and structures. Whether it is population growth, poverty, the economic situation, the environmental crisis, the spread of disease, the breakdown in social institutions, or ethnic and racial unrest, there is a sinking feeling that the world system may not prove equal to the challenge. It is not only political processes, economic ideologies, social conventions and environmental practices that are being severely tested. More fundamentally, the whole conceptual and theoretical system, which humanity has evolved over the centuries to preserve some semblance of order and stability, is on trial.

The moon shot dealt a devastating blow to the present world system. It did so by destroying the vision on which the present world system is based; namely, that material opulence and leisure time are attainable on earth through the technological exploitation of resources elsewhere in the universe. The moon shot proved three things without a doubt: first, there are few resources on the moon capable of human utilization; second, it may be decades before the resources that do exist on the moon can be brought back to earth in quantities large enough to be significant; and third, human habitation on the moon is impossible as a means of alleviating population pressure on earth. Recent explorations in outer space appear to confirm that what is now known about the moon also holds true for other planets.

Hence the uncertainty about the present situation. While technology has liberated humankind from many traditional dependencies, it has simultaneously increased humanity's dependence on 'Spaceship Earth'. It is now clear that humanity is going to have to use all its collective ingenuity and creative potential to ward off the Malthusian spectre and prevent the Utopian dream of material abundance and leisure time from turning into a nightmare. Indeed, wars over resources, international chaos and the ultimate catastrophe may be inevitable if humanity is unable to create a more effective world system.

The Search for a New World System

Given the anxiety about the present world system, more and more people are turning to the search for a new one.

It is a compelling search—one that is universal in scope. Not only is it affecting young and old, women and men, but also it is touching every continent. It is as much the concern of the farmer in Africa, the statesman in Asia and the scholar in Latin America as it is of the labourer in North America and the housewife in Europe. Furthermore, no stone is being left unturned in the quest to uncover it. Everything is being turned topsy-turvy: ideas, values, theories, life styles and ideologies. Excavations are even under way in the catacombs of history to see if there is anything in the past that can provide the key to a more promising future.

There are many different views and opinions about the kind of world system this should be. For some, it should be a new economic system, one capable of redistributing income and wealth on a more equitable basis, creating a new international monetary mechanism, and solving alarming industrial, labour and unemployment problems. For others, it should be a new environmental system, one capable of conserving resources, controlling pollution, protecting the biosphere, and radically altering attitudes and practices with respect to nature, the natural environment and other species. For still others, it should be a new moral, social, legal, political or religious system, one capable of fashioning new ethical structures and legal codes, stabilizing diplomatic relations, promoting the spread of democracy, or drastically reducing the production of arms and nuclear weapons. And finally, for still others, it should be a new information or communications system, one capable of dealing with the shift from verbal to visual literacy, phenomenal accumulations of data, global networking, internets, the computer revolution, electronic highways, cyberspace, and mind-boggling changes in communications.

But herein lies a difficulty. Each group has a specialized way of looking at the problem, and hence a specialized view of how the problem should be solved. Slowly but surely, it is becoming evident that the specialized way of looking at the world system may be the cause of the present predicament. Individuals and institutions have become so caught up in some particular aspect of the world system that it is difficult to see and deal with the world system as a whole. As a result, the solution to one problem is often the cause of another, more serious problem. Economic solutions are advocated which have a devastating effect on the environment. Political and military interests are pursued that threaten the entire global ecology and life on earth. Technological advances that play havoc with social and human values are promoted. In the modern world, it is hard to stop long enough, *or step back far enough*, to view the world system for what it really is: a complex entity composed of countless interdependent and interactive components.

Clearly, the specialized perspective has become so ingrained in public consciousness and perceptions that it is difficult to see the world system in holistic terms. Yet, this is precisely what may be required if humanity is to extricate itself from the present situation and cross over the threshold to a more compelling future.

Many would agree that fundamental changes are needed in the way the world system is perceived but argue that changes in perception are not really all that crucial in terms of coming to grips with the fundamental problems confronting humanity. However, when Fritjof Capra claimed that all the difficult economic, environmental, social, political and human problems of our times are 'different facets of one and the same crisis, and that this crisis is essentially a crisis in perception',[2] he put his finger on the crux of the problem. He underlined the quintessential importance of 'seeing' as a prerequisite to effective problem solving. Perhaps this is why Goethe said towards the end of his life that 'it was with the eye more than with all the other organs that I learned to comprehend the world'.[3]

Why is cultivation of 'the art of seeing' so essential? It is so because the ways in which people see the world determine largely how they interpret and act in the world. If one thing has been lost in the modern world, surely it is the ability to see the world and the world system, and all that is contained in them, in holistic terms. Existing perspectives seem fragmented and limited. This makes it difficult, if not impossible, to bring about those fundamental changes in perceptions, principles, values and lifestyles necessary for laying down the foundations of a more effective world system in the future.

Culture: Key to the Future

Where should the search be commenced for the holistic perspective that is needed for the future? It is natural to turn first to the major institutions of modern times—corporations, governments and educational institutions. But herein lies a difficulty. These institutions have become so caught up in some particular aspect of the world system that they seldom are able to look at the world system as a whole. Where attempts have been made—such as with interdisciplinary studies—success has been limited.

It was this basic perceptual problem that Alexander King had in mind when he said:

Nearly all contemporary social problems, whether national or global, are interrelated and exceedingly complex, a tangled mass of individual threads connected in ways which are only dimly understood, so that attempts to solve a specific issue have repercussions on many others. Furthermore, each problem has many elements, technical, economic, social, political and human and can seldom be resolved by the politician, scientist, engineer or economist in isolation. With the increasing interdependence of nations and the emergence of so many problems of global dimension, many disciplines have to be called simultaneously into play. Yet multidisciplinary action is difficult to achieve, for society is organized essentially on a vertical basis.[4]

If it is not possible to find the holistic perspective that is needed in the network of contemporary institutions, the next place to look is in the realm of ideas. Fortunately, it does not take too much exploration here to ferret out exactly what is required. For there exists in the realm of ideas an idea that does have the holistic capability required, and that is the idea of culture.

It should be made clear that 'culture' is not being used here in a restrictive sense as the arts, the legacy from the past and the cultural industries of publishing, radio, television, film, video and sound recording—that is to say the way most governments use the term today. Nor is it being used in its broader sociological sense as a set of shared symbols, values, customs and beliefs. Rather it is being used in its holistic sense as a 'dynamic and organic whole'.[5] When culture is visualized and dealt with in this way, it possesses the potential to see the world and the world system in holistic rather than specialized terms. Visualized in this way, the development of the world can be seen as 'the development of culture and civilization'.[6]

If culture only possessed a holistic quality, it might be dismissed more readily as an indispensable asset for the future. However, culture possesses a number of other qualities that make it of crucial importance to the future. Foremost among these qualities is the capacity for holism, context, value, identity, criticism, vision, creativity and power. While these qualities relate to culture and cultures as concepts as well as realities—*and can be used or abused depending on how they are dealt with*—it is on qualities such as these that humanity should seek to create a more effective world system in the future.

The key to creating this system lies in making culture and cultures the centrepiece of global activity and human affairs. With the necessary safeguards and precautions, this would make it possible to create a world system according to culture's highest, wisest and most enduring principles, rather than its basest and crudest practices. Included among these principles are: the quest for equality, justice and truth; the love of beauty, knowledge and wisdom; the need for stability, order and diversity; the importance of co-operation, caring and sharing; recognition of the rights and freedoms of others; and the search for the sublime.

If culture's potential to lay the foundation for a more equitable and effective system is to be realized, a much more harmonious association will have to be achieved between human beings, nature, the natural environment and other species. Such an association should be based on unity with nature rather than supremacy over nature. This would enable humankind to take a more restrained and sustainable approach to the natural environment. The concern should be for conservation, renewal, and never taking more from the environment than is necessary for survival, rather than exploitation and spoliation. This would not only enable humanity to treat the natural environment and other species with the dignity and respect they deserve, but would also permit people to enjoy decent living styles without straining the environment to the breaking point.

More compelling worldviews, values and value systems are needed if this association is to be forged. They should be based on the realization that the challenge lies in living a full life, not in the sense of a life filled with consumer indulgences and materialistic practices, but in the sense of a life filled with creative activity, spiritual fulfillment, personal integrity and ethical ideals. Worldviews, values and value systems predicated on these convictions confirm the fact that the honest expression of feelings and emotions, artistic creations, learning, scientific discovery, spirituality, friendship and human love are the most essential things in life—the things that are remembered long after everything else is forgotten. These things not only tend to reduce the drain and strain on scarce resources, thereby holding the key to the environ-mental crisis, but also, they tend to bring about real fulfillment in life, thereby solving the riddle, of maldevelopment or spiritual poverty in the midst of plenty.

Of all the prerequisites for a more effective world system, none may be more demanding than the need to interpret history along more accurate, equitable and authentic lines. In the execution of this task, one objective should transcend all the rest. It is the objective of truth. The world cannot afford major transfers of power or the retracing of political and geographical borders if they are based on the substitution of one distorted view of history for another. If reinterpretations of history are to have any meaning, they must be based on truth. Where interpretations and reinterpretations of history are objective and honest, they should prove capable of confronting some of the greatest injustices of modern times—injustices that stand in the way of planetary progress.

As matters now stand, injustices are being done to many countries and peoples, particularly aboriginal people, marginal groups, ethnic minorities and African, Asian and Latin American nations, as a result of the one-sided account of the process of historical evolution. While much progress has been made in this area in recent years, these injustices will only be eradicated when the contributions that all people and all countries have made and continue to make to national and international development are recognized. A cultural interpretation of history could provide a way of balancing the scales of historical and contemporary justice in this sense.

Reinterpretations of history are also needed to correct some serious conceptual flaws and operational shortcomings. During the last two or three centuries, historical interpretations have been dominated largely by western countries in general and by economics, technology and politics in particular. This has had the effect of promoting worldviews, values, value systems and renderings of the historical process which are western in orientation, thereby suppressing alternative models available in other parts of the world. Here again, a cultural interpretation of history could help to focus the spotlight on worldviews, values and value systems that may be more in tune with the direction in which the world and humanity should be headed in the future.

As culture's potential to lay the foundation for a more effective world system unfolds, it is certain to spawn new concepts of the individual, the community and the state. In keeping with culture's capacity for holism, this could cause the focus to shift from preoccupation with the component parts of the individual, the community and the state to the individual, the community and the state as 'wholes'. For the individual, this would mean greater emphasis on the integration of all the physical, mental, emotional, intellectual, and spiritual dimensions of the personality to form the 'whole person'. For the community, it would mean greater emphasis on the development of the community as a comprehensive and coherent entity, as well as on the cultural statement the community makes to itself and the rest of the world. As for the state, it would mean greater emphasis on bringing together all the determinants of development to form an 'integrated whole'. While insufficient attention has been given to these holistic requirements over the last few centuries, they are of utmost importance to the future because they relate so fundamentally to what individuals, communities and nations are about.

These developments at the individual, community and national level should be matched by developments at the international level. Indeed, nothing short of a transformation in international relations will suffice to pave the way for a world system based on a more effective set of principles and practices. Here, the focus should be on more equitable distributions of resources and wealth, as well as on the creation of an indivisible world. Such a world should be based on reciprocal exchanges and collaborative arrangements among all the nations and peoples of the world.

In the creation of a more equitable system of international relations, a crucial role should be reserved for the cultural heritage of humankind. In the final analysis, world progress does not consist of the fashioning of individual works, the building up of specific institutions, or the development of particular nations. Regardless of how important these things are—and there is no intention of diminishing or denigrating their importance here—they are really means towards a much more enthralling end: the creation and diffusion of a treasure-trove of cultural achievements from all parts of the world for use by all citizens. As the shining star which is clearly discernible amidst the rise and fall of specific cultures and civilizations, this treasure-trove of cultural achievements is the real measure of humanity's progress down through the ages. Not only is it the product of all peoples and countries, but also it is the birthright of all citizens, regardless of their education, socio-economic status or geographical location in the world.

Why is it so essential to project this living legacy of hope into the foreground? It is so because it will not be possible to solve the *transnational* problems of modern times—overpopulation, pollution, poverty, disease, resource shortages, income inequality, and the constant threat of a nuclear catastrophe—without full familiarity with, and collective sharing of, this universal storehouse of cultural accomplishments. The great Indian sage Rabindranath Tagore foresaw this day when he said 'We must prepare the field for the cooperation of all the cultures of the world where all will give and take from others. This is the keynote of the coming age.'[7] This is what makes the diffusion and utilization of the cultural heritage of humankind by all people and all countries the real hope for human survival and planetary progress in the future.

Is it realistic to assume that culture can play the role visualized for it here? Surely it is. In an historical sense, the power of culture is easily recognized, particularly when the appropriate precautions and safeguards were taken to ensure that culture was directed to positive rather than negative ends. Entire periods of history—the Classical Age, the Renaissance, the Enlightenment, and Romantic period—are recognized for the cultural transformations they brought about.

Reflection on the potential that culture possesses to transform the world situation brings to mind Erasmus' reputed comment about 'the dawning of a new world' at the sunrise of the modern era. What was it about this remarkable man that caused him to see the future so clearly? Was it his ability to see that a cultural renaissance was in the making—a cultural renaissance that was transforming the entire conceptual and operational basis of society?

Perhaps that is what is needed today. Perhaps a cultural renaissance is needed capable of drawing its inspiration from all countries, and bringing hope, dignity, equality and justice to all people. If so, it would be a cultural renaissance well worth the effort.

2. Culture as a Concept

In sum, though the concept of culture was first defined in print in 1871 by E. B. Tylor, after all these years it still lacks the rigorous specificity which characterizes many less revolutionary and useful ideas.[1]

Edward T. Hall

If culture's capacity to improve the world system and create the conditions for a better world is to be realized, much more will have to be known about culture. Not only will knowledge of culture's nature, scope and subject matter have to be enlarged, but also a general understanding will have to be reached on what is meant by this elusive but evocative term.

This is an extremely difficult task in view of the enormous amount of confusion and controversy over the term 'culture'. Is culture the arts? Is it publishing, radio, television and film? Is it the legacy from the past or leisure-time activity? Is it shared values, symbols and beliefs, a state of mind, a way of life, or a means of interacting with the natural environment? Is it the organizational forms and structures of different species? Or is it all of these things? Little wonder that culture is the cause of so much confusion, controversy, suspicion and misunderstanding. It can be stretched in many directions and used to justify all sorts of diverse and often devious practices, and there is virtually no agreement among individuals and institutions throughout the world today on how culture should be conceived and defined. Indeed, when Alfred Kroeber and Clyde Kluckhohn, two distinguished American anthropologists, set out to clarify the nature and meaning of culture several decades ago, they ended up writing an entire book on the subject. Entitled *Culture: A Critical Review of Concepts and Definitions*, it identifies over a hundred different definitions of culture and is essential reading for anyone interested in plumbing its depths.[2]

It behooves anyone proposing that culture and cultures be made the centrepiece of the world system of the future to confront this situation head-on by dealing first and foremost with the thorny problem of conceptualizing and defining culture. In order to do this, culture must be dealt with *as a concept* before it can be dealt with in other ways. On the one hand, this means coming to grips with the many different concepts and definitions of culture that have appeared in the historical literature and are in active use throughout the world today. On the other hand, it means evolving an understanding of culture that is in tune with both the rapidly changing nature of reality and the direction in which humanity appears to the headed in the future. In other words, it means evolving a way of conceiving and defining culture that is consistent with historical experience, contemporary reality, linguistic practice, present trends and future needs.

Various Approaches to Culture

How is it possible to proceed when there are so many different concepts and definitions of culture from which to choose? While many approaches to the problem are possible, four in particular stand head and shoulders above the rest. They are: the institutional approach; the practical approach; the theoretical approach; and the conceptual approach. While each approach has its strengths and shortcomings, each also contributes to broadening and deepening our understanding of culture as a concept.

Of the four approaches, the institutional approach is the most logical and straightforward. It involves examining the way in which culture is conceived and defined by governments, corporations, foundations and educational institutions.

While a great deal of work is needed in this area, a valuable step was taken several years ago when a group of researchers from Finland analyzed the way in which member states of Unesco employed the term 'culture' for purposes of their contributions to Unesco's series of studies and documents on cultural policies.[3] The findings of this study revealed that while some member states of Unesco include science, education, broadcasting, the mass media, religion and other activities in their definition of culture, all member states include the arts in their definition of culture.[4] This would appear to be consistent with the way in which many educational institutions, foundations, corporations and governments define culture, as well as the institutional trend that appears to be emerging throughout the world towards defining culture for administrative, policy, planning, funding and trade purposes as 'the arts, heritage and cultural industries of publishing, radio, television, film, video and sound recording'.

While the institutional approach has a number of strengths, it also has some obvious shortcomings. Not only do governments, corporations, foundations and educational institutions often conceive and define culture narrowly, usually for the purpose of operationalizing, managing and controlling it, but also history is filled with examples of the political, corporate and intellectual use of culture for propagandistic, imperialistic or commercial purposes. While this subject will be revisited later when attention is shifted from culture as a concept to culture as a reality, suffice it to say that no greater mistake could be made than to use the institutional approach as the point of departure for the investigation into culture as a concept.

The practical approach focuses on the way people use the term 'culture' in public and private discourse. This is most readily revealed by listening to conversations, as well as by examining the way the term is employed in articles, books, journals and other documents. Even cursory attention to this matter will quickly confirm what Alfred Kroeber and Clyde Kluckhohn discovered: there is a bewildering array of different concepts of culture used in conversation. This helps to explain why culture is the subject of so much confusion, ambiguity, controversy and misunderstanding.

This problem is compounded when attention is shifted from conversation to articles, books, journals, and other documents concerned with culture. Here, the term 'culture' is used many times with reference to other species as well as the human species. The use of such terms as horticulture, silviculture, permaculture, the bee culture, the ant culture, and the bacterial culture suggests that human beings believe that what they deem to be culture is not limited to themselves, but is omnipresent throughout the entire domain of nature. This explains why the term is used frequently in disciplines like ecology, biology, botany and zoology.

While the practical approach expands people's understanding of the scope and orbit of culture, it is of limited usefulness in determining how culture should be conceived and defined, or in exposing the qualities and properties that make culture relevant to the world of the future.

The theoretical approach to culture proves helpful here. Rather than focusing on the way culture is used in institutions, discourse or literature, it focuses on culture as an abstract idea or archetype. This represents a valuable step forward in terms of broadening and deepening our knowledge and understanding of culture because, as indicated earlier, culture must be dealt with first and foremost as a concept. While 'manifestations of culture' like books, art objects, records, tapes and products can be touched and seen and take physical form, culture itself is largely a theoretical term that is imposed on reality in order to explain, comprehend, and deal with reality.

No sooner is the theoretical approach taken than it is apparent that culture can be conceived and defined in many different ways. It can be defined broadly or narrowly, loosely or tightly, directly or indirectly as a platonic form, ideal, product, process, system, structure, living organism, artifact, myth, or civilization. Moreover, it can be imbued with all sorts of qualities and characteristics—positive and negative, functional and dysfunctional, realistic and idealistic. While this gives culture a great deal of malleability, flexibility and elasticity, it also increases its susceptibility to a variety of uses and abuses.

Although the theoretical approach has the advantage of building up a conceptual understanding of culture through logic, observation, application and analysis, the fact remains that culture is primarily a product of the human mind and can be stretched in many directions to achieve different results. This means that the theoretical approach also suffers from a number of shortcomings. Since theorists conceive of and define culture differently, this results in a bewildering array of different perceptions and definitions of culture.

This problem is overcome somewhat when the conceptual approach is employed. This is the approach that Alfred Kroeber and Clyde Kluckhohn used when they set out to shed light on the complex enigma posed by culture several decades ago.[5] By classifying the many different definitions of culture that are evident in discourse and the historical literature according to the basic *theme* that is inherent in them, a profuse and bewildering array of different 'definitions of culture' can be reduced to nine basic 'concepts of culture'. This is because many definitions are variations on the same or a similar theme.

The nine basic concepts are: philosophical, artistic, educational, psychological, historical, anthropological, sociological, ecological and biological. While these are not the only concepts of culture that appear in the historical literature or are in use throughout the world today, most definitions of culture can be classified under one or another of these concepts.

Since each concept contributes a great deal to a collective understanding of the nature, scope, subject matter, complexities, intricacies and idiosyncrasies of culture, it pays to examine them in turn. This effort is doubly rewarded when these concepts are examined according to the time they appear in history. For when this is undertaken, it is possible to trace the historical evolution of culture *as a concept* over a history that spans some two thousand years. Moreover, and much more importantly, it makes it possible to derive certain conclusions and identify trends which have the greatest significance for the way culture might be conceptualized, defined and dealt with in the future.

Historical Evolution of Culture

Of the nine basic concepts of culture, the philosophical concept is the oldest. It was formulated two thousand years ago when Cicero equated culture with the philosophy or cultivation of the mind.

Clearly, Cicero's intention was to link culture to the intellectual development of the individual, and hence to the acquisition of knowledge, wisdom and understanding. While philosophers see culture today as something significantly broader than a mental, intellectual and individual activity, many people continue to think of culture in personal terms and consider a 'cultured person' to be informed, intelligent and knowledgeable.

What is equally fascinating about the philosophical concept of culture is its emphasis on *cultivation*. This is not surprising in view of the fact that the term culture derives from the Latin verb 'colo' meaning 'to till' or 'to cultivate'. Here, culture is seen as a process that requires constant tending and nurturing—a process not unlike the cultivation of a garden. Not only does this help to explain why terms like horticulture, agriculture, silviculture and permaculture have worked their way into the lexicon on culture, but also it serves to underline the fact that there is an intimate connection between culture, cultivation and nature stretching back two thousand years—a connection that has largely been lost in the modern era and is only now being rediscovered as a result of the environmental movement. However, if the emphasis on culture as cultivation is important, so is the emphasis on culture as a *process*. In fact, viewed from this perspective, culture is much more a process than a product. This figures prominently in the distinction that is often made between culture and civilization: culture being viewed as the progressive movement towards an end product; and civilization being viewed as the end product itself.

Like the philosophical concept of culture, the artistic concept of culture is centuries old. It can be traced back to the Middle Ages and the Renaissance, where culture was associated with literature and the arts through terms like *cultura literarum humanorium* and *cultura bonarum artium*. Whereas culture was intimately connected with the Muses in those days, particularly those of epic and lyric poetry, music, tragedy, sacred song, dance, and comedy, today it is generally believed to embrace the performing arts (music, drama, opera, dance, mime, puppetry); the literary arts (poetry, literature, creative writing); the visual arts (painting, sculpting); and often the environmental arts (architecture, town planning, urban design, landscaping) and the material arts or the crafts (weaving, pottery, enamelling, engraving and the like). While there is broad agreement in most parts of the world on what is included in the artistic concept of culture, there are exceptions. What is considered art in one country may not be considered art in another country. In Japan, for example, tree dwarfing and flower arranging are art forms, just as calligraphy is in Japan and China and tattooing is in Tanzania. Then there is Bali, which is rich in the arts and elevates many activities to art forms because everything is done 'to the best of one's ability' according to the old adage.

As indicated earlier, virtually every country in the world today employs some variation of the artistic concept of culture as the basis of its official definition of culture. There are compelling reasons for this. Most countries consider the arts to constitute the very essence of their culture. In fact, the arts have long been recognized as seminal sources of creativity, excellence, perfection, beauty, truth, and inspiration—qualities that go a very long way towards giving countries their distinctive identity.[6] It is not surprising that the first thing most countries do when they subdue other countries is expropriate or destroy their art objects and artifacts. For the arts have long been recognized for their mythological, symbolic and communicative value. They can easily be used to galvanize people and lift them to incredible heights, something political and military leaders have known from time immemorial.

Of all the qualities the arts possess, none may be more essential at the present juncture in history than the quest for creativity and the search for truth. In an age where illusion rather than reality has become the norm, the artist's ability to cut through illusion and strike at the heart of the matter is needed more than ever if truth is to triumph over falsehood and honesty and justice are to prevail over dishonesty and injustice. Moreover, it is far from coincidental that creativity is commonly regarded as the lifeblood of artistic activity. It is the artist, never satisfied with existing ways of doing things but always probing, exploring, experimenting and innovating, who often provides the impetus for discovering new and better ways of doing things. As such, it is the artist who is responsible for providing much of the fuel that is needed to propel societies to higher and higher levels of achievement.

While the arts are often cordoned off and set apart from the general process of development, ultimately municipal, regional, national and international development is inconceivable without a healthy and vigorous artistic life. While political, business and bureaucratic leaders may often be loath to admit it, economic, commercial, industrial and political development often depends on healthy injections of artistic insight and imagination, the kind of insight and imagination that springs from the artist's desire to fashion new images, concepts, contexts, styles and techniques. Perhaps this helps to explain why artists are often regarded as 'the antennae of the race'.

Of all the areas where the arts make a significant contribution to society, none may be more important to the world of the present and the future than the contribution they make to national identity and international understanding. The arts contribute substantially to the visibility and credibility of all countries in the world, thereby yielding countless economic, social, political and diplomatic benefits. Furthermore, by communicating across geographical and political frontiers in profound and often moving and humane ways, the arts have a monumental role to play in promoting peace and understanding throughout the world.

Just as the artistic and philosophical concepts of culture are centuries old, so is the educational concept. In the original Chaldean sense, culture was Ur or light— the light within the individual as well as throughout society. It was education and learning in the best and fullest sense of the term: illumination of the mind and the spirit through exposure to the vast reservoir of accumulated knowledge and wisdom.

This kind of education and learning is not limited to formal education: far from it. It embraces not only all aspects of elementary, secondary, post-secondary, continuing, adult, and special education, but all forms of non-formal and informal education and learning as well. Perhaps the closest approximation to it is 'life-long learning' or 'education for life', encompassing all theoretical and practical learning from the cradle to the grave. In other words, it is education and learning based on the joys of exploration and discovery for their own sake, rather than on preparation for a job or indoctrination into the biases, norms and mores of a specific society.

Despite the fact that the philosophical, artistic and educational concepts of culture surfaced in classical, medieval and early modern times, it was not really until the nineteenth century that interest in culture started to intensify and take shape. It is interesting in this regard that towards the middle of the nineteenth century, the educational, artistic and philosophical concepts of culture were fused to produce a kind of 'psychological concept of culture'. Culture was then associated not so much with the cultivation of the mind through exposure to philosophy, the arts, education and learning, but rather with the cultivation of the human being through the pursuit of perfection and exposure to the vast reservoir of accumulated knowledge, wisdom, artifacts and accomplishments.

Matthew Arnold, the nineteenth century British scholar, was in the forefront of this movement. His vision of culture was set out in *Culture and Anarchy*, which appeared in 1869. In this publication, Arnold likened culture to:

a pursuit of total perfection by means of getting to know, on all the matters which most concern us, the best which has been thought and said in the world…culture has one great passion, the passion for sweetness and light…He who works for sweetness works in the end for light also; he who works for light works in the end for sweetness also.[7]

For Arnold, culture, or the pursuit of perfection through sweetness and light or the arts and education, was a highly personal affair. It was an inward condition of the mind, the body and the spirit, not an outward condition of mechanical and material civilization. It was an inward condition that must be constantly directed towards the harmonious expansion of *all* the powers that comprise human nature. Not only was Arnold committed to preventing the development of any one of these powers to the exclusion of the others, but also he was committed to ensuring that culture was an active rather than a passive affair. It was not sufficient for the individual to merely observe, see, learn and understand—to absorb, in effect, without giving something back in return. It was also necessary for the individual to ensure that the best knowledge, wisdom, and understanding *prevailed*, in the sense that it was made accessible to fellow citizens and future generations and fully incorporated into the development of societies. Thus, there was a moral imperative to culture not only in terms of pursuing perfection but also in promoting and acting on it. This is what Arnold had in mind when he talked about 'the cultured person'. It is also what separates the philosophical concept of culture proposed by Cicero from the psychological concept of culture developed by Arnold:

The great men of culture are those who have had a passion for diffusing, for making prevail, for carrying from one end of society to the other, the best knowledge, the best ideas of their time; who have laboured to divest knowledge of all that was harsh, uncouth, difficult, abstract, professional, exclusive; to humanize it, to make it efficient outside the clique of the cultivated and learned, yet still remaining the *best* knowledge and thought of the time, and a true source, therefore, of sweetness and light.[8]

Like the other concepts of culture, the psychological concept has a great deal of relevance to the world of the future. Its emphasis on the pursuit of perfection, the constant striving for improvement, sharing, and the universal diffusion of all that is most worthwhile in the arts, sciences, humanities and education, make it of vital importance to all individuals and societies in the years and decades ahead.

About the same time that Arnold was giving culture a personal face through the psychological concept of culture, others were busy giving it a material face through the historical concept of culture. The two are intimately connected, since both are concerned with the legacy from the past and the present. The one looks at this legacy from the standpoint of the individual whereas the other looks at it from the standpoint of material reality.

Several German authors were in the forefront of the movement to create the historical concept of culture. One was Johann Christoph Adelung, who published his *Essay on the History of Culture of the Human Species* in 1782. It covered the history of human and social development from its origins until the end of the eighteenth century. Another was Dr Gustav Klemm, who published the first volume of his ten volume *Cultural History of Mankind* in 1843. It was devoted to a study of the gradual development of humankind as a species. This was followed, in 1854 and 1855, by his two volume *Science of Culture* which focused on the history and science of culture. In these works, great tribute is paid to Voltaire, who, according to Klemm, was the first author to set aside dynasties, kings' lists and battles in order to study culture *per se*, even if he did not use the term itself.

In effect, there are actually two versions of the historical concept of culture. The broader one embraces *all* accumulations from the past, large and small, old and new, relevant and irrelevant. It makes no distinction whatsoever between the importance or unimportance of objects and artifacts: it is the total legacy from the past that is important. In contrast, the narrower version includes only those accumulations from the past that have withstood the test of time and are highly valued by individuals, societies and nations in the present. Clearly both versions of the historical concept of culture are present in the following definition:

culture in general as a *descriptive* concept means the accumulated treasury of human creation: books, paintings, buildings, and the like; the knowledge of ways of adjusting to our surroundings, both human and physical; language, customs, and systems of etiquette, ethics, religion, and morals that have been built up through the ages.[9]

The historical concept of culture also possesses many qualities that are relevant to the overall understanding of the complexities and intricacies of culture as a concept. It emphasizes the fact that human beings are the inheritors of a profuse historical legacy representing the summation of all the hopes and fears, dreams and deeds, knowledge and wisdom, insights and ideas, objects and artifacts, and tangible and intangible accomplishments of their ancestors. This legacy is available to present and future generations in order to help them understand and differentiate between right and wrong, relevant and irrelevant, simple and profound, timely and timeless. By giving the present and the future a past, the past exercises an enormous influence over the present and the future.

It is clear that this priceless legacy from the past has a crucial role to play in the world of the future. Not only does it help to anchor humanity in reality, thereby ensuring continuity and creating an intimate bond between the past, the present and the future, but also it contributes substantially to identity and solidarity. In so doing, it speaks directly to individuals and societies about the things they hold most dear to themselves, thereby giving people in general and countries and societies in particular a sense of rootedness, cohesion, coherence and continuity. These qualities may be needed more than ever in an age characterized by globalization and rapid and relentless technological change.

While the historical, artistic, educational, and psychological concepts of culture held sway through much of the nineteenth century, significantly broader concepts of culture were making their appearance and taking their place alongside the narrower and more traditional ones towards the century's end. While culture was still very much associated with the arts, sciences, philosophy, education and history, and while 'the cultured person' was still very much seen as the person conversant with the finer things in life and the legacy from the past, nevertheless a number of scholars were manifesting a desire to visualize culture in much more expansive terms. The process whereby this came about is elucidated by Raymond Williams in his book *Culture and Society 1790–1950*:

Before this period, it (culture) had meant, primarily, the "tending of natural growth", and then, by analogy, a process of human training. But this latter use, which had usually been a culture of something, was changed, in the eighteenth and early nineteenth century, to culture as such, a thing in itself. It came to mean, first, "a general state or habit of the mind", having close relations with the idea of human perfection. Second, it came to mean "the general state of intellectual development, in a society as a whole". Third, it came to mean "the general body of the arts". Fourth, later in the century, it came to mean "a whole way of life, material, intellectual and spiritual".[10]

The most expansive of these broader concepts of culture, and in retrospect the one which has had the most powerful impact on contemporary thinking, is the anthropological concept of culture. It was originally propounded in 1871 by Sir Edward Burnett Tylor, one of the world's first anthropologists. In his *Origins of Culture*, Tylor set out what has since become the classic definition of the anthropological concept of culture:

Culture or Civilization, taken in its wide ethnographic sense, is that *complex whole* which includes knowledge, belief, art, morals, law, custom, and any other capabilities and habits acquired by man as a member of society.[11]

Ever since it was first propounded, the anthropological concept of culture, and especially Tylor's formulation of it, has had a profound effect on scholarly and popular thinking. Not only has it had a substantial impact on contemporary notions regarding the nature, scope, meaning and substance of culture, but also it has acted as a watershed in the historical evolution of concepts and definitions of culture. Whereas all concepts of culture prior to Tylor's time were partial concepts, parts of the whole so to speak, here was a concept of culture deemed to be total. Virtually all well-known anthropologists since Tylor's time, including Benedict, Boas, Mead, Linton, Lowie, Malinowski, Kroeber and others have tended to view culture as: 'that *complex whole* which includes *all* the habits acquired by man as a member of society', 'the sum of *all* activities in a society', '*all* manifestations of a community', 'the *totality* of material and non-material traits', the '*sum total* of ideas, conditioned emotional responses and patterns of habitual behaviour', and 'the *total* body of belief, behaviour, knowledge, sanctions, values, and goals that mark the way of life of any people'.[12]

Like all the other concepts of culture, the anthropological concept of culture reveals a great deal about the nature and meaning of culture. By focusing on the sum total of human experience, the anthropological concept of culture provides a significantly broader and more all-encompassing way of looking at culture. This yields a number of benefits. In the first place, it makes culture the product of all classes of society and not just certain classes of society, thereby making culture a more egalitarian and populist affair. Second, it focuses attention on culture as a *whole*, as well as the complex interrelationships that exist between and among the component parts of the whole. And finally, it emphasizes the relative as well as the absolute nature of culture,[13] thereby paving the way for the realization that concepts and definitions of culture vary greatly from one part of the world to another and one period of time to another.

About the same time that anthropologists were busy weaving a web of definitions around the idea of culture as 'the complex whole', sociologists started to weave a web of definitions around the idea of culture as 'shared values, symbols, beliefs, and behavioural characteristics'. Over time, these definitions have coalesced to form the sociological concept of culture:

Culture, a word of varied meanings, is here used in the more inclusive sociological sense, that is, to designate the artifacts, goods, technical processes, ideas, habits and values which are the social heritage of a people. Thus, culture includes all learned behaviour, intellectual knowledge, social organization and language, systems of value—economic, moral or spiritual. Fundamental to a particular culture are its law, economic structure, magic, religion, art, knowledge and education.[14]

A number of qualities embedded in the sociological concept of culture should not be allowed to escape our attention. First of all, there is the idea of values, value systems, patterns and themes, which is exceedingly pertinent to the overall understanding of culture in general and cultures in particular. Viewed from this perspective, not only is the totality of activities in itself important, but also the way in which these activities are combined. Clearly, cultural experiences are configured and organized differently in different parts of the world, largely because they are based on different perceptions, preferences, and possibilities. The noted anthropologist Frobenius, for instance, contended that European cultures are organized around intellectual patterns and themes whereas African cultures are organized around emotional patterns and themes.[15]

If the emphasis on values, value systems, patterns and themes is important, so also is the emphasis on *shared* symbols, beliefs and behavioural characteristics. It is impossible to become a member of any group, be it a family, a community, an ethnic group, a class, a society or a race without sharing certain values, symbols and beliefs in common and acquiring certain ways of acting and behaving. T. S. Eliot, for example, identified a number of distinctive and shared symbols which comprise 'English culture' and set it apart from other cultures. These he identified as 'Derby Day, Henley Regatta, Cowes, the twelfth of August, a cup final, the dog races, the pin table, the dart board, Wensleydale cheese, boiled cabbage cut into sections, beetroot in vinegar, nineteenth-century Gothic churches and the music of Elgar.'[16] Surely it is all this and much more.

Race, ethnicity, class, gender, identity and identities are exceedingly germane to the sociological concept of culture. This makes it essential to study the insights and findings of sociologists in these areas very carefully, as race, ethnicity, class, gender, identity and identities have assumed great importance in the modern world. The same is true for language and communication. For it is through communication and language that the bonds are developed—or not developed—which bind people and societies together. In the modern world, it is the mass media, or the so-called 'cultural and communications industries' of publishing, radio, television, film, video, sound recording, the computer and the like, which facilitate the act of communication most readily. It is far from coincidental that books, records, tapes, videos, radio and television programmes, computers, internets, electronic highways, films, dialogue and discourse are generally regarded as the lifeblood of modern communication, for these are the things used to transmit the images, messages, impressions, signals and symbols needed to enable people in different parts of a country, or in different countries, to share information, ideas, perceptions, patterns, and beliefs. Little wonder there is growing concern about who owns, operates and controls these vehicles of communication, as well as what messages are transmitted through them. Failure to exercise adequate control and ownership of the modern instruments of communication can pose serious problems for countries in terms of cultural expression, identity, sovereignty and survival.

While the sociological and anthropological concepts of culture have a great deal to recommend them, they both suffer from one fundamental problem. By focusing attention on the human species and the products of human creation, they tend to downplay, assume or take for granted other species and the realm of nature. In recent years, this has generated interest in a number of even broader concepts of culture, such as the ecological and biological concepts of culture, where the idea of culture is not limited to the human species but is extended to other species and the entire domain of nature. This requires a quantum shift in thinking about the nature and meaning of culture. It is not unlike the shift that occurred when Tylor broke with the long tradition of defining culture in terms of 'the parts' and started defining culture in terms of 'the whole'.

Rather than thinking of culture as the sum total of human creation, the ecological concept of culture may be viewed as a symbiotic relationship between human beings and the natural environment. Seen from this perspective, culture is an interactive process involving human beings and nature. In many ways, the ecological concept of culture is an outgrowth of the environmental movement. In one form or another, this movement has made people aware of the fact that technology, which is often regarded as the crowning achievement of human creation, has not liberated humanity from its traditional dependency on nature but has increased its dependency on the natural environment through depletion and pollution of the globe's renewable and non-renewable resources. As this happens, there is much greater appreciation of the role that nature plays in shaping culture, as well as the incredible dependency that human beings have on all forms of plant, animal, vegetable and mineral life.

With the introduction of the ecological concept of culture, the doors are opened to even broader concepts of culture. One is the biological concept of culture. It is predicated on the belief that culture is not limited to the human species but includes other species as well. Viewed from this perspective, all species have culture. This not only makes sense of a vast panorama of terms like agriculture, horticulture, silviculture, permaculture, aquaculture, the bee culture, the oyster culture, the ant culture, and the bacterial culture which must be accounted for if the complexities and idiosyncrasies of culture as a concept are to be understood, but also it confirms the fact that what is perceived as culture by human beings is not limited to the human species but encompasses other species as well.

Support for the biological concept of culture has been slow to materialize. This may be due to the fact that there are many people, particularly those who view culture as the crowning achievement of the human species, who are reluctant to extend the concept of culture to other species. Such people contend that culture is the very thing that sets human beings apart from nature and other species. Nevertheless, the biological concept of culture is slowly but surely gaining ground and winning converts, primarily because of the environmental movement and a growing recognition of the fundamental link between human beings and other species. While it still requires more precise formulation, the biological concept of culture is implicit in the following statement by Ortega y Gasset:

We can now give the word, culture, its exact significance. There are vital functions which obey objective laws, though they are, inasmuch as they are vital, subjective facts, within the organism; they exist, too, on condition of complying with the dictates of a régime independent of life itself. These are culture. The term should not, therefore, be allowed to retain any vagueness of content. Culture consists of certain biological activities, neither more nor less biological than digestion or locomotion...Culture is merely a special direction which we give to the cultivation of our animal potencies.[17]

While the biological concept of culture requires more precise formulation, it is steadily evolving through numerous advances in the natural, botanical, zoological and biological sciences. These advances suggest that every species, be it animal, vegetable or human, has its own functions and forms of cultural creation inherent in the structures, systems, behavioural characteristics, traits, patterns and preferences it manifests. Take the bee culture as an example. Like the human culture, it possesses a highly complex and intricately-designed system of social and economic arrangements. This system, with its well-defined caste structure of queen, drone and worker bees, its rigid hierarchy and division of labour, its finely-tuned communications network, its sensing capabilities and productive apparatus, acts to ensure the survival of bees as a species, as well as to guarantee a continuous supply of products. These products, such as honey, wax, the beehive and the honeycomb, are much in demand in the human realm and have both a functional and aesthetic significance. The beehive and the honeycomb, for example, are intricately-designed cultural creations, comparable in their way, style, design, function, and complexity to many of the cultural creations fashioned by human beings. And what is true for the beehive, the honeycomb, and more generally for the bee culture, is equally true for all other forms of animal and plant life. Each has its own forms of cultural creation, including its distinctive methods of procreation, habitat, social arrangement, community organization, and consumption and production activity. Interestingly, modern advances in the botanical and biological sciences are even revealing that plants, like animals and human beings, have feelings and emotions and experience pain and, what is more, respond very much the way people do when confronted with such unpleasantries.

The more scientists learn about plant and animal cultures, the more is known about the various qualities which are deeply embedded in the biological concept of culture. This very expansive view of culture confirms the fact stated earlier that culture is not only a *product*, but also a *process*. It is an evolutionary and organic process—a process which is constantly evolving and changing over time in response to new conditions and altered circumstances. As such, it yields valuable information about the organization and conduct of all forms of plant and animal life. This information may prove to be exceedingly important in the future. It is clear, for example, that many animal species—ants, bees, insects and the like—have developed modes of social organization and collective behaviour which manifest an intimate understanding of the way large populations are organized and regulated when resources are scarce and space is limited. Viewed from this perspective, the biological concept of culture may represent one of the most important concepts of culture of all.

By depicting culture as an evolutionary process, the biological concept of culture offers an ideal opportunity to understand the complexities and intricacies of other species, for cultures are subject to continuous adaptation and change, not only in terms of their general systems and structures, but also in terms of their specific functions, characteristics, and interrelationships. One of the best ways of understanding and dealing with the cultural life of human beings, therefore, may be to study the cultures of other species more intensively. This may prove helpful in terms of anticipating and preventing unfavourable occurrences, reversing certain trends, and forecasting problems. Careful study of the reasons for the survival, extinction and transformation of non-human cultures, for example, may provide valuable clues in dealing with such human challenges as overpopulation, migration, resource conservation, and environmental degradation.

With consideration of the biological concept of culture, the examination of the nine basic concepts of culture that have appeared in the historical literature and are in active use throughout the world today is complete. Looking back over the course of this encounter, what conclusions can be drawn and trends identified that are helpful in determining the way in which culture might be conceived, defined and dealt with in the future?

An initial conclusion is obvious. While the formulators of the nine concepts of culture may have drawn on cultural experiences, theories or practices prevalent in other parts of the world, all the nine concepts are products of the western mind and the western intellectual tradition. This fact should be constantly borne in mind, since how culture is conceived and defined *as a concept* has a powerful impact on how it is applied and practiced *as a reality*. Clearly there is a pressing need for concepts of culture that originate in non-western societies, particularly when culture is becoming such a crucial force in human affairs.

A second conclusion is equally obvious. Culture is a dynamic concept. It has experienced a number of fundamental shifts and turning points over the course of its history, such as the shift that occurred in the latter part of the nineteenth century to the anthropological and sociological concepts of culture and the shift that appears to be occurring today to the ecological and biological concepts of culture. These shifts have been necessary in order to keep culture *as a concept* in tune with the rapidly changing nature of reality. They also serve as a reminder that concepts of culture change; people and countries in all parts of the world should be extremely careful to use concepts of culture that are best suited to their own circumstances and needs.

A third conclusion is also apparent. There is a large gulf between the way culture is conceived and defined by scholars and theorists compared to the way it is conceived and defined by institutions, especially governmental and commercial institutions. Whereas many scholars and theorists conceive and define culture in expansive terms, especially in the contemporary era, most governments and corporations conceive and define it in narrow terms, most often as the arts, heritage, and cultural industries of publishing, radio, television, recording, film and video. This tends to marginalize culture and make it an insignificant priority in the affairs of political and commercial institutions.

A final conclusion is also evident. Culture is an evolutionary concept. Just as it has been constantly changing over time in order to remain in tune with the rapidly-changing nature of reality, so it has been steadily evolving in some very specific and highly discernible directions. These directions are revealed as soon as attention shifts from the concepts of culture themselves to the trends inherent in the historical evolution of culture as a concept.

One such trend is the trend towards conceiving culture more broadly. This trend is immediately apparent as soon as the earlier philosophical, artistic, educational, historical and psychological concepts of culture are compared with the anthropological, sociological, ecological and biological concepts of culture gaining currency today.

The trend towards conceiving culture more broadly is intimately tied up with the trend towards conceiving culture in comprehensive terms. Looked at from this perspective, the nine concepts of culture are not really separate or mutually exclusive. On the contrary, they are interconnected and comprise larger and larger conceptions of reality, since the ones that came earlier in historical time tend to be incorporated in the ones that came later in historical time. For example, the anthropological concept of culture incorporates the philosophical, artistic, educational, psychological and historical concepts of culture, as well as a great deal else, just as the biological concept of culture incorporates all the concepts of culture that precede it in historical time as well as in the entire domain of nature. While this is a generalization subject to certain exceptions—the artistic concept of culture does not 'incorporate' the philosophical concept of culture for example— it means that there has been an identifiable trend over the past two thousand years towards conceiving culture in more all-encompassing terms. This trend makes it possible to depict the historical evolution of culture *as a concept* as a series of continuously expanding and ever more inclusive concentric circles, with the narrower, older and more specific concepts of culture at the centre and the broader, newer and more expansive ones at the outer rim.

More and more people throughout the world appear to be conceiving culture in broader, more comprehensive terms. When people talk about being 'the products of their culture', for example, they often mean they are the products of everything that exists in their culture, or their culture *as a whole*. This includes economic activities, media experiences, educational endeavours, political processes, social conventions, religious values and interactions with the natural environment as well as art forms, the finer things in life and the legacy from the past.

It is not only individuals who are conceiving culture in broader and more comprehensive terms. Specific institutions appear to be adopting this practice as well. After several decades of conceiving and defining culture as the arts, the finer things in life and the legacy from the past, Unesco has started to conceive culture in significantly broader and more comprehensive terms. This was revealed most recently when the member states of Unesco adopted the following definition of culture at the second World Conference on Cultural Policy in Mexico City in 1982:

Culture ought to be considered today the whole collection of distinctive traits, spiritual and material, intellectual and affective, which characterize a society or social group. It comprises, besides arts and letters, modes of life, human rights, value systems, traditions and beliefs.[18]

The arguments for adopting this significantly broader and more comprehensive understanding of culture were set out even more forcefully in the planning documents and working papers for the World Decade for Cultural Development:

Reflection on the subject of cultural development finally led to what was almost a new definition of culture by the participants at the Mexico City Conference. Without neglecting the importance of creativity as expressed in intellectual and artistic activity, they considered it important to broaden the notion of culture to include behaviour patterns, the individual's view of him/herself, of society, and of the outside world. In this perspective, the cultural life of a society may be seen to express itself through its way of living and being, through its perceptions and self-perceptions, its behaviour patterns, value systems and beliefs.[19]

The impetus for adopting this expansive understanding of culture is not only coming from individuals and institutions like Unesco. It is also coming from aboriginal groups, ethnic minorities and colonized countries. The reason for this is not difficult to detect. As long as nations, peoples, and groups are in no danger of losing their culture, it is easy to define culture in narrow and specialized terms. However, as soon as culture is threatened or there is a real danger of losing it, there is often a sudden realization of the broad and comprehensive nature of culture. Clearly there is nothing quite like the threat of foreign domination or cultural extinction to bring about a rapid realization of the expansive character of culture.

It is impossible to conceive of culture in broad and more comprehensive terms without extending it to include all groups, peoples, classes, institutions and activities in society. Culture is egalitarian rather than élitist in this sense. It is popular music as well as classical music; science as well as art; blue collar workers as well as white collar workers; corporations as well as film agencies; gardening as well as post-secondary education. Clearly culture is the business of all citizens, institutions and societies when it is conceived in this way.

If it is possible to detect a trend towards conceiving culture in broader and more comprehensive terms, it is also possible to detect a trend towards conceiving culture in holistic terms. This trend is most conspicuous after Sir Edward Burnett Tylor broke with the long tradition of conceiving culture in terms of 'the parts' and started conceiving and defining culture in terms of 'the whole'. For Tylor, and many anthropologists, the whole is visualized as everything that is created by human beings or acquired by human beings as members of society. With the emergence of the more expansive ecological and biological concepts of culture, the whole is expanded to include everything created or acquired by other species as well.

This completes the examination of the way culture has evolved as a concept over a history spanning some two thousand years. What stands out most clearly is the fact that culture possesses *breadth* and *depth* as a concept. In breadth, all human beings and even other species possess culture, depending on whether culture is conceived and defined in an anthropological, ecological or biological sense. In depth, culture is concerned with much of what is most valuable and worthwhile in life. Evidence of this fact may be found in the philosophical, artistic, historical, educational, psychological and sociological concepts of culture.

Is it possible to reconcile these two seemingly contradictory ideas? Is it possible, for example, to evolve a concept of culture taking into account the fact that culture is concerned with many of the most valuable and worthwhile things in life while simultaneously accounting for the fact that all human beings and even other species possess culture?

The answer appears to lie in the development of a 'holistic concept of culture'. As will be demonstrated momentarily, this holistic concept makes it possible to recognize the fact that culture is concerned with 'the whole,' 'worldview' and 'worldviews', as well as with 'values' and 'value systems'. This capitalizes on the broader and more comprehensive concepts of culture gaining currency in the world today, while simultaneously recognizing that culture is concerned with much of what is most worthwhile and valuable in life.

The key to fashioning this holistic concept of culture lies in exploring the connection that exists between culture and cosmology. For although culture and cosmology have evolved in very different ways in the past, and conjure up entirely different images at present, there is an intimate bond between them. This makes it possible to open the doors to a way of conceiving and defining culture which is not only consistent with historical experience, discernible trends, linguistic requirements and contemporary practice, but also with future needs.

A Holistic Concept of Culture

Culture and cosmology. Cosmology and culture. Complex words. Compelling words. While these two words appear to share little in common, they actually share a great deal in common. Like culture, cosmology has a long history. It can be traced back to the earliest civilizations, to the first peoples and their need to interpret and understand the universe in order to cope with it.[20] This would not have been possible without the creation of very specific cosmological theories about how the universe came into existence and how it functions in fact:[21]

One of the characteristic, persistent, and irrepressible needs of the human mind is to have a cosmology. It consists in the interest of being able to describe and understand the large-scale, global structure of the universe in which we live. An interest in cosmology...is to be found in virtually every period and culture of recorded history.[22]

It is clear from this that cosmology is concerned with the creation of a systemic and coherent picture of the universe as a 'worldview'. In the process of creating this worldview, cosmology seeks to answer a number of the most profound and pressing questions imaginable: What are the origins of the universe? How did the universe come into existence? Does the universe have a beginning and an end? Is the universe constant in size or is it continuously expanding? How is the universe structured and what are its principal elements? Is there a basic set of organizational principles or laws explaining how the universe functions? Is there an ultimate purpose to the universe? Does the universe have a specific life span? Many of these questions, *albeit in a very altered form*, are similar to the basic questions with which culture is equally concerned: questions of origin, structure, function, purpose, organization, and evolution. They also underline the fundamental importance of 'worldview' to both cosmology and culture. It is this concern with worldview that makes cosmology a highly holistic and integrative discipline:

Cosmology is the study of universes. In the broadest sense, it is a joint enterprise by science, philosophy, religion, and the arts that seeks to gain understanding of what unifies and is fundamental...Cosmology is the one science in which specialization is rather difficult. Its main aim is to assemble the cosmic jigsaw puzzle, not to study in detail any particular jigsaw piece. While all other scientists are pulling the universe apart into more detailed bits and pieces, the cosmologists endeavour to put the pieces together in order to see the picture on the jigsaw puzzle.[23]

Unfortunately, cosmology is often confused with astronomy, with which it shares certain concerns. However, whereas astronomy is concerned with the functioning of stars, planets and solar systems in the universe, cosmology is concerned with the nature and functioning of the universe *as a whole*:

Cosmology is thus the all-embracing science, for it deals with the structure and evolution of the entire universe—everything that we now observe and that we can ever hope to observe in the future. Astronomy, by contrast, deals with the properties of individual objects, such as stars and galaxies.[24]

Cosmology's interest in the universe *as a whole* gives it its holistic character. Clearly this is not 'the whole' in an anthropological, ecological or even biological sense. Rather it is 'the whole' in a cosmological sense, or what is often referred to as 'the cosmic whole'. While the cosmic whole can never be seen, known or understood because of its infinite complexity, vastness and totality,[25] humanity appears to be deeply committed to the quest to try to understand it, regardless of how inadequate or deficient the effort might be. This is because there appears to be a deep psychological need in human beings to see and understand the universe and all that is contained in it as a totality. Presumably this is why all the world's greatest philosophers, scientists, theologians and religious leaders have endeavoured to understand the holistic and unitary nature of the universe and reality.

One of the most recent scholars to tackle the need for cosmic understanding in this sense was the cultural philosopher and historian Wilhelm Dilthey. H. P. Rickman comments here on Dilthey's insights into the holistic and unitary nature of reality:

Underlying all, was his assumption that reality is a whole of interrelated parts (and not an agglomeration of independent pieces) and that philosophy must make us aware of that unity...In his analyses of literary works, cultural systems, social groupings, historical phenomena or whole ages, he invariably emphasized that they were complex entities embedded in even more complex contexts. Isolated phenomena, unconnected facts or independent mental acts were, for him, hypothetical constructions, because what we encounter in experience is invariably part of an enormously intricate web.[26]

According to Dilthey, 'the whole' is much more than a collection of parts. The parts are always ordered or configured in very specific arrangements. They may be ordered or configured well or badly, loosely or tightly, intelligently or unintelligently, but they are always ordered or configured in the first place.

In an historical sense, this idea manifested itself in the classical Greek notion of the universe '*as an ordered whole*'. In fact, in a strictly etymological sense, the term cosmology derives from two Greek words: 'kosmos' meaning 'the universe as an ordered whole'; and 'logos' meaning 'discourse' or 'logic'. In a purely linguistic sense then, cosmology is discourse or logic about 'the cosmic whole' or the universe as an ordered whole.[27]

With the introduction of the idea of the universe as an ordered whole, the link between worldview, the whole, and the ordered whole starts to become clear. For the idea that the universe is not only a whole, but an ordered whole, is in effect a very particular type of worldview. It is a worldview espoused by the ancient Greeks and other philosophical, theological and religious leaders who contend that some divine authority or supernatural power is responsible for configuring the universe in such a way that it forms an integrated and harmonious entity. Clearly a complex set of cosmological, theological and metaphysical beliefs, convictions and assumptions is at work here to explain how the universe was originally created and how it functions in fact.

With the growth of modern science, other types of cosmological theories, worldviews and interpretations of the cosmic whole have emerged to rival the more traditional and classical ones. One such theory is the 'big bang' theory. It is based on the belief that the universe is the product of a 'kick-start' which occurred millions and millions of years ago when two or more random elements collided with one another, rather than the product of some divine creation or grand design. Another such theory is the 'cosmos as chaos' theory. Here, the universe is seen not so much as an 'ordered whole' but rather as a 'disordered mess'. In this case, some form of human intervention may be required to impose order on chaos. Even the Marxian theory, which has traditionally been viewed as an economic theory, is in reality a kind of cosmological theory because it posits a very specific worldview based on the conviction that all societies are 'wholes' divided into material and nonmaterial components. By contending that economics is the central organizing principle of all societies and advocating that this is true for all times and in all places, Marx proposed a very specific way of looking at and interpreting history and the world based on economic necessity rather than divine intervention.

What these and other cosmological theories demonstrate is just how dependent human beings are on worldviews in general and interpretations of the creation and functioning of the universe in particular. For worldviews and cosmological theories are created in very specific physical settings and social situations when people come together for the express purpose of living together in the world and eking out their existence in the world. In the process, they evolve very specific worldviews or 'cosmologies' that attempt to explain how the universe was originally created, how it functions in fact, and what concrete skills and practical techniques are needed to function effectively in the universe. Viewed from this perspective, the intimate connection between culture and cosmology starts to become clear:

Culture is the socially determined mental framework in which we live. It is our *Weltanschauung*, our worldview, our abstract conception of reality…Every society has thus invented a *cosmology*: an explanation of how the universe came into being and why humans came to be in it…Each cosmology thus provides a distinctive vision about who people are, where they stand in the universe, what their responsibilities are, and how they ought to behave.[28]

It follows from this that culture in a fundamental sense is every bit as much concerned with 'worldview' as cosmology. It is the cornerstone of culture in a holistic sense because it is concerned with how human beings perceive and interpret the world. And how human beings perceive and interpret the world has a profound bearing on how they act in the world.

Every human being is compelled to develop a 'personal worldview' or 'cosmology' in this sense, comprised of thoughts, opinions and ideas on how the universe was created, how it functions, how the individual positions himself or herself in the universe, how life is lived in the universe, and what life is all about:

"World view" attends especially to the way a man, in a particular society, sees himself in relation to all else. It is the properties of existence as distinguished from and related to the self. It is, in short, a man's idea of the universe. It is that organization of ideas which answers to a man the questions: Where am I? Among what do I move? What are my relations to these things?[29]

We wish to know our "place", where we fit in among all the other entities that make up the universe. What forces, powers, and causes brought us into existence and sustain us? What should be our goals, purposes, and values? Is there some cosmic design of which our lives are a part?[30]

Just as individuals are compelled to develop personal worldviews or cosmologies, so groups, societies and cultures are compelled to develop collective worldviews or cosmologies which explain the operations of the universe and their role, purpose, place, and *modus operandi* in it:

Every culture, every people, every society must [discover and] rediscover its own interior cosmology, must arrive at a coherent account of its being in the world, must be able to locate itself in a recognizable world and find for itself the organizing principle of its world.[31]

If culture and cosmology share a mutual interest in worldview, they also share a mutual interest in 'the whole'. Whereas the concern of cosmology is with 'the whole' in a cosmic sense, the concern of culture is with 'the whole' in an individual, institutional, group, community, national, international, environmental or species sense, as terms like personal culture, corporate culture, community culture, African culture, western culture, global culture, ecological culture, bee culture and plant culture imply. Here the focus is not so much on the parts of the whole, important as these may be, but rather on the whole itself. The role that mind and concepts play in this process is immediately apparent:

Culture is learned as a child, and as children we each learned from those around us a particular set of rules, beliefs, priorities and expectations that molded our world into a meaningful whole. *That is our culture.*[32]

It is not difficult to determine why culture is so concerned with 'the whole'. For the whole determines the parts according to an age-old philosophical truth. Ruth Benedict, the noted American anthropologist, illustrates why this must be so through her use of the example of making gunpowder:

The whole determines its parts, not only their relation but their very nature…The whole, as modern science is insisting in many fields, is not merely the sum of all its parts, but the result of a unique arrangement and inter-relation of the parts that has brought about a new reality. Gunpowder is not merely the sum of sulphur and charcoal and saltpetre, and no amount of knowledge even of all three of its elements in all the forms they take in the natural world will demonstrate the nature of gunpowder. New potentialities have come into being in the resulting compound that were not present in its elements, and its mode of behaviour is indefinitely changed from that of any of its elements in other combinations.[33]

As it is for gunpowder, so it is for culture. Culture in the holistic sense is concerned with 'the whole' before anything else. No amount of studying the individual parts of the whole will ever result in an understanding of the whole since, as Ruth Benedict observed, the whole is greater than the sum of its parts by virtue of the fact that new potentialities have been added and brought into being that were not in the parts.

It is this concern with the whole that explains why cultural scholars have been so preoccupied with deciphering the codes or recipes that are used to create and recreate the whole in this sense. Since the whole is composed of myriad parts, the parts always have to be arranged or configured in very specific combinations and arrangements. It follows from this that a very distinct recipe or code is used to bring the parts into a meaningful relationship with each other. As T. S. Eliot observed, 'just as a man is something more than an assemblage of the various constituent parts of his body, so a culture is more than the assemblage of its arts, customs, and religious beliefs. *These things all act upon each other, and fully to understand one you have to understand all.'*[34]

The recipe, code or process used to bring the component parts of the whole into meaningful relationship with one another has been variously described as a 'system of shared values, symbols and beliefs', 'a value system', 'a value hierarchy', or 'a hierarchy of values'. Jerzy Wojciechowski comments on the role that this hierarchy plays in the creation of the whole in a cultural sense:

It should be pointed out that the hierarchy of values underlying each culture is the principle of internal cohesion of a culture, which bonds the various elements of a culture together and structures them into an organized whole composed of interdependent parts.[35]

The hierarchy of values used to determine the cultural whole makes it possible to talk about the cultural whole as 'an ordered whole'. Here the link between culture and cosmology is very much in evidence. For just as cosmology is concerned with the ordered whole in a cosmic sense, so culture is concerned with the ordered whole in a cultural sense. This whole can be defined in terms of individuals, institutions, groups, communities, regions, countries, continents, the world, cultures, the human species or other species depending on the specific unit under investigation. However, the concern is always the same: What hierarchy of values has been used to order the whole and how does this affect the perception and understanding of the whole itself?

If the hierarchy of values is the key to understanding the whole as an ordered whole, it is also the key to understanding the whole as 'worldview'. Here again Jerzy Wojciechowski provides valuable insights:

The hierarchy of values underlying a culture integrates elements of knowledge into a world view, determines to a large extent attitudes and reactions to life situations, and offers a general framework for man's conscious presence in, and relationship to, the world. Central to each culture are convictions about the universe and about man, about his nature, his relation to the external world, his place in the universe, the meaning of human life, the supreme values, and the distinction between right and wrong, good and evil.

The sum of these convictions forms in each case a unique and distinctive system, differing from culture to culture, even though some of its elements are similar in different cultures.[36]

While culture as a concept is concerned with value hierarchies, the whole, the ordered whole and worldview, it is important to point out that these are always created within 'the cosmic whole'. In other words, how the cosmic whole is perceived, visualized and interpreted has a fundamental bearing on the whole, the ordered whole, worldview and value hierarchies in a cultural sense. Robert Redfield illustrates this point by focusing on the fundamental link existing between the culture of a people and its conception of the whole in this broader cosmic sense:

The culture of a people is, then, its total equipment of ideas and institutions and con-
ventionalized activities…The "world view" of a people…is the way a people charac-
teristically look outward upon the universe…"world view" suggests how everything
looks to a people, "*the designation of the existent as a whole*".[37]

Here we have it then: the primary reason for the intimate link between
culture and cosmology. Just as the artistic concept of culture is concerned
largely with excellence and creativity, and the sociological concept of culture
is concerned primarily with shared values, symbols, ideologies and beliefs, so
the holistic concept of culture is concerned with the whole, the ordered
whole, worldview, worldviews, values and value systems. Not only are these
the same basic concerns of cosmology, albeit in a cultural rather than cosmological sense, but also they are conceived, defined and formulated within the
larger framework of the cosmic whole.

Given these considerations, are there grounds for linking culture with
cosmology and proposing a holistic concept of culture at this particular
juncture in history? Indeed there are. By focusing attention on the whole, the
ordered whole, values, value systems and particularly worldview and
worldviews, the holistic concept of culture shines the spotlight directly on one
of the most important areas of all human activity. Albert Schweitzer's early
encounters with the great philosophical systems as well as the need for
worldview and worldviews are revealing in this regard:

Even as a student I used to be struck by the fact that the history of thought was always
presented as the history of philosophical systems, not as that of a struggle for a worldview…

Our only possibility of progress lies in thorough comprehension of and
immersion in the problem of world-view.[38]

Culture in the holistic sense in which the term is employed here addresses
this need. By focusing attention on the idea of worldview and worldviews,
culture makes it possible to engage in a thorough consideration of the
problem of worldview and worldviews in the most concrete and practical
terms imaginable. On the one hand, it emphasizes the fundamental
importance of the way in which people perceive and interpret the world as a
prerequisite to the way they act in the world. For human beings, this places
the emphasis squarely on a broad range of cosmological, philosophical, metaphysical, theological and religious factors that are often assumed or taken for
granted in the modern world. On the other hand, it emphasizes the need to
create worldviews that are more appropriate to the future. Many of these
worldviews may well come from African, Asian and Latin American nations,
aboriginal groups and ethnic minorities whose ways of looking at and interpreting the world have been marginalized and suppressed. For in the process
of asserting the superiority of the western worldview, many worldviews of
importance to the world of the future have been ignored or neglected.

If the preoccupation of the holistic concept of culture with worldview is important, so is its preoccupation with 'the whole', for this is what gives culture its holistic capacity. Fritjof Capra comments on the need to cultivate this holistic capacity in terms of the world of the future:

Today we live in a globally interconnected world in which biological, psychological, social and environmental phenomena are all interdependent. To describe this world appropriately we need a new paradigm, a new vision of reality—a fundamental change in our thoughts, perceptions and values. The beginnings of this change, or the shift from the mechanistic to the holistic conception of reality, are already visible.[39]

The crucial role that culture appears destined to play in this process is immediately apparent. Not only has culture been concerned with 'the whole' and 'holistic perception' ever since Sir Edward Burnett Tylor broke with the traditional practice of defining culture in terms of the parts and started defining culture in terms of the whole, but also it is clear that concern with 'the whole' is at the core of many cultural issues and concerns.

While there are many reasons for this, surely the main reason has to do with the fact that the parts too often dominate the whole. Not only is this contrary to the age-old philosophical truth that the whole should take precedence over the parts, but also it strikes at the heart of many of the most debilitating and demanding difficulties of modern times. The world is filled with examples of the parts dominating the whole, such as political interests dominating society; economic interests dominating development: military interests dominating global concerns; and commercial and technological interests dominating life. While concern with the whole cannot eliminate these practices, it can provide a more effective perspective on these practices and reveal exactly why it is that they are playing havoc with the world situation.

If preoccupation with 'the whole' is of crucial importance to the world of the future, so is preoccupation with 'the ordered whole'. For it is not only the whole that is important, it is also how the whole is structured and put together.

It is impossible to focus on 'the ordered whole' without focusing on values and value systems for, as indicated earlier, they indicate how the component parts of the whole are weighed and valued in relation to one another. They also reveal how the parts are linked together to form a whole. If they are linked wisely, the outcome will likely be harmonious and beneficial. However, if they are linked badly, the outcome will likely be chaotic and destructive.

In much the same way that new worldviews are needed to guide global development and human affairs, so new values and value systems are needed to guide human action and behaviour. Given the rapid expansion of the human population and the growing scarcity of renewable and non-renewable resources, many of these values and value systems will have to be based on different relationships between human beings, the natural environment and other species. Activities that consume resources are going to have to be curtailed, while activities that conserve resources are going to have to be encouraged. Likewise, activities that respect the rights of other species and future generations are going to have to be condoned, while activities that do not respect these rights and generations are going to have to be condemned. Here again, there is much to be learned from values and value systems prevalent in African, Asian and Latin American countries, as well as from aboriginal peoples and marginalized groups.[40]

If there is one place where the holistic concept of culture's concern with worldview, the whole, the ordered whole, values and value systems comes to rest, surely it is in the idea of *unity*. For when culture is given the holistic casting it is here, it is concerned with bringing things together rather than splitting them apart.

If it is the role of philosophy according to Dilthey to make humanity aware of the unity and the connectedness of all expressions of being, it is the role of culture to provide humanity with the conceptual and practical means to do this. It does so by directing attention to the unifying capability that is inherent in the holistic understanding of culture. Without this, humanity may be destined to treat the world and all that is contained in it in a fragmented, disjointed, and specialized way rather than a unified, holistic, and harmonious way. This will exacerbate even more the basic divisions existing between human beings, nature, people, ethnic groups, other species, countries and cultures.

Several decades ago, the environmentalist Barbara Ward observed that everything is linked. But if everything is linked, what provides the thread that links all things together? Culture may provide this thread. Perhaps this is why Wole Soyinka, the recent Nigerian Nobel Laureate for Literature, prefers to speak of culture as 'source'. In a speech to the International Conference on Culture and Development in Washington he said:

We need therefore to constantly reinforce our awareness of the primacy of Source, and that source is the universal spring of Culture. It is nourished by its tributaries, which sink back into the earth, and thereby replenish that common source in an unending, creative cycle.[41]

By travelling back to source in this fundamental cultural sense, humanity may be able to come to grips better with the host of environmental, economic, social, political, ethnic and human problems which typify modern times.

It is the unifying property in culture when it is perceived and defined in holistic terms that makes it very different from endeavours like economics, political science, psychology, physics, chemistry, or astronomy. Whereas these latter endeavours are highly specialized, designed to enhance knowledge and understanding of particular parts of wholes, culture is a unifying endeavour designed to enhance knowledge and understanding of wholes themselves. To perform this function effectively, it is necessary to provide a perspective on human wholes, *however limited, inadequate or incomplete this perspective may be*, and to reveal what it is about wholes which is unifying and fundamental.

Although the idea of adopting a holistic concept of culture and more generally accepting the intimate connection between culture and cosmology sounds strange, it really isn't. It can be traced back to the ancients and the Greeks and their need to understand the cosmos and all that is contained in it as a unitary entity if true knowledge, understanding and enlightenment are to be achieved:

The ancients explored nature [through cosmology] not to dominate her, certainly not to exploit her, but to become wise. The aim was understanding: and the view was often expressed that without understanding and knowledge, peace of mind and happiness are unattainable.[42]

Unfortunately, somewhere along the long march of history, contact has been lost with this classical gem of wisdom. Progressive specialization and fragmentation, coupled with preoccupation with the human species, has caused humankind to lose touch with the unequivocal connection that exists between human beings and nature. Thus, of all the manifold benefits to be derived from a holistic concept of culture, none may be more valuable to the world of the present and the future than culture's unifying property and integrative potential.

By defining culture in an expansive and unifying sense, a holistic concept of culture breaks with the separation of human beings from nature as well as the centredness of the human species. With introduction of the cultural forms and manifestations of other species, the focus shifts from preoccupation with the human species and its creations to all species and their creations. While this idea has numerous advantages in view of the apparent discord and lack of harmony between human beings, nature and other species, it necessitates a profound shift in consciousness about the character of culture in general and the focus of cultural inquiry in particular. After several centuries of thinking that culture is the very thing that separates human beings from nature and other species, thereby giving human beings supremacy over them, it is going to take a profound change in perception and conceptual thinking to accept the fact that culture may be the very thing that binds all species together in a unitary relationship. It is this shift that necessitates a quantum leap in consciousness.

Flesh has started to appear on the bare bones of a holistic concept of culture. By way of recapitulation, the investigation commenced with a review of the main concepts of culture that have appeared in the historical literature and are in active use throughout the world today. This resulted in the identification of nine basic concepts of culture—philosophical, artistic, educational, psychological, historical, anthropological, sociological, ecological, and biological—each of which contains indispensable clues to the overall understanding of culture as a concept. When these nine concepts were viewed in chronological context, it was possible to identify a relentless historical trend towards conceiving culture in broader and more comprehensive terms. This led to the formulation of a holistic concept of culture, where culture was linked to cosmology in general and worldview, worldviews, the whole, the ordered whole, values and value systems in particular.[43] In one form or another, these ideas are closely linked to the idea of unity because they relate so fundamentally to the interdependent nature of reality and the cosmic condition.

A Holistic Definition of Culture

Now that a concept of culture has been evolved which is consistent with historical experience, present realities, linguistic practice and future needs, it is possible to confront the problem of defining culture.

Like the problem of conceiving culture, the problem of defining culture cannot be ignored. It must be confronted and dealt with for what it really is: a necessary step along the road to broadening and deepening understanding of the nature, meaning, scope and subject matter of culture in general and cultures in particular. Fortunately, the task is made somewhat easier by the fact that there is now a specific concept of culture with which to work. For it is through a holistic concept of culture that it is possible to evolve a holistic definition of culture.

The key to this definition lies in notions of the whole, the ordered whole, worldview, worldviews, values and value systems, since how people perceive and interpret the world has a fundamental bearing on how they live and act in the world. Viewed from this perspective, people no sooner come together in association than they are compelled to confront a whole host of complex and difficult problems. How are the universe and the world visualized and interpreted? How is survival assured? How is the need of food, shelter, accommodation and creative expression dealt with? How is procreation and nurturing handled? How are groups and communities organized? How is production, distribution and consumption addressed? How is the quality of life improved? How is geographical space occupied? And how are relations conducted with other species and the world at large? By organizing these questions around the central themes that are inherent in them, it is possible to construct a holistic definition of culture. Addressed in this way, culture is 'an organic and dynamic whole which is concerned with the way people see and interpret the world, organize themselves, conduct their affairs, elevate and enrich life, and position themselves in the world'. Each component part of this holistic definition of culture contributes a great deal to the overall understanding of the content, characteristics and complexity of culture and cultures.

How people see and interpret the world deals with all the deeper philosophical, cosmological, theological, mythological, ethical and ideological beliefs and convictions which people possess. These beliefs and convictions constitute the cornerstone of culture and cultures because they provide the axioms, principles and assumptions on which culture and cultures are based. Not only do they determine the way in which people visualize and interpret the world, but also they shape the way in which people act in the world. As a result, they are intimately connected to the environmental situation, the global predicament, the human and cosmic condition, the relationship between mind and matter, and changing perceptions of time, space and the universe.

How human beings organize themselves deals with all the decisions people make with respect to economic, social and political systems, technological and scientific endeavours, military pursuits, defense installations, environmental policies and ecological practices, not to mention the development of towns, cities, regions, countries, cultures and all forms of human settlement. These 'macro elements' of cultural life are undergoing profound change at the present time as a result of shifting trading practices, globalization, rapidly-changing demographic patterns, and new economic and political realities.

How human beings conduct their affairs deals with the character of people's lives, and with it, decisions about consumer expenditure and behaviour, daily living arrangements, child rearing, family life, and personal preferences and practices. These 'micro elements' of cultural life are intimately connected to the macro elements of cultural life, or how people organize themselves and their affairs.

How human beings elevate and embellish life deals with people's education and training, aesthetic and scientific preferences and ideals, religious and spiritual practices, moral values, and all those things that make life a deeper, richer, and more meaningful affair than it might otherwise be.

How human beings position themselves in the world deals with people's geographical location, geopolitical situation, and territorial manoeuvering in the world. These factors play a crucial role in determining the way in which people relate to their physical surroundings and other species, as well as to each other as members of groups, countries, cultures, and continents. Clearly the potential for conflict and confrontation is always present at these *cultural contact points*, particularly as a result of rapidly-changing demographic, economic, political, technological and social conditions.

When culture is defined in this holistic sense, it can be visualized as a gigantic tree with roots, trunk, branches, leaves, flowers and fruits.

Metaphorically speaking, myths, religion, ethics, philosophy, cosmology and aesthetics comprise the roots; economic and military systems, technological practices, political ideologies, social structures, environmental policies, and consumer practices constitute the trunk and branches; and educational systems, literary works, art objects, spiritual beliefs, moral practices and the like constitute the leaves, flowers and fruits.[44] This provides a very useful way of thinking about and conceptualizing culture. Not only does it deal with culture as a totality, thereby relating to culture's holistic and egalitarian nature, but also it highlights the complex interrelationships that exist between and among the component parts of culture.

Of all the complex interrelationships that comprise the domain of culture, seven in particular stand out above all the rest because they are so intimately related to the world system, the human condition, the environmental crisis, global survival and cosmic realities. These are: the relationship of people to themselves; to each other; to the objects, artifacts and systems they create; to the particular culture in which they are embedded; to other cultures; to the natural environment; and to the supernatural.

The relationship of people to themselves bears on the innermost psychological states and spiritual well-being of people. The relationship of people to each other bears on the bonds that exist, *or do not exist*, between relatives, friends, neighbours, foreigners, races, communities, countries and continents. The relationship of people to the objects, artifacts and systems they create bears on the technological and material circumstances of people's lives, as well as on the economic, political, social, artistic and scientific policies that govern people's lives. The relationship of people to the culture in which they are embedded bears on the sense of identity and belonging or alienation and estrangement that people experience in specific cultural contexts. The relationship of people to other cultures bears on the total spectrum of associations and exchanges that people have with other societies and cultures. The relationship of people to the natural environment bears on the complex ecological association that people have with all forms of plant, animal and mineral life. And the relationship that people have to the supernatural bears on the religious, theological, mystical and mythic association that people have with supreme forces and divine beings.

It is clear from these relationships that culture is concerned with questions and issues of the greatest importance to humanity.

How are the universe and the world visualized and interpreted at the present time and how should they be visualized and interpreted in the future? What concepts, theories and ideas are needed to strengthen the bond between human beings, nature, races, ethnic groups, and other species? What environmental practices and policies are necessary in an age characterized by unprecedented levels of pollution, population growth and ecological contamination? How are human affairs conducted so that famine, malnutrition, genocide, violence, human rights abuses and premature deaths are minimized, or if possible, eliminated? How are the complex economic, social, political and technological problems that typify modern times resolved? How is the gap closed between affluence and poverty, between African, Asian and Latin American nations on the one hand and European and North American nations on the other hand? How are wars and the ultimate nuclear catastrophe prevented? How is respect for the values, rights, traditions, and beliefs of others garnered? And, perhaps most importantly, how is it possible for all the globe's inhabitants to live healthy, meaningful and fulfilling lives? These are the immensely practical and pressing questions with which culture is concerned when culture is conceived and defined in holistic terms—questions of the greatest relevance and utmost urgency to humanity.

It is clear from the nitty-gritty nature of these questions that culture is concerned with all aspects of reality and the human condition. In fact, it is impossible to think of a subject more concerned with reality and the human condition than culture, for it is concerned with both sides of the equation: the conflict, violence, manipulation and enslavement as well as the ideals and principles; the negative as well as the positive; the past as well as the present and the future; the problems as well as the possibilities. It is local as well as global; individual as well as collective; theoretical as well as practical; emotional as well as spiritual. Culture is, in effect, reality and the human condition in their endless profusion of pains and pleasures, prejudices and potentialities, adversities and accomplishments.

The intention here is not to imply that culture can deal successfully with all the problems encountered in reality. It is, rather, to imply that culture is concerned with all of these problems and can play a valuable role in addressing them, primarily by providing fruitful approaches and fertile avenues for coming to grips with them. It does so by providing an effective framework for understanding and confronting problems, particularly when it is conceived and defined in holistic terms. By focusing not only on problems themselves, but also on the container within which problems are situated, as well as the complex interconnections and interrelationships existing among them, culture makes it possible to take into account the trade-off effects and consequences of different courses of action. It is in the domain of culture that consumption demands are brought into line with environmental realities, economic and technological interests are tempered with social, ethical and human concerns, and political and military excesses are subjected to critical analysis and detailed scrutiny.

Culture as a Discipline

What is the purpose of conceiving and defining culture in holistic terms? Is it to engage in theoretical debates and metaphysical discussions about the ultimate nature of culture and reality? Decidedly not. Regardless of how important these things are, and however much they stand behind the very concept of culture proposed here, the real reason for conceiving and defining culture in holistic terms is to attempt to come to grips with the host of conceptual and practical problems playing havoc with people's lives and threatening to rip the world apart: the environmental crisis; a divided world; growing shortages of renewable and non-renewable resources; escalating violence and terrorism; increased potential for wars and the ultimate catastrophe; and the growing gap between rich and poor countries and rich and poor people.

While culture provides a valuable tool for approaching and confronting these problems, ultimately the full potential of culture to contribute to the realization of viable solutions to them may only be unleashed when culture becomes a field of theory and practice in its own right. The reason for this is apparent. Although culture has gained immeasurably from its rich historical association with the arts, anthropology, sociology, philosophy, history, ecology, economics, geography, biology and the like, culture needs to be treated as a distinct discipline if its full potential is to be realized and its full contribution is to be made to the realization of a better world.

The examination of the way culture has evolved as a concept over the last two thousand years has revealed that at no time in the past has culture been treated as a distinct discipline. Invariably it has been treated as an adjunct to, or sub-component of, other disciplines. This poses a very serious problem for culture at the present time, for it makes it difficult to reach a common under-standing on the nature, meaning, scope, subject matter and definition of culture, as well as to develop a methodology suitable for culture as a field of theory and practice in its own right.

These difficulties are aggravated by the fact that culture tends to be treated as a minor branch on the tree of knowledge. The upshot of this is that culture is conspicuous by its absence from most government decisions, corporate matters, labour-management negotiations and educational endeavours. Even a cursory review of the activities of the most powerful insti-tutions of modern times—governments, corporations, international organi-zations, foundations and the like—will reveal that culture is either neglected or relegated to a secondary rather than primary position.

As long as culture remains in this situation, it will not possess the status or stature needed for it to become a vital force in public and private affairs. Nor will it possess the freedom and flexibility it needs to draw on many if not all disciplines in the search for viable solutions to the world's most pressing problems.

While all disciplines and fields have a valuable contribution to make to the realization of culture as a distinct discipline, cosmology, philosophy, theology, anthropology sociology, economics, ecology, biology, history, geography and the arts have a particularly important role to play. Not surprisingly, these are the disciplines with which culture has had the closest historical connection and intellectual affiliation.

From cosmology, philosophy and theology, there is insight into worldview, worldviews, holism, and the relationship between the parts and the whole. From anthropology, there is insight into the formation of cultures as wholes, as well as into cultural patterns and themes. From sociology, there is insight into values, value systems, symbols, beliefs, identity, race, class, ethnicity and gender, as well as into the bonds and tools of communication needed to bind cultures together. From ecology, there is insight into the interactive process that is constantly going on between the human species and other species, as well as the entire domain of nature. From biology, there is insight into the nature of organic processes, as well as into the evolutionary character of cultural life and the cultures of other species. From history, there is insight into the organization and evolution of culture over time, as well as into the rise and decline of different cultures and civilizations. From geography, there is insight into the organization and evolution of culture in space, as well as into the nature of human settlements. And from the arts, there is insight into creativity, excellence, the pursuit of beauty and truth and the search for the sublime.

Obviously all of these disciplines, and others, contain indispensable clues to unlocking the secrets of culture as a discipline and seeing where culture as a discipline should be headed in the future. They also contain indispensable clues to developing a methodology for culture as a field of theory and practice in its own right. Rather than being grafted on to culture from other disciplines, however, this methodology should evolve naturally and organically from the quest to establish culture as a distinct discipline. In order to achieve this, it should be an authentic and indigenous methodology; one which necessitates a great deal of creative thinking in its design and scholarly co-operation in its execution.

In the creation of this methodology, it is imperative to recognize the intellectual and historical traditions on which culture is based. On the one hand, this means recognizing the contributions that have been made by many disciplines and fields to culture. On the other hand, it means recognizing the contributions that have been made by countless scholars and thinkers. Included among these scholars and thinkers, in addition to numerous others, are: anthropologists such as Boas, Mead, Benedict, Malinowski, Frobenius, Kroeber, Linton, Geertz, White, Hall and Harris; historians such as Voltaire, Klemm, Guizot, Vico, Lamprecht, Burckhardt, Huizinga, Spengler, Williams, Ki-Zerbo and Toynbee; sociologists such as Sorokin, Weber and Mannheim; and philosophers, artists, writers and thinkers such as Dilthey, Arnold, Alisjahbana, Tagore, Senghor, Solinka, Nandi, Paz, Mazrui, Malraux, Nettleford, Linzheng, Kothari, Girard, Masini, Sardar, Goonatilake and

Inayatullah. Not only should the quest to establish culture as a field of theory and practice begin with an examination of the works of these and other scholars, but also it is on their thoughts, ideas, insights and research findings that attempts should be made to create a methodology suitable for culture as a distinct discipline.

It is a discipline that may prove capable of providing the multidisciplinary link needed to bring many fields together in the collective search for viable solutions to humanity's most difficult problems. Perhaps this is why culture is being seen more and more as a common denominator for many if not all fields, as evidenced by the use of such terms as economic culture, social culture, political culture, corporate culture, material culture, spiritual culture and environmental culture. Not only does this serve to underline culture's holistic property and integrative potential, but also it serves to indicate that culture may be one activity that most if not all disciplines share in common.

3. The Character of Culture

For even the small children were collaborators in an undertaking that transcended both me and them—the attempt to understand enough about culture so that all of us, equally members of humankind, can understand ourselves and take our future and the future of our descendants safely in our hands.[1]

Margaret Mead

The time has come to put the concept of culture to work. This is achieved most effectively by examining culture's capacity for holism, context, value, identity, conflict, criticism, vision, creativity and power. It is through an exploration of these qualities that an intimate understanding of culture's character is gleaned and the doors are opened to an examination of culture as a reality.

Culture as Holism

It is often said that the more expansive a concept is, the less useful it is as a device for comprehending reality, confronting problems, and dealing with challenges. Looked at from this perspective, the holistic concept of culture has no utility whatsoever, since it is concerned with providing an extremely expansive view of reality and its constituent ingredients. In the minds of many, therefore, culture in the holistic casting it is given here may be too broad, vague, general or abstract to serve a useful purpose.

It is difficult to concur with this point of view, particularly at the present juncture in history. Given the inability of humanity to deal with the vast and interconnected nature of reality, as well as the complexity and interrelatedness of contemporary issues and problems, nothing may be more essential to the world of the present and the future than culture's capacity for holism. This capacity makes it possible to see 'the big picture', as well as to focus attention on the complex interrelationships and interconnections that exist between and among the component parts of the big picture.

This need for holism serves to highlight the battle that is being waged at present over two seemingly contradictory ways of seeing. On the one hand, there is the specialized way of seeing. Here, the universe and all that is contained in it is viewed as a collection of parts, fit largely for detailed study and scientific analysis. Predicated on the belief that it is better to have specific and detailed knowledge of the parts than it is to have general and abstract knowledge of the whole, the specialized way of seeing is microscopic, and it focuses on the parts rather than the whole. On the other hand, there is the holistic way of seeing. Predicated on the belief that it is better to see things in holistic rather than partial terms, it is a macroscopic way of seeing, and it focuses on the whole and on the complex interrelationships and interconnections that exist among the component parts of the whole.

It is clear that the specialized way of seeing has the upper hand at present. One consequence of this is that solutions to problems are almost always deemed to exist *in the same field* as the problems themselves. Hence, economic solutions are sought for economic problems, political solutions are sought for political problems, and environmental solutions are sought for environmental problems. It is too seldom recognized that the solution to environmental problems may lie in changes in economic behaviour, just as the solution to political problems may lie in changes in social and human relationships.

It is becoming steadily more apparent that preoccupation with the specialized way of seeing obstructs humanity's ability to see, understand, and deal with the totality, complexity and interrelatedness of problems. This is producing a dangerous state of affairs in the world, because it produces a situation where some parts dominate other parts as well as the whole.

The world is replete with instances of this. For example, there are political and military leaders who exercise control over social classes and entire populations, subjecting them to their will. Many totalitarian governments and fascist regimes use repressive measures and propagandistic devices to manipulate specific parts of the whole in order to dominate it and direct it to their own ends, thereby compelling humanity to remain ever watchful and mindful of the actual and potential abuses of the parts of the whole. In much the same way, certain classes and interest groups are often able to dominate the whole and subject it to their will. In this way, economic, corporate and technological concerns are often able to dominate environmental and human concerns, the rich are able to dominate the poor, and commercial and business interests are able to monopolize societal interests. In all these cases, and others, there seldom seems to be the ability to focus on the larger picture or overall container within which these interests and concerns are located. To this extent, the old adage that it is impossible to see the forest for the trees may represent more than a cliché, but rather a tragic comment on the nature of the contemporary predicament.

As it is visualized here, the holistic way of seeing is not an alternative to the specialized way of seeing. Rather, it is a more all-encompassing and integrated way of seeing—a way of seeing that incorporates the specialized way of seeing in its grasp. Whereas the specialized way of seeing is essentially a one-step process focusing on a part or parts of the whole, the holistic way of seeing is a four-step process commencing with the cosmic whole, continuing with 'cultural wholes' within the cosmic whole, moving on to a consideration of the parts within cultural wholes, and concluding with a refocusing on cultural wholes and the cosmic whole.

A clue to this particular way of seeing is revealed by Giles Gunn in *The Culture of Criticism and the Criticism of Culture*:

We cannot understand the parts of anything without some sense of the whole to which they belong, just as we cannot comprehend the whole to which they belong until we have grasped the parts that make it up. Thus we are constantly obliged to move back and forth in our effort to understand something "between the whole conceived through the parts which actualize it and the parts conceived through the whole which motivates them" in an effort "to turn them, by a sort of intellectual perpetual motion, into explication of one another".[2]

The starting point for the holistic way of seeing is the cosmic whole. Despite the fact that the cosmic whole can never be seen, known, or understood in totality because of its vastness and infinite complexity, it provides the context or container within which everything is situated: animal, vegetable and mineral; organic and inorganic; tangible and intangible; human and non-human.

Within the cosmic whole, it is possible to identify a number of quite specific and fundamental 'cultural wholes', such as individuals, families, ethnic groups, social classes, communities, regions, countries, cultures, continents, the world, the human species, and other species. These cultural wholes are 'wholes' in the sense that they are discrete entities. These entities often exert a great deal of influence and control over their own development and evolution, even though they are strongly influenced by external factors, such as worldviews, values and the cosmic container in which they are situated. While these are not the only entities that can be treated as cultural wholes, they represent the basic building blocks of culture as a concept and as a reality because they relate so fundamentally to culture's holistic quality and capacity for holism.

Next to cultural wholes, there are the specialized parts that make up these wholes. Every species, culture, community, ethnic group, family or individual is composed of myriad, interdependent parts, which constitute the principal preoccupation of the specialized way of seeing.

Finally, there is the cosmic whole and cultural wholes again, but this time at a deeper and more profound level of analysis. This is because deeper under-standing of the parts has led to a deeper understanding of the cosmic whole and cultural wholes within the cosmic whole.

Clearly the holistic way of seeing is a dynamic rather than a static process. This is due largely to the fact that all the ingredients of which it is comprised are in a constant state of flux. They are like the shifting sands of time: every change that takes place in them, regardless of how large or small it might be, alters their composition, character and configuration. The fact that each ingredient in the holistic way of seeing is in constant flux and change means that they are all variables in a complex cultural system.[3] A change in any one of these variables can set off a chain reaction throughout the entire system.

Clearly much more needs to be known about this system and the way it functions, even if it can never be known in total terms. Much more needs to be known, for example, about how the system functions *as a system*, how its various parts are composed, and how they interact and impact on one another. In the language of systems analysis, much more needs to be known about how a change in any one of the variables affects all variables in the system, and hence the system itself. At the present time, this is most imperative in terms of the relationship between human beings, nature and other species, economics and the environment, individuals and groups, groups and communities, communities and nations, nations and continents, and the world and the universe. Nothing may be more essential to the world of the future than the need to understand, and more importantly deal with, the causes and consequences of these complex relationships.

If the holistic way of seeing provides a key to understanding culture as a system, it is essential to give consideration to the way it is most effectively cultivated. This is best achieved by examining those disciplines concerned primarily with 'the whole' and the development of the holistic perspective. For it is through these disciplines that culture's capacity for holism can be cultivated most effectively in the future.

There is much to be learned from philosophy and cosmology in this regard. As indicated earlier, philosophy and cosmology are concerned with seeing the universe and all that is contained in it as unitary and interdependent systems composed of myriad interrelated and interconnected parts.

As demonstrated earlier, anthropology has been concerned with holism and the holistic perspective ever since the writings of Edward Burnett Tylor. Since that time, anthropologists have been concerned with broadening and deepening the knowledge and understanding of culture as a whole and cultures as wholes, as well as cultivating the mode of perception which is necessary for this.

There is also much to be learned about holism and cultivation of the holistic way of seeing from the arts. Every work of art is an organic whole requiring constant awareness of the overall container within which specific parts are situated. The artist, always conscious of this, is constantly moving around a work of art—stepping back and forth and from side to side—in order to view it from a holistic perspective. Moreover, the artist knows from situating objects in their proper location and viewing them from a holistic perspective that the solution to one problem is often the cause of other problems. Thus, for example, a change in the colour of the hair may cause a change in the appearance of the face. This is because works of art are holistic entities—integrated systems in which a change in one part may necessitate changes in other parts as well as in the whole.

Although scientists have been preoccupied largely with specialization and specialized issues over much of the last two centuries, holism and the holistic mode of perception underlie every type of scientific endeavour. Biologists, botanists and ecologists, for example, treat the cosmos as a system or complex organism, just as physicists and astronomers treat the universe as a single, interconnected entity. Likewise, mathematicians have made frequent attempts throughout the history of mathematics to devise a set of simultaneous, interacting equations that explain the functioning of the universe as an integrated and interdependent whole. While these efforts and endeavours have not always been as publicized or conspicuous as they might have been, they are of vital importance to the future.

Synthesis of the scientific and artistic modes of perception could go a long way towards refining the four-step, holistic way of seeing. While the scientist's mode of perception is focused and specific, the artist's mode of perception is more all-encompassing and free-ranging. It is far from coincidental that the scientist's basic tool is the microscope, whereas the artist's basic tool is the canvas, for the scientist is a focal perceiver and the artist is a peripheral perceiver. In a work of art, the whole is seldom sacrificed to the parts. Excesses and imbalances are permitted, yes, but only in relation to the whole and seldom for their own sake.

What is slowly emerging here is a way of looking at and thinking about cultural systems and all that is contained in them as totalities. They are totalities in which there is always a dynamic interplay going on between the whole and the parts because the whole is in the parts and the parts are in the whole. Nothing is taken for granted or ignored, regardless of how small or large it might be, because one never knows how important it is in the total scheme of things or how it impacts on other elements in the system.

Culture as Context

Culture's capacity for holism and holistic perception makes culture a highly contextual discipline. It is impossible to see the world, the world system and cultural systems in holistic rather than specialized terms without seeing things in context rather than in isolation.

Humanity is paying a real price at the present time for its inability to see things *in context*. For example, failure to give sufficient consideration to the fact that nature and the natural environment provide the context within which human activity takes place is leading to destruction of the globe's natural ecosystem, depletion of the world's renewable and non-renewable resources, increased pollution, and contamination of the biosphere. Likewise, failure to give sufficient consideration to the fact that culture provides the context within which economic and technological developments take place is leading to equally disturbing results, since these developments are being achieved at great psychological, social, ethical, environmental and human cost. Not only are economic and technological developments causing a great deal of disorientation and difficulties, but also they are having a fundamental impact on social structures and moral and spiritual values.

As these examples illustrate, there is a price to be paid whenever decisions are made without sufficient consideration given to the context in which they are situated. This is having a debilitating effect on the world since priority is often given to the parts over the whole. The consequences of this are clear. The system of checks and balances needed to prevent excesses and imbalances is breaking down. Hence the need to cultivate the contextual capacity provided by culture.

It is impossible to cultivate this capacity without being aware of the trade-off effects of different courses of action. By focusing on the potential consequences of actions before decisions are taken—economic, environmental, technological, social, political, moral, and most of all human—decision-making processes could be improved. Moreover, by flagging problems before they occur, it is possible to avoid taking a 'crisis-response approach' to problem-solving. If applied on a large scale, culture's capacity for context in this sense could result in a more methodical, systematic and deliberate attack on national and international problems, as well as a more effective and efficient allocation of scarce resources.

There could be other benefits as well. Attention could be shifted from symptoms to causes. This would make it possible to deal with the root causes of problems rather than secondary issues and side effects. For what culture provides here is a contextual framework within which problems can be analyzed, evaluated, and understood. Without this, it is impossible to attach sensible weights and priorities to problems, or give sufficient consideration to the contextual consequences of actions.

Culture as Value

If culture's capacity for holism and context is essential, so is its capacity for value.[4] Alfred Kroeber and Clyde Kluckhohn asserted the crucial importance of values and value systems for culture in general and cultures in particular when they said:

Values are important in that they provide foci for patterns of organization for the materials of cultures. They give significance to our understanding of cultures. In fact, *values provide the only basis for the fully intelligible comprehension of culture, because the actual organization of all cultures is primarily in terms of their values.* This becomes apparent as soon as one attempts to present the picture of a culture without reference to its values.[5]

It is this same point that the Indian authority on culture, Prem Kirpal, had in mind when he penned the following passage:

In general, the culture of a particular society is comprised of three distinct elements: ideas, aesthetic forms and values...Of these three elements of culture, the values are of the greatest importance; values develop the precious assets of wisdom and discrimination in a specific culture; and they also provide the dynamism for action and change, and impart vitality and quality to the life of the people.[6]

While not a prerequisite to the creation of values and value systems, the process of valuation is very much enhanced when consideration is given to the context or container within which values and value systems are situated. This is because values and value systems are determined by comparing one element against another in order to determine the relative weight or comparative worth of each. When elements are ignored, overlooked or missed, valuations can still take place, but they are far less meaningful than they might otherwise be.

Like worldview and worldviews, values and value systems are of crucial importance to human survival and global well-being. It is becoming increasingly apparent that many of the world's most debilitating problems will not be dealt with effectively without the creation of values and value systems capable of redistributing wealth on a more equitable basis, preserving and protecting the natural environment, reducing the consumption of the world's renewable and non-renewable resources, and asserting the importance of 'the human factor in development'. While many may cling to the view that the ecological problems of contemporary times can be dealt with effectively by environmental clean-ups after the fact, it is clear that the real solution lies in the creation of values and value systems capable of making fewer demands on scarce environmental resources.

It goes without saying that there is an *approach* to value theory buried deep in the holistic concept of culture. This approach is consistent with the holistic mode of perception set out earlier. Generally speaking, narrower cultural considerations should always be evaluated within the context of broader cultural considerations.

This approach provides a useful *point of departure* to the problem of value creation. At the present time, for example, it is fitting that the interests of specific countries, cultures and communities should be evaluated within the broader context of the natural environment, the world and the world system, just as the interests of industry, trade, commerce and technology should be evaluated within the broader context of specific countries, cultures and communities. While many problems will obviously be encountered in the development and practical application of this approach, it does provide a way of tackling the problem of value creation which could prove helpful in coming to grips with the matrix of difficult and demanding problems comprising 'the global problematique'.

It should also prove helpful to cultures. As noted earlier, every culture is 'an ordered whole' within an ever-widening constellation of cultural wholes and the cosmic whole. In this case, the component parts of cultures are individuals, institutions, groups, communities, regions, economic systems, political structures, environmental resources, religious and educational institutions, artistic and social associations, commercial organizations, and the like. The key questions are exactly the same for cultures as they are for culture. On what basis are the component parts of cultures ordered and reordered, and who decides how they are ordered and reordered? In other words, what values and value systems prevail, and who are the actual and potential decision-makers? Answers to these questions will determine in no uncertain terms how cultures as wholes are ordered and put together, as well as who actually directs and controls them.

Considerable care should be exercised with respect to how the values and value systems of different cultures are analyzed and assessed. If the purpose is to gain knowledge, understanding, appreciation and insight into differences in values and value systems, there is no real problem. However, if the purpose is domination or judgment, there is a very real problem indeed. This is particularly true with respect to comparing the values and value systems of different cultures. Alfred Kroeber and Clyde Kluckhohn comment on the difficulties involved in this:

Comparisons of cultures must not be simplistic in terms of an arbitrary or preconceived universal value system, but must be multiple, with *each culture first understood in terms of its own particular value system and therefore its own idiosyncratic structure.* After that, comparison can with gradually increasing reliability reveal to what degree values, significances, and qualities are common to the compared cultures, and to what degree distinctive.[7]

The problem of comparing values and value systems constitutes one of the most difficult problems in the cultural field. Comparisons between cultures are often made on the basis of one or two criteria or forms of valuation, such as gross national income, income per capita, level of education, technological attainment, or extent of capital formation. This leads to numerous problems and injustices, especially where highly problematic forms of valuation and measurement are used to label some countries primitive, backward and underdeveloped while other countries are labelled advanced, developed and sophisticated. To avoid this, cultures should not be directly valued or compared in this way. Rather, they should be valued according to the aims and objectives they have set for themselves, or the contributions they have made to humanity as a whole.

It is impossible to raise the question of values and value systems without raising the related question of absolute and relative values. Are all values relative, or is there a set of absolute values to which all people and all societies should aspire? Like value comparisons, this is also one of the most difficult and complex challenges confronting culture in general and cultures in particular. To conclude that all values are relative is to open the doors to a vast panorama of possibilities, both positive and negative. On the positive side, it helps to combat centrism, or the belief in the superiority of one country's, group's or culture's values. Without this, the worst kinds of oppression, suppression and coercion are possible. On the negative side, however, it opens the doors to real abuses of power, since virtually anything a leader, group, country or culture does can be justified in terms of the legitimacy of relative values and value systems.

While the right of individuals, groups, societies, countries and cultures to define their own values and value systems must be upheld, the abuse of values and value systems under the guise that 'all values are relative values' must be condemned whenever and wherever it is encountered. One of the best ways to do this is to identify an absolute set of values to which individuals, groups, societies, countries and cultures should aspire, such as the quest for equality and creativity, the pursuit of justice and truth, the love of beauty, the sanctity of life, the legitimacy of freedom, respect for the rights and needs of others, and the need for peace. These values are worth striving for, even if they are seldom achievable in fact and there are markedly different views and opinions about what they mean, for in the process of striving to achieve them, individuals, social groups, countries and cultures may be compelled to live life on a higher plane of existence.

Culture as Identity

It is difficult to travel down the road of culture very far without encountering the problem of identity. For identity is essential to human existence and survival: people simply cannot live without it, either as individuals, groups, communities, regions or nations. As such, it is deeply ingrained in the human psyche and cultural condition.

There can be no identity without similarities, since, in part, identity is achieved through recognition of the common bonds and shared experiences that bind people together. Likewise, there can be no identity without differences, for too much sameness can obliterate identity by destroying its unique nature and distinctive character. Thus, identity is achieved—and maintained—by walking the tightrope between similarities and differences.

It is a balancing act that is fraught with difficulties. A slip in the direction of too much sameness can cause people to rebel, if only to protect themselves from the numbing effects of standardization, homogenization and uniformity. A slip in the direction of too many differences can be equally disastrous, since people mistrust and fear what they are unable to understand. This makes finding the right mixture of sameness and distinctiveness, or unity in diversity, one of the greatest challenges of all.

Few problems are more difficult than the problem of identity. There are a number of reasons for this, but three in particular predominate. First, many peoples and cultures are losing their identity, due to the erosion of their values and traditions, and breakdowns in their social structures and political systems. Second, contemporary developments in technology and the mass media, particularly developments in television, radio, film, video and computers, are having a homogenizing influence on cultures and peoples everywhere in the world. Finally, globalization, the emergence of larger trading blocks, the creation of powerful 'superstates', and increased concentration of power in fewer and fewer hands is resulting in a loss of identity for more and more people, not to mention a growing sense of powerlessness and alienation.

Demands for sovereignty, autonomy and independence, as well as ghettoism, ethnocentrism and racism, are the consequences of this. The more power becomes centralized, concentrated and global, the more people rebel and demand control over the decision-making processes affecting their lives[8]—in other words, the more they clamour for identity and the right to assert it in the social and cultural settings they find themselves in.

Culture as Conflict

It is the assertion of identity in general and 'cultural identities' in particular which constitutes one of the world's most formidable problems, for as much as identity and the assertion of cultural identities are a necessary part of living and the expression of beliefs, convictions, attitudes, rights and responsibilities, they can degenerate into conflicts and confrontations very quickly. In today's world, this is probably more true within countries than it is between countries, as recent experiences in the former U.S.S.R., the former Yugoslavia, Central Africa, Sri Lanka and many other parts of the world demonstrate. Indeed, it is difficult to think of a country anywhere in the world that has not had its own painful encounter with the assertion of identity and cultural identities in one form or another. While this can often lead to positive results in the long-run, resulting in new forms, new structures and new ways of doing things, it is usually an exceedingly bitter experience and painful process in the short-run.

It is difficult to know how to resolve this problem. While broadening and deepening our knowledge and understanding of culture, cultures, and especially the reasons for cultural differences helps, it is no guarantee that viable and lasting solutions to this problem can be found. Indeed, what is needed in these circumstances is nothing short of a major transformation in the way people and groups relate to one another, and therefore in cross-cultural dialogue, communication, exchange and fertilization. Not only should there be many more opportunities for ethnic and racial groups to come together and interact, but also there should be phenomenal developments in the field of cultural integration, for cultural integration is closely linked to identity and the assertion of cultural identities. Whereas identity and the assertion of cultural identities is concerned with the sense of belonging and togetherness that particular groups and minorities have in common, cultural integration is concerned with the cohesion and bonding necessary across ethnic groups and racial minorities. The arts, artists, artistic and social organizations and the mass media have a particularly important role to play here in terms of creating the signs, symbols and images necessary to bring ethnic groups and racial minorities together when other forces are operating to split them apart.

Countries characterized by disintegration rather than integration are unlikely to overcome the forces which fragment them. If these forces are allowed to fester too long, they can degenerate into disillusionment and despair, thereby increasing the risk of ruptures, conflicts and confrontations between different groups of people as well as society as a whole.

There are a number of ways in which cultural integration can be achieved. One is to ensure that all citizens and groups share enough signs, symbols, beliefs and values in common to bind them together in a cohesive sense. Another is to provide citizens and groups with opportunities for 'collective experiences'—experiences that give them a sense of common purpose and participation in a worthwhile cause. Still another is to create the public institutions, programmes and policies that give people a feeling that they can preserve personal values and individual and group identities while at the same time participating in the larger task of community development and nation-building. A final way, and perhaps the most effective way of all, is to ensure that people are able to participate fully in the creation of a shared culture—a culture experienced, enjoyed and created by all groups and all people.

Culture as Criticism

If problems as difficult and demanding as the problem of identity and the assertion of cultural identities are to be dealt with effectively, it will not only be necessary to cultivate culture's capacity for integration. It will also be necessary to cultivate its capacity for criticism. For criticism, like integration, depends on people's ability to scrutinize themselves and their actions carefully and evaluate their behaviour and practices with an objective and critical eye. Ruth Benedict explains why the capacity for criticism is so essential, but also so difficult to achieve:

There is, however, one difficult exercise to which we may accustom ourselves as we become increasingly culture-conscious. We may train ourselves to pass judgment on the dominant traits of our own civilization. It is difficult enough for anyone brought up under their power to recognize them…They are as familiar as an old loved homestead. Any world in which they do not appear seems to us cheerless and untenable. Yet it is these very traits which by the operation of a fundamental cultural process are most often carried to extremes.[9]

It should be clear that the term 'criticism' is not being used in this context as a synonym for complaining or fault-finding: tearing something down without offering something constructive in return. Rather it is being used in the sense of 'critical evaluation', or assessing something as objectively and impartially as possible in order to improve, enhance or curtail it. Needless to say, this requires the ability to stand on the perimeter of situations, issues or problems in order to evaluate them with a detached and dispassionate eye, much as the anthropologist does when assessing the strengths and shortcomings of cultures and civilizations.

This capacity for critical evaluation should be developed to the point where it provides a running commentary on human actions in general and the economic, social, spiritual, environmental and human consequences and implications of actions in particular. In the final analysis, it is only in this way that human beings will develop the critical faculties needed to detect flaws, fallacies and deficiencies in their cultural behaviour, practices and ways of life.

In the development of these faculties, particular attention should be paid to the way in which cultural behaviour and ways of life are transmitted and reinforced. As scholars like Edward Hall have consistently pointed out, cultural behaviour and ways of life can be transmitted and reinforced through verbal and non-verbal communication.[10] As important a device as verbal communication is for transmitting and affirming cultural behaviour and ways of life, non-verbal communication—body language, intuition, empathy and psychic communion and the like—may constitute even more compelling and forceful devices for cultural transmission, dissemination and affirmation. In most cultures, for example, identity is more often felt than said, sensed than seen. In such cases, it may be exceedingly difficult to bring about cultural change because this is the way things have always been and there is little or no impetus to change them, even if they are inappropriate or undesirable:

A value system serves to fuse individuals into a socially cohesive whole, which then survives and evolves as a unit. Once such a social system develops, it tends to be conserved, changing only gradually over time. Its values are maintained by customs, rituals and beliefs, that both guide the individual and give meaning to her or his life…Most members of a society accept its norms, its rules and regulations, not because they are coerced but because 'that is how things *ought* to be'.[11]

It is probably for reasons such as these that humanity has found it difficult to develop the critical faculties needed for the present and the future. Inability to examine critically the environmental consequences of certain lifestyles and behavioural practices, for example, combined with inability to analyze dispassionately the limitations of economic and technological systems and ideologies, has produced intolerable levels of environmental pollution, resource consumption, aesthetic degeneration and human exploitation. Unfortunately the existing system has a way of forcing everyone to become so caught up in the process of coping with the system that little time or energy is left over to examine the system with a critical eye. Even institutions whose historical role it has been to evaluate society's actions with a critical and impartial eye, such as universities and institutions of higher learning, are having a difficult time with this. Thus the burden of critical evaluation falls on people who have the determination and courage to speak out against the major shortcomings and injustices of modern times.

This is why culture's capacity for criticism is so essential. By prompting humanity to become aware of the consequences of its actions before they happen, as well as instilling in people a willingness to examine generic causes rather than secondary symptoms, it forces humanity to make adjustments in its behavioural characteristics and practices before they prove too injurious to the world, the environment and society as a whole.

It is here that the difference between culture as an ideal and culture as a reality shows up most clearly. As an ideal, culture is concerned with developing the critical faculties necessary to correct deficiencies and short-comings in specific cultural practices and characteristics. If specific cultural practices and characteristics are not in the best interests of humanity, the environment or the world as a whole, they should be challenged and changed regardless of how this affects particular interests. In culture as a reality, however, cultural practices and characteristics that are not in the best interests of humanity, the environment and the world as a whole are often condoned. This is frequently due to the fact that they are so deeply ingrained in a culture that they are taken for granted and go unchallenged.

Acute threats to human life and global survival should cause humanity to cultivate culture's capacity for criticism and critical evaluation to the utmost. It is clear where the main problem lies in this regard. It lies in the relentless expansion of human numbers compared to the availability of renewable and non-renewable resources and the carrying capacity of the earth. This problem was pinpointed very precisely two centuries ago by Thomas Robert Malthus when he drew attention to the devastating consequences of overpopulation in terms of poverty, famine, pestilence, war and premature deaths,[12] as these are the only ways, other than through preventive checks such as birth control and abstinence, in which excessive numbers can be brought into line with environmental realities. Consciousness of this fact should cause humanity to cultivate the capacity for critical evaluation to the fullest extent. Failure to do so could have a debilitating effect on the world, the world system and humankind in the future.

Culture as Vision

If culture's capacity for criticism is essential, so is culture's capacity for vision, which depends partly on the capacity to critique people's and society's behaviour in order to determine where it is going off the rails. In large measure, however, it depends on the capacity to ascertain what is needed to set things right. In other words, it depends on the ability to cast an objective and discerning eye over the human condition in order to determine more appropriate and compelling directions for the future.

In the final analysis, people find it difficult to alter their cultural behaviour for two reasons. First, they find it difficult because there is little or no desire to interfere with the established way of doing things. Second, they find it difficult because there is no compelling vision on which to predicate behaviour in the future. Where there is no vision to lift people to higher heights, societies quickly atrophy and sink into oblivion. The old adage, 'without a vision, the people perish', may be a cliché, but it has been a fundamental realization since biblical times.

It is vision that determines the lifeline and longevity of cultures. For just as a culture's identity is determined by walking the tightrope between uniformity and diversity, similarity and difference, so a culture's lifeline and longevity is determined by walking the fine line between tradition and modernity, permanence and change. Cultures too wedded to tradition and permanence often find that the world has passed them by, largely because they have been unable to create new and exciting images of the future. Cultures too obsessed with modernity and change often experience difficulties because their image of the future is too disconnected from historical roots and traditions. Thus, how cultures visualize their future, particularly in relation to the present and the past, is instrumental in determining life expectancy and their overall survival in the world.

Viewed from this perspective, the important questions confronting cultures are not when they came into existence, how they arrived at the present point, or what their major shortcomings and deficiencies are, but rather whether they can create dynamic and enticing visions around which to orchestrate behaviour and instigate action in the future. This requires the participation of countless individuals and institutions, as well as a great deal of creative thinking about new directions in economics, technology, the arts, sciences, religion, the environment and human affairs generally.

It is visionary thinking, particularly when it is achieved on a societal scale, that yields the worldviews, values, value systems, concepts, ideas and behavioural patterns needed to cross over the threshold to a more exhilarating future. This ray of hope and spur to action should come from culture's quest to improve life for every member of the human family. It is a quest that is concerned not only with what culture is, but more importantly, what culture can become when it is developed to its fullest extent. It is an eternal quest, one which represents humanity's ceaseless efforts down through the ages to reach above and beyond itself in the search for the sublime.

Despite the fact that this quest has seldom if ever been achieved, it is a quest worth persevering with none the less. Many societies, cultures and civilizations have distinguished themselves in their attempt to realize culture's highest ideals, including those of the Greeks, Romans, Chinese, Indians, Incas, Mayas and Elizabethans.[13] While these societies, cultures and civilizations have all possessed numerous shortcomings and deficiencies, they have also incorporated many of culture's highest, wisest and noblest qualities, including the striving for excellence and perfection, the love of beauty, the commitment to creativity, the need for order, and the pursuit of truth. In other words, they have opened up a commanding place for culture's highest, wisest and noblest values in general, and the arts, the humanities, sciences, education and learning in particular, at the very core of their cultural life. Values and activities such as these, especially when judiciously blended in their proper proportions and skilfully incorporated into a compelling and coherent whole, make it possible to raise culture's capacity for vision to the level of an art.

Culture as Creativity

Without doubt, creativity is humanity's most valuable asset. Time and again, it has rescued humanity from disasters and provided people with the means to deal with the most complex challenges and difficult circumstances imaginable. Creativity, therefore, will bring forth the new theoretical ideas and ideals and practical tools and techniques needed to deal with the problems and possibilities that combine to comprise the global situation. Humanity will have to draw on culture's capacity for creativity to the utmost extent if this situation is to be dealt with effectively in the future.

In effect, there are two types of creativity. First, there is the creativity that reinforces a culture. Second, there is the creativity that redirects a culture. The first type of creativity occurs when people are largely satisfied with the worldviews, values and norms of their culture, and are content to make contributions that embellish and fortify these worldviews, values and norms. While these creative contributions may go unheralded because they do not have an abrasive or disruptive quality, it is essential to emphasize that they are creative none the less. The second type of creativity results when people are dissatisfied with the worldviews, values and norms of their culture and feel compelled to express themselves in ways that redirect their culture along a different path. Destruction often precedes construction in this case; old structures must be torn down before new ones can be created. This is what makes this particular type of creativity so threatening when it is occurring, but often so exhilarating after it has run its course.

The highly provocative and iconoclastic nature of this second type of creativity explains why it has dominated human consciousness. This has resulted in two very specific developments. First, creativity is often seen as the preserve of a small and select group of people, most notably artists, scientists and scholars. Second, creativity is usually viewed in absolute rather than relative terms.

Fortunately, the walls which have been built up around these two notions of creativity are breaking down. The more creativity is analyzed and understood, the more it is realized that each and every individual is creative to a degree. And the more the works of artists, scientists and scholars are studied, the more it is realized that a great deal of the form, content and inspiration for their creativity derives from the creativity of the common man. One only has to study the writings of Gandhi and Shakespeare, the paintings of Van Gogh and Gauguin, the poetry of Tagore and Senghor, or the music of Brahms, Beethoven and Villa Lobos to realize this. When George Gershwin said that there would be no classical music without popular music, he was merely using a specific example to express a profound general truth. For the truth of the matter is that an intimate bond exists between all the different types of creativity, reinforcing and redirective, which comprise culture.

It follows from this that the time has come to adopt a much broader understanding of creativity that casts its net so widely that it incorporates the creativity of many different types of individuals and institutions, as well as all sectors of society. Such a theory must be classless, boundless and timeless, as capable of doing justice to the creative contributions of citizens in general as it does to the diverse segments of society in particular.

A 'cultural theory of creativity' possesses this breadth, depth and complexity. On the one hand, it recognizes the fact that all individuals and institutions are creative to a degree, and therefore make legitimate and valuable contributions to societal progress. In so doing, it erases the traditional view that only a very small and privileged group of individuals and institutions is creative. On the other hand, it recognizes that there are varying degrees of creativity. In so doing, it preserves the integrity of creativity and prevents it from being dragged down to its lowest common denominator and denuded of all its importance.

Such a theory of creativity extends the scope and orbit of creativity well beyond the arts, sciences and humanities to encompass economics, politics, technology, social affairs, business, and every other field of endeavour. Moreover, it broadens the base of creativity beyond artists, scientists and scholars to include farmers, fishermen, businessmen, labourers, housewives, and every other type of individual and profession. As a result, it compels humanity to recognize that the billions of people who inhabit the earth represent a valuable resource to be tapped rather than a curse to be endured.

This creative mine exists everywhere. It is practical as well as theoretical, commonplace as well as esoteric, African, Asian and Latin American as well as North American and European. How familiar are people with the rich mine of creativity that exists in their own society, let alone with the creativity of other societies? At the same time that steps should be taken to ensure that people become much more conversant with the creative contributions of their own society, steps should also be taken to ensure that they become more conversant with the creative achievements of other societies. Familiarity with these achievements should open a vast panorama of possibilities, including new ways of thinking, modes of life, multicultural activities and celebrations, religious and artistic practices, economic and scientific possibilities, customs and values, and perceptions of time, space and the universe.

The mass media and modern instruments of communications—satellites, computers, videos, tapes, films, books, slides, television programs, internets, electronic highways and the like—have a particularly important role to play here. With innovative planning and a willingness to share, an international communications system could be fashioned capable of acquainting people in all parts of the world with the creative achievements and historical and contemporary accomplishments of all countries and all cultures. Every country in the world possesses a rich cornucopia of creative achievements in this sense: inventions, artifacts, ideas, sacred shrines, tribal relics, rare stories, myths, legends, songs, dances and expertise. This innovative outpouring constitutes the very essence of cultural life—the pinnacle of human accomplishment down through the ages. Not only should it be protected from the ravages of time, but also it should be made accessible to all citizens and all generations. Due to phenomenal advances in contemporary technology and communications, the *means* exist for the first time in history to expose people in all parts of the world to the finest and noblest the world has to offer. What is needed now, and needed more than ever, is the *will* to create the global networks and universal bridges which are essential in order to link the whole of humanity together in this fundamental sense. It is here that culture's capacity for creativity joins forces with its capacity for vision. Whereas the latter is concerned with the visualization of a shared fund of universal achievements, the former is concerned with the practical wherewithal to make this a reality.

Culture as Power

Of all the capabilities culture possesses, none is more awesome or dangerous than the capacity for power. It is neglected to humanity's peril.

In an historical sense, culture's power is recognized in cultural transformations like the Renaissance, the Reformation, the Enlightenment and Romanticism. In the modern world, however, it is more difficult to detect. Nevertheless, one only need think of the 'cultural revolutions' that have taken place in the twentieth century to recognize the awesome power culture possesses to bring about unprecedented change.

It is clear that culture possesses the potential for infinite good and infinite evil in this sense. The very force that has brought so much goodness to the world is equally capable of bringing about a great deal of violence, suffering, brutality and oppression.

It all depends on how cultural power is used. If it is used in positive, constructive and imaginative ways, it can be a source of considerable joy and fulfillment, since, in one form or another, it is responsible for much of what is most valuable in life and the world. However, if it is used in negative, destructive and counter-productive ways, it can be a source of considerable injustice, since, in one form or another, it is responsible for vengeance, exploitation and inequality.

History is replete with examples of this. Numerous tyrants, dictators and military leaders have been able to impose their wills on people and subject them to the most brutal and appalling atrocities imaginable, largely because they have learned how to manipulate culture in general and worldviews, values and value systems in particular, and deflect them to their own devious ends. In some cases, this is achieved through military force, as is the case when military rule is imposed on a country by brute force, or one country marches into another country and takes it through sheer aggression. In other cases, it is achieved in more seductive and subtle ways, such as when the worldviews, values, value systems, lifestyles and cultural practices of one group or one country are imposed on other groups and countries. The exercise of cultural power in these cases is often far less overt and conspicuous. Nevertheless, its consequences can be equally as deplorable, especially if they result in enslavement of one segment of society by another or one country by another.

Given the actual and potential uses and abuses of cultural power, it is imperative to establish numerous safeguards, countervailing measures and protective devices to ensure that cultural power is used in positive and constructive rather than negative and destructive ways. Included among these safeguards, measures and devices, in addition to others, are the democratization of cultural institutions, the decentralization of cultural resources and opportunities, the establishment of cultural agencies at arm's length from government and the political process, and commitment to democratic ideals and freedom of expression. Without such precautions, there is a need to remain ever watchful and mindful of the exercise of cultural power.

The Challenge of the Future

Recognition of the actual and potential uses and abuses of cultural power is helpful in coming to grips with the central challenge of the future. For when it is viewed from a *cultural perspective*, the challenge of the future is to make culture and cultures the centrepiece of the world system of the future, but do so in such a way that the world system is designed and developed in accordance with culture's highest, wisest and most enduring values rather than basest and crudest practices. For this is the only way it will be possible to ensure that culture and cultures are used in benevolent and constructive rather than malevolent and destructive ways.

This will be no easy matter. It will require a great deal of energy and effort on the part of individuals, institutions, groups and countries in all parts of the world. Domestically, it will be necessary to ensure that too much power is not concentrated in too few hands. Internationally, it will be necessary to ensure that communities, groups, regions, countries and continents maintain sovereignty, control and independence over their own affairs.

As illustrated earlier, many of culture's highest, wisest and noblest values are buried deep in the philosophical, artistic, educational, historical and psychological concepts of culture. Pressing these values to the forefront of human consciousness and global development at this time could prove valuable. As Herman Hesse observed:

World history is a race with time, a scramble for profits, for power, for treasures. What counts is who has the strength, luck or vulgarity not to miss the opportunity. The achievements of thought, of culture, of art are just the opposite. They are always an escape from the serfdom of time, man crawling out of the muck of his instincts and out of his sluggishness and climbing to a higher plane, to timelessness, liberation from time, divinity.[14]

This climb is impossible without becoming much more immersed in culture and cultures in general and the arts, sciences, humanities, education, ethics and spirituality in particular. These are the activities that help to expand consciousness of the internal world of the heart, the soul, the mind and the spirit, as well as the external world of reality. They also lift people to higher levels of creativity and accomplishment. In so doing, they represent much of what is worthwhile in life. It is to the arts, sciences, humanities, ethics, education, spirituality and the like, therefore, that humanity should look for the clues necessary to realize culture's noblest and most enduring ideals. For as Takdir Alisjahbana, the distinguished Indonesian cultural scholar, said, 'culture in the last analysis represents the human aspiration to realize the highest form of life'.[15]

4. Culture as a Reality

In a world of exceedingly rapid social change, whether driven by development or not, questions of the preservation, regeneration and adaptability of cultures assume great urgency. When, for example, does adaptation lead to loss of identity, or preservation to stagnation? It is necessary to begin the attempt to answer these sorts of questions with a recognition of the complexity of human cultures.[1]

Soedjatmoko

The concern thus far has been with culture as a concept. Viewed in holistic terms, culture as a concept is concerned with the way human beings visualize and interpret the world and act in the world, and therefore with matters of great importance to humanity.

Now the time has come to examine culture as a reality. This is achieved by analyzing the way in which culture manifests itself most readily in the world, namely through the creation and development of cultures. Hence the object of this chapter. It is designed to broaden and deepen understanding of cultures as complex entities or organic wholes. This will make it possible in subsequent chapters to deal with such issues as a cultural interpretation of history, the role of culture in the life of the individual, the community, the state and the world, and the art of cultural development and policy.

The Nature of Cultures

Few subjects require more attention at the present time than the subject of cultures. This is not only because cultures differ so much from each other and one part of the world and another. It is also because the world is characterized more and more by interactions between cultures. Without a vastly improved understanding of cultures, the prospects for improved cultural understanding and interaction are bleak indeed.

Clearly cultures differ very much from each other and one part of the world and another because people in different cultures and parts of the world see the world differently and act in the world differently. These differences may be large, small, subtle or distinct depending on a variety of factors, including origins, needs, environmental conditions, geographical location, historical development, customs, traditions, and relations with other cultures. For example, the differences between Chinese, Indian and American cultures are very pronounced, and are generally perceived and accepted as such by people living inside and outside these cultures. In contrast, the differences between Canadian and American culture—to cite one example from many— may be much less pronounced and visible to the naked eye. Indeed, they may only be apparent to people living in these cultures, and even then they may be difficult to detect.

Regardless of whether the differences between cultures are large or small, subtle or distinct, there is no doubt that religion and religious outlooks and beliefs play a key role in shaping cultures.[2] This is true everywhere in the world, and has been particularly true during the formative stages of the development of most cultures. Takdir Alisjahbana makes this point in talking about the role that religion and religious outlooks and beliefs played in the formative stages of the Indonesian culture:

Like other early traditional cultures in history, the Indonesian people, prior to the arrival of Indian culture, had evolved a style of thinking at once complex, all-inclusive, and highly intuitive. This style of thought was closely bound up with the enormously important position of religion in the cultural life of Indonesian society. A belief in spirits and supernatural powers pervaded all aspects of individual and communal life.[3]

While the diverse religions of the world have played an exceedingly important role in making and shaping cultures, it should not be assumed that this is merely a traditional role. It is also a very contemporary role. Despite the schism which has occurred between the secular and sacred in many parts of the world, religions like Christianity, Hinduism, Islam, Buddhism, Judaism, Confucianism, Taoism, Shintoism and others exert an extremely powerful influence on cultures.[4] This influence may increase in the future whenever and wherever there is a revival of interest in religious fundamentalism.

If religion has played and continues to play a powerful role in making and shaping cultures, so do philosophy, cosmology and mythology. As indicated earlier, not only are these factors located at the roots of cultures, but also one does not have to travel back far along the continuum of time to realize that they are basic elements in the compendium of ideas, convictions, beliefs, values and worldviews which comprise all cultures.

While these factors play a crucial role in making and shaping cultures, specific mention should be made of the role that myth and mythology play in this process. Joseph Campbell expanded human awareness of the incredible power of myth and mythology in this regard.[5] The problem is that mythology and myth, like other cosmological, theological and philosophical factors, are often so commonplace that they are taken for granted and ignored. Ronald Wright explains why this is so:

Most history, when it has been digested by a people, becomes myth. Myth is an arrangement of the past, whether real or imagined, in patterns that resonate with a culture's deepest values and aspirations. Myths create and reinforce archetypes so taken for granted, so seemingly axiomatic, that they go unchallenged. Myths are so fraught with meaning that we live and die by them. They are the maps by which cultures navigate through time.[6]

For cultural scholars like Alisjahbana, it is impossible to overstate the importance of the natural environment, nature and landscape in the creation and development of cultures. For the size, variety, flora and fauna, and distinctive features of nature, the natural environment and landscape have a profound bearing on how people visualize and interpret the world and act in the world:

The landscape which enters consciousness through the senses evokes a precept of the landscape. The human mind sees the landscape as an organized, meaningful configuration...We can also say that the landscape evokes in the bearers of culture a certain basic attitude, which gives to their behaviour a constant tendency characteristic of the value system of the culture.[7]

Obviously cultures close to the Arctic and Antarctic have a very different quality and feel about them than cultures located at or near the Equator. Moreover, where a culture is situated in terms of physical proximity to oceans, lakes, rivers, mountains and natural resources is of principal importance in determining the specific details and characteristics of the culture and all aspects of cultural life. There is a vast difference, for example, between land-locked cultures like the Swiss or Paraguayan cultures and water-dominated cultures like the British, Indonesian or Japanese cultures. Furthermore, where cultures are located in relation to other cultures—what is often called their geopolitical position—is also exceedingly important in determining the specific nature of cultures and their outlook on the world. Cultures close to a superpower will have a different character and outlook on the world than cultures surrounded by secondary or tertiary powers.

Like geographical location and geopolitical circumstances, physical terrain plays an important role in determining the specific nature of cultures. There is hardly a single aspect of a culture's cultural life which is not deeply affected by it, including economic and educational systems, political processes, social conventions, communications activities, art forms, ecological relationships, and spiritual values.

In one form or another, every culture must come to grips with its specific physiology and work out a suitable accommodation with it. In some cases, this accommodation will be very difficult and demanding. Where land is parched and water is scarce, the development of cultures is an extremely painful and protracted process, much as it is for many African cultures. In other cases, such as where cultures enjoy a surfeit of arable land and fresh water, the development of cultures is a far less demanding and difficult affair. In all cases, however, people are compelled to work out a symbiotic relationship with their physical terrain. Where this relationship is based on sensitivity and respect, the outcome is likely to be positive and harmonious. Where it is based on insensitivity and disrespect, the result is likely to be negative and unsatisfactory, for nature has an uncanny way of striking back when it is abused or exploited.

In the modern world, with its complex communications mechanisms and production and distribution machinery, interactions with other cultures may play as important a role in shaping cultures as cosmological, metaphysical, mythological, religious, geographical and physiological factors.

Interactions with other cultures can occur in a number of ways, and be peaceful or violent. On the one hand, they can occur when some cultures impose their wills on other cultures. As history reveals, these impositions usually only last as long as the dominant cultures maintain their power and control over subservient and oppressed cultures. On the other hand, they can occur when cultures willingly accept the worldviews, values and ideologies of other cultures. This happens most readily when worldviews, values and ideologies of other cultures are seen to be preferable or desirable, usually because they hold out a ray of hope for a better way of life in the future.

Interactions between cultures are intensifying rapidly in the modern world. They are also taking on new directions and meanings. There are numerous causes of this. As the world shrinks in psychic terms and takes on more and more of the characteristics of a 'global village'—to use McLuhan's evocative phrase—communications devices like television, film, radio, video and the computer play an increasingly important role in molding cultures and heightening the potential for cultural borrowing and imitation. Clearly these modern counterparts to the book, the picture, and the photograph are having a profound impact on cultures and the international transmission of worldviews, values and lifestyles everywhere in the world.

Contemporary modes of communication are not the only devices for moving worldviews, values and lifestyles from one part of the world to another. The actions of multinational corporations, financial interests and élites who have been educated in one part of the world but are now living in another part of the world are also having a crucial effect.

While cultures are being altered by contemporary developments in all these areas, it would be a mistake to underestimate the influence that history and tradition play in all this, for history and tradition provide the reference points that people need to maintain their sense of identity and integrity. Not only do they provide people with the collective memory which is indispensable as cultures evolve in space and time, but also they provide the continuity that is necessary to create a continuous link between the past, the present and the future.

Ultimately cultures are affected by all the forces and factors that go into their make-up and composition. It is this fact which makes cultures highly complex and unique. The breakthrough in exposing the complexity and uniqueness of cultures came when anthropologists and sociologists began studying cultures on the ground. Suddenly what appeared to be simple or similar when viewed from afar became complex and distinct when examined up close. Not only did anthropologists and sociologists discover fundamental differences between cultures in terms of their cosmologies, worldviews, values and value systems, but also they discovered basic differences in their beliefs, rituals, kinship relations, forms of economic, social and political organization, and modes of communication.

These differences exist in all parts of the world and persist to this day. For example, examine the way in which any African, Asian, Latin American, North American or European culture is composed and it is instantly apparent that there are numerous differences in the way people visualize and interpret the world, organize themselves, conduct their affairs, elevate and embellish life, and position themselves in the world.

When people talk about cultures being distinctive and unique because they are based on different ways of visualizing and interpreting the world and acting in the world, they are talking about cultures as wholes. Jan Christiaan Smuts, one of the world's foremost proponents of holism, had this to say about the nature and evolution of wholes, and hence about the nature and evolution of cultures:

Wholes are therefore composites which have an internal structure, function or character which clearly differentiates them from mere mechanical additions and constructions...

It is very important to recognise that the whole is not something additional to the parts: it *is* the parts in a definite structural arrangement and with mutual activities that constitute the whole.[8]

It is this 'definite structural arrangement' which makes cultures as wholes greater than their parts. For while the whole is in the parts and the parts are in the whole, it is the fact that the parts have been brought together in very specific combinations and arrangements that means that something has been created which is not in the parts.

Perhaps the best way to illustrate this is to use the example of the jigsaw puzzle. Every piece in a jigsaw puzzle is a piece in its own right, possessing its own specific characteristics and unique design. However, it is only when the pieces are brought together in a very specific and meaningful arrangement that it is possible to form the picture of the jigsaw puzzle as a whole. As it is for jigsaw puzzles, so it is for cultures. Cultures are wholes which are composed of countless economic, social, political, artistic, scientific, technological and religious parts. It is only when these parts are brought together in a meaningful relationship that cultures as wholes are created. This fact makes it essential to focus on cultures as wholes, as well as the codes or recipes that

have been used to create these wholes. Edward Hall, author of numerous publications on culture and cultures, talks about the difficulty of describing and
understanding cultures as wholes, particularly if one is unfamiliar with the
code or recipe that has been used to construct them or one is looking at them
from the outside:

Because cultures are wholes, are systematic (composed of interrelated systems in
which each aspect is functionally interrelated with all other parts), and are highly
contexted as well, it is hard to describe them from the outside. A given culture cannot
be understood simply in terms of content or parts. One has to know how the whole
system is put together, how the major systems and dynamisms function, and how they
are interrelated.[9]

This emphasis on how cultures as wholes are structured and put together
is of crucial importance. While a great deal is known about the component
parts of cultures, largely because of the specialized age of the present, unfortunately far less is known about how the component parts of cultures are
combined together and impact on one another. For example, inability to
understand the connections and relationships that exist between the economy
and the environment, ethnic and racial groups, materialism and ethics,
human beings and other species—to cite only a few of the most obvious
examples—is having a profound effect on cultures and people everywhere in
the world. This makes understanding the codes or recipes used in composing
cultures as dynamic and organic wholes a basic prerequisite for the future.

It is impossible to achieve this without asking what it is that keeps cultures
together. This question of 'integration' preoccupied Pitirim Sorokin and
eventually gave rise to his theory of different types of cultures—sensate,
idealistic, ideational and mixed.[10] Sorokin poses the question of integration in
no uncertain terms:

Is every culture an integrated whole, where no essential part is incidental but each is
organically connected with the rest? Or is it a mere spatial congeries of cultural
objects, values, traits, which have drifted fortuitously together and are united only by
their spatial adjacency, just by the fact that they are thrown together, and by nothing
more?[11]

What makes cultures dynamic and organic wholes rather than collections
of disintegrated or disordered parts is the fact that every culture possesses a
cohesive property making it possible to bind all the diverse elements of the
culture together. This property—which is being taxed to the limit today in
many cultures—has been variously described as a central organizing
principle, unifying theme or dominant technology.

James Feibleman calls it the 'dominant ontology' of a culture. It is the
bundle of beliefs and principles needed to bind the component parts of a
culture together and give them cohesion in space and time. More often than
not, this dominant ontology, like the cosmological, mythological, philosoph-

ical and theological factors that underline and shape it, is implicit rather than explicit. It becomes so ingrained in a culture that it is taken for granted and passed from one generation to another without reservation or qualification:

The implicit dominant ontology, then, is the subconsciously accepted belief of the majority of the members of a social group respecting the ultimate nature of reality. It is their philosophy, more particularly their ontology, of which they are only partly conscious, if at all. They betray it rather than assert it, and follow it in their actions most often when they least know that they do so.[12]

This implicit dominant ontology is often deemed to constitute 'the ethos', 'spirit' or 'soul' of a culture. Thus, in much the same way that individuals are assumed to have souls, so cultures are assumed to have souls. And just as the soul of an individual is deemed to be that mysterious something that constitutes the essence of the individual, so the soul of cultures is deemed to be that mysterious something that constitutes the essence of cultures. In effect, it is the central organizing principle or unifying theme around which everything else is galvanized and coalesced. It is like a huge magnet that draws everything to it. When it is said that 'the centre cannot hold', it usually means that the soul of cultures cannot prevent the parts from flying off in all directions.

For Oswald Spengler, there are two basic types of cultural souls: the Apollonian soul; and the Faustian soul.[13] Whereas the Apollonian soul manifests itself in the need for order and harmony, the Faustian soul manifests itself in the need for conflict, struggle, and the search for the infinite or the sublime. The concern of the former is largely with balance, stability and synthesis, or occupying the middle ground in such a way that all things remain in a state of equilibrium or rest. The concern of the latter is primarily with polarities and opposites, or reverberations between extremes in order to achieve higher and higher levels of achievement. Whether cultures possess an Appollonian soul, a Faustian soul or any other kind of soul, there can be little doubt that integration around a soul, spirit, ethos or theme is essential for survival in a dynamic and rapidly-changing world. For integration provides the cohesion, coherence, solidarity and continuity needed to bind cultures together when other forces are operating to split them apart.

Whereas scholars like Feibleman and Spengler view the cohesive substance that binds cultures together as a central organizing principle, a dominant ontology, a spirit or a soul, Harold Innis regards it as a dominant technology.[14] In his Introduction to a book by Innis, Marshall McLuhan comments on Innis' belief that it is the particular mode of communications technology, such as paper, print, radio or television, that provides this cohesive property:

Once Innis had ascertained the dominant technology of a culture he could be sure that this was the cause and shaping force of the entire structure...At a stroke he had solved two major problems that are forever beyond the powers of the "nose-counters" and of statistical researchers. First, he knew what the pattern of any culture had to be, both psychically and socially, as soon as he had identified its major technological achievements. Second, he knew exactly what the members of that culture would be ignorant of in their daily lives. What has been called "the nemesis of creativity" is precisely a blindness to the effects of one's most significant form of invention.[15]

This equating of the cohesive substance that binds cultures together with the dominant technology or form of communication is extremely germane to the contemporary world, for it focuses attention on the powerful role that technology and modes of communication play in determining the structure and substance of cultures. It is a role that can be expected to increase and intensify in the future as the modern means of communication proliferate in number and become more pervasive in character.

Knowledge of Cultures

No sooner are cultures defined as dynamic, organic, and as wholes than a profound problem arises. How is it possible to 'know cultures' as wholes when they are composed of so many different elements and ingredients and are so vast and complex?

There are four major dimensions to this problem which must be addressed. First, it is impossible for people to know *all* of the elements and ingredients which go into making up cultures because there are far too many of them. Second, not all elements and ingredients have the same importance or weight; some are much more important than others. Third, it is never possible to know and understand all the myriad relationships which exist between and among the component parts of cultures because they result from very complex connections and interconnections. And finally, and perhaps most importantly, there is the dilemma of the parts and whole: too much focus on the parts can cause people to lose sight of the whole, just as too much focus on the trees can cause people to lose sight of the forest.

Despite these difficulties, it is imperative to persevere with the *quest* to know and understand cultures as wholes. Not only does the pursuit of knowledge, understanding and insight into cultures demand it, but also the challenges confronting humanity necessitate it. For failure to understand the way in which cultures operate and function in the world will not only make it impossible to develop the forms, structures, practices, values and worldviews which are needed to ensure human survival and environmental well-being in the future, but also it will make it impossible to deal with the causes and consequences of cultural conflict and confrontation.

An important step in the right direction is taken by developing 'reasonable approximations' of cultures as wholes. This is achieved by probing more deeply into the idea that cultures are dynamic and organic wholes composed of a variety of complex and interrelated parts. As indicated earlier, knowledge and understanding of cultures comes largely from knowledge and understanding of the interplay that is constantly going on between the parts and the whole.

For Robert Redfield, who spent his life studying cultural and human wholes, the best place to start is with individuals who are concerned in their work with communicating knowledge and insights into wholes, rather than with individuals who are preoccupied with analysing or understanding the parts of wholes:

Still farther from where we just now stand are those who study the relations of parts to parts, of elements abstracted out from the whole in strict and limited relationship to each other, generally described…

Over there, on that other side, are all those who strive to present the concrete reality of each human whole as each, in itself, is. They are a various group. Included are novelists, philosophers, historians, philosophers of history, literary people, critics of literature and of art, historians of art, and writers of personal reminiscence. These people describe human wholes—personalities, civilizations, epochs, literatures, local cultures—each in its uniqueness.[16]

This capacity to communicate information, insights and ideas about wholes places these people in an extremely important position in society. Through their use of a variety of devices like signs, symbols, impressions, images, similes, metaphors, myths, stories and the like, such people communicate a great deal of information about cultures as wholes. The old adage 'a picture is worth a thousand words' is a cliché, but it speaks volumes about the ability of creative people to communicate an incredible amount of knowledge and information about the holistic nature of cultures which cannot be communicated at all in any other way, or cannot be communicated nearly as effectively using any other device.

This capacity for 'portraiture', as Redfield calls it, places artists, arts organizations and the arts in a particularly crucial position in society. For they speak to people about what is most essential in their cultures, as well as to lay bare their essence:

The characterizations of the artist…are of course not precise at all; but very much of the whole is communicated to us. We might call them all portraits. They communicate the nature of the whole by attending to the uniqueness of each part, by choosing from among the parts certain of them for emphasis, and by modifying them and rearranging them in ways that satisfy the "feeling" of the portrayer.[17]

People interested in learning more about the holistic nature of cultures should immediately turn their attention to the works of contemporary and historical artists and arts organizations, as well as the legacy of inherited artistic works. Here they will find a rich cornucopia of materials related to the holistic nature of cultures, as well as the way cultures are best understood as wholes. In other words, they will discover cultures as realities as well as concepts.

While artists, arts organizations and the arts are the best vehicle for exposing the holistic nature of cultures, they are not the only vehicle. The 'cultural industries' of publishing, radio, television, film, video and sound recording are extremely important because they provide the communication channels and distribution mechanisms which are necessary to make the works of artists, arts organizations and the arts known and accessible to the public. Anthropological, sociological and historical studies are important because they tend to deal with cultures as wholes, and therefore with the overall patterns, themes, worldviews, values, value systems, behavioural characteristics, social structures, and interrelationships which comprise cultures. Personality studies are important because, as Ruth Benedict observed, cultures are often personalities writ large. Philosophical studies and religious treatises are important because they often deal with the totality of human conduct and hence with the overall nature and meaning of cultures. And finally, ecological, economic, geographical and historical studies are important because they reveal how cultures have imprinted their holistic nature on the natural, historical and global environment. All these activities serve a valuable purpose because they help to expose the basic contours of cultures as wholes, as well as put enough flesh on them so that cultures can be understood in all their complexity and inter-relatedness.

As indicated earlier, cultures are wholes in the sense that some unifying theme or central organizing principle is needed to link the component parts of cultures together to form wholes. An examination of these themes and principles is imperative, therefore, in acquiring knowledge of the holistic nature of cultures.

So is looking at the way cultures achieve and maintain order, since, without order, cultures can degenerate into disorder and chaos. Scrutinize any culture, for example, and countless ways of achieving and maintaining order will be revealed, such as through legal arrangements, laws, customs, traditions, behavioural characteristics, consumer practices, and habitual patterns of work and leisure. Values are also important for achieving and maintaining order because they establish definite relationships between the component parts of cultures, thereby establishing a kind of pyramidal structure or pecking order which helps to stabilize cultural situations and control change. Power is obviously another tool that is used to achieve and maintain order in cultures because it gives some individuals and institutions authority over other individuals and institutions. And finally, education is important because it prepares people for citizenship and participation in cultural life. All these various devices, and others, are designed to preserve some semblance of order in cultures, thereby keeping them together in space and time and preventing them from flying off in all directions.

Examining cultures as wholes and the order that is required to maintain them should not be taken as an end in itself, but rather as a means to more intensive forays into the acquisition of knowledge and understanding of cultures in a deeper and broader sense. This is achieved by examining the worldviews, values and value systems that underlie cultures and form the basis of all cultural life.

As indicated earlier, culture as a concept is concerned with worldviews, values and value systems because how people see and interpret the world determines in large measure how they live in the world. As a result, there is a whole set of cosmological, philosophical, mythological, metaphysical, aesthetic, scientific and theological factors which must be examined and understood if the object is to comprehend specific cultures in a functional, operational or practical sense.

To understand any African, Asian, Latin American, Middle Eastern, North American or European culture, it is necessary to plunge deeply into an examination of these deeper and more profound factors. How do people in African, Asian, Latin American, Middle Eastern, North American and European cultures visualize and interpret the world? What roles do cosmology, religion and philosophy play in shaping specific attitudes towards life and outlooks on the world? What are the great myths and legends, and what role do they play in shaping aesthetic and scientific preferences, perceptions and relations with the natural, historical and global environment? Answers to these questions should reveal in no uncertain terms how these cultures originated, how they have evolved over time, where they stand at present, and where they are headed in the future.

Just as the arts, philosophy, history, anthropology, sociology and the like can be used to broaden and deepen knowledge and understanding of cultures as wholes, so economic, political, and religious systems can serve a similar purpose. One of the first scholars to focus on this was Max Weber. In *The Protestant Ethic and the Spirit of Capitalism*,[18] Weber demonstrated how a religious system like Puritanism, which manifested itself in industry, thrift, hard work, frugality, saving and investment, gave rise to the capitalist economic system and a very particular outlook on the world. Taking a cue from this, it does not prove difficult to see how economic, political, and religious systems like capitalism, communism, socialism, liberalism, conservatism, Christianity, Islam, Buddhism and others reveal a great deal about the functioning of particular cultures and the way specific groups of people visualize and interpret the world and act in the world.

While this knowledge and understanding can never constitute more than a close approximation or surrogate of the real thing—with all this implies in terms of shortcomings and limitations—it is essential to persevere with the quest to expand knowledge and understanding of cultures as dynamic and organic wholes. Failure to do so will heighten the potential for conflict and confrontation between cultures, as reasons for differences will not be understood. It will also make it impossible to bring about those fundamental changes in worldviews, values and value systems of cultures necessary for the future.

The Development of Cultures

Of all the questions confronting knowledge and understanding of cultures, no question is more relevant or timely than the question of how to develop cultures. The reason for this is not difficult to detect. The world is changing so rapidly that a great deal of consideration will have to be given in all parts of the world to the way in which cultures are evolved most effectively in the future.

Viewed from the holistic perspective proposed here, cultures should be *comprehensive, coherent, cohesive, humane* and *positioned* properly in the natural, historical, domestic and international environment if they are to cope with all of the changes that are going on in the world.

In order to be comprehensive, all the component parts of cultures will have to be developed and not just certain components. This includes legal and ethical codes, social structures, ethnic groups, subcultures, scientific and artistic endeavours, educational programmes and spiritual requirements as well as economic, political and technological systems.

If cultures should be comprehensive, they should also be coherent. In order to achieve this, meaningful relationships will have to be established between the various components of cultures, as well as between the various components of cultures and culture as a whole. In the modern world, this will require much more emphasis on *cross-cultural* communication and *links* between the various sectors and segments of cultural life.

Cultures that are coherent stand a good chance of being cohesive. In other words, they stand a good chance of being bound together effectively because harmonious relationships will have been established between the component parts of which they are comprised. Cultures that are not bound together effectively in this sense run the risk of becoming unglued and splitting apart. On the one hand, they can fall prey to communications problems, especially when geographical size or formidable terrain make communication difficult or impossible. On the other hand, they can fall prey to ethnic, racial and linguistic tensions, such as many cultures are doing today as a result of difficult changes going on in economics, demographics and society generally. This makes it imperative to develop the collective programmes, communications devices and social bonds necessary in order to provide for cohesion in cultures, thereby making it possible for them to maintain their identity through integration and inclusion rather than separation and exclusion.

Cultures should also be humane. In order to achieve this, they need to place a high priority on the human factor in development, caring and sharing, compassion, co-operation, respect for the rights and the traditions of others, and commitment to justice, equality and diversity. Without this, cultures can fall prey to partisan interests, political manipulation and special interest groups. For cultures, like culture and all other powerful forces, can cut in two directions. On the one hand, they can be sources of fulfillment, liberation, enjoyment and happiness. On the other hand, they can be sources of brutality, oppression, injustice and enslavement.

Cultures which are humane are likely to be positioned properly in the natural environment. The reason for this is clear. It is impossible to be humane without developing the sensitivities and sensibilities needed in order to achieve this. Initially, these sensitivities and sensibilities may be focused on human beings, thereby making it mandatory to stamp out human rights abuses and other forms of injustice whenever and wherever they are found. Ultimately they should be focused on future generations, other species and the natural environment, for humanness in this broader and deeper sense requires compassion and caring for the self and the other, the human and the non-human. In other words, it requires humanity, humility and sustainability in space, which is what properly positioning cultures in the natural environment is about.

Just as environmentalists and ecologists have riveted attention on the need to position cultures properly in space or the natural environment, so the aboriginal peoples and minority groups have riveted attention on the need to position cultures properly in time or the historical environment. Many cultures were originally founded and nurtured through the formative stages of development by groups of people who have an entirely different ethnic origin or skin pigmentation than the groups in positions of power today. Proper positioning of cultures in time, therefore, requires recognition of the seminal contributions of these people in an official, public sense and unofficial, private sense in all constitutional arrangements, educational practices, pedagogical and historical narratives, institutional actions and societal practices. Failure to do this results in long-standing feuds and deep-seated hostilities—feuds and hostilities that can fester in the side of cultures for centuries and remain there until they are set right.

Cultures should also be properly positioned in the domestic and international environment. This serves to highlight the fact that the development of cultures ultimately depends on two inter-related factors. The first is internal: what goes on within a culture. The second is external: what goes on between cultures.

If cultures are to mature and ripen properly, both the domestic and international dimensions will have to be given a great deal of consideration. In domestic terms, people will have to be actively involved in all aspects of cultural life. In international terms, cultures will have to be exposed to a great deal of scrutiny and attention. If this fails to happen, cultures can easily become parochial, provincial, nationalistic. However, it is impossible to blossom effectively and evolve high standards of creation and performance if cultures are unable to benefit from maximum citizen participation and international scrutiny of their efforts. For domestic and international exposure are the best defenses of all against nationalism, parochialism and provincialism.

The importance of domestic and international positioning was emphasized by T. S. Eliot when he said that the development of cultures depends on two factors: the ability to go back and learn from domestic sources; and the ability to receive and assimilate influences from abroad.[19] Mircea Malitza, the Romanian scholar and statesman, had the same sentiment in mind when he talked about the need for interaction between the domestic and international dimensions of cultures:

> Cultures in watertight compartments are doomed to oblivion. Dialogue is essential. The choice between the development of a national culture and an increase in exchanges with the outside world is a false one. Interdependence cannot be denied. The cultures which have blossomed are those which have had the advantage of innumerable influences, received and transmitted in accordance with a process of unceasing enrichment.[20]

If cultures are to be comprehensive, coherent, cohesive, humane and properly positioned in the natural, historical, domestic and international environment, they will have to maintain a great deal of control over their decision-making processes. Not only will people have to possess the autonomy and independence they need to decide for themselves how they want the component parts of their cultures to be ordered and orchestrated, but also they will have to be able to determine for themselves how they want to structure and organize their cultures as dynamic and organic wholes. Achieving and maintaining autonomy and independence in this larger and more all-encompassing sense is not only the key to a vital, active and dynamic cultural life. It is also the key to survival in a complex, difficult and demanding world.

This world is increasingly characterized by 'world cultures', or cultures that are integral parts of the global village, and are strongly influenced by all the modern modes of communication. To say that many cultures are 'world cultures' in this sense, however, is not to say that all cultures share similar beliefs, perceptions, characteristics, worldviews and values, especially when nothing could be farther from the truth. Rather it is to say that the modern instruments of communications have become so powerful, pervasive and persuasive that it is impossible to tune out what is going on in other parts of the world.

Hence the importance of achieving and maintaining sovereignty and control over all matters related to modern communications. Without full control over publishing, radio, television, film, recording, video production, computers, satellite communications, electronic highways and the like, cultures run the risk of becoming the victims of standardization, homogenization, colonization, imperialism and globalization. To prevent this, people and governments in all parts of the world should be acting to ensure that control over communications industries is in domestic rather than foreign hands, and a reasonable portion of cultural programming is domestic rather than international. What may be at stake here is the survival, independence and viability of cultures in the future.

The Necessity of Cultural Education

If cultures are to develop effectively in the modern world, a great deal of consideration will have to be given to cultural education in general and comparative cultural education in particular. Unfortunately, many educational systems throughout the world devote little time and attention to cultural education and comparative cultural education. This is a cause for concern, since much more needs to be known about cultures as wholes, as well as the reasons for differences between cultures, if cultures are to develop effectively and cultural conflict and confrontation are to be avoided.

Most educational systems devote a great deal more time and attention to preparing people for participation in one culture than they do to understanding different cultures. This is understandable in view of the fact that people are compelled to function first and foremost in their own culture. However, without adequate exposure to, and knowledge and understanding of, other cultures, people will progressively become intolerant of other cultures and other people. This will fan the flames of fear, suspicion and misunderstanding, and make it more difficult for people to understand the strengths and shortcomings of their own culture and the reasons for differences between cultures.

Knowledge and understanding of one's own culture is enriched by exposure to other cultures, for this exposure acts like a mirror: it permits people to see themselves and their own culture more clearly, as well as at a much deeper and more profound level of analysis. The Russians contend 'all is known by comparison', and perhaps this is why. Comparison makes it possible to broaden and deepen individual and collective understanding of one's own reality and the reality of others.

Comparative cultural education represents one of the best vehicles for achieving this, for it helps people to see and understand the strengths and shortcomings of their own culture, as well as the reasons for similarities and differences between cultures. This latter aspect is particularly important if the capacity for cultural harmony, peace and understanding is to be properly cultivated in the future.

While there is a fair amount of agreement that knowledge and under-standing of one's own culture is enriched by exposure to other cultures, there is much less agreement on whether it is really possible to know and understand other cultures. This is largely because of the limitations and con-ditioning of one's own culture. Antonio Alonso Concheiro, the Mexican authority on culture, explains why knowledge and understanding of other cultures is such a difficult and demanding process:

...we generally assume that cultures are simply different modes of adaptation to nature, different codes for the same fundamental purposes...We seldom recognize that in this manner we are only studying and classifying cultures which we invent through our own cultural framework and not the cultures themselves. In other words, we generally reach for and obtain only ethnocentric visions of other cultures.[21]

Regardless of the difficulties involved in getting to know and understand other cultures, no greater mistake could be made than to abandon the attempt; for despite the fact that people may never know other cultures in an ultimate, ontological sense, even if they live in other cultures for many years, the very fact that people make an effort to know and understand other cultures enhances the potential for tolerance, acceptance and appreciation of cultural differences.

Realization of this fact should open the doors to much more cultural education and especially comparative cultural education. Through an intensive commitment to education of this type—the type of commitment that commences in the earliest years of elementary school and extends throughout life—people will be exposed to worldviews, values, value systems, philosophies of life and concepts of space and time which are different from their own. Surely the world would be a better place as a result of this commitment.

5. The Cultural Interpretation of History

> Our own past is moving away from us at frightening speed, and if we want to keep open the lines of communication which permit us to understand the greatest creations of mankind we must study and teach the history of culture more deeply and more intensely than was necessary a generation ago...If cultural history did not exist, it would have to be invented now.[1]
>
> E.H. Gombrich

Now that culture and cultures have been examined as concepts and realities, it is tempting to plunge into a consideration of the role they should play in the world of the future. Such a temptation must be resisted, at least until time has been taken to examine the past. For if the present situation is proving difficult to cope with, and if the future is filled with anxiety and uncertainty, it is probably because insufficient consideration has been given to the past. Strange as it may sound, it is to the past that humanity should turn for the clues which are necessary to lay a more effective and equitable foundation for the future.

The Power of Interpretations of History

For people who believe the past possesses an awesome power, interest in history is gratifying. It is history, more than any other discipline, that humanity looks to for answers to many of its most profound questions: Where did human beings come from? Why have human beings evolved the way they have? Where do they stand at present? Where do they go from here? Moreover, it is history that human beings turn to in times of adversity to cope with life's instabilities and uncertainties. In one way or another, humanity is a prisoner in the web of history.

Given the importance of history, care must be taken to distinguish between history as fact and history as interpretation. History as fact embraces all events and activities which have occurred in the past. Whether these events and activities occurred at random, or are the result of some grand design or inexorable law, is impossible to tell. Indeed, short of some divine revelation, the mysteries of history may never be revealed in this sense.

Then there is history as interpretation. All written and oral history is of this type, since some form of human intervention and involvement is required to size up historical events and give them meaning. Here, a complex problem arises. If it was possible to approach these events free of biases and beliefs, it would be possible to get an impartial account of the past. But this is more than human beings can expect, since it is impossible for them to transcend the very thing that makes them human. The most humanity can hope for, and indeed must demand, is that interpretations of history are as accurate, authentic and truthful as possible. Such interpretations must be as free as possible from personal biases and subjective beliefs. What must be guarded against are interpretations of the past that seriously distort the truth, or are designed to manipulate and condition human behaviour in the present and the future.

As a rule, the greater the historian, the greater the need for historical interpretation. What may start out as an honest attempt to assess the past from an objective and impartial perspective can end up as an exercise in subjective interpretation, if only because historians must engage in matters of reconstruction and meaning. Moreover, like all people, historians have their hopes, dreams and fears, and history often becomes the vehicle they use to translate these hopes, dreams and fears into reality. This is not being hard on historians; it is merely commenting on a fundamental problem in historical interpretation. To say that historians construe the events and activities of history to satisfy their own theories and ideas is not to say that they are dishonest or diabolical. They are trying to do something extremely worthwhile and constructive for humanity.

Unfortunately, the distinction between history as fact and history as interpretation is seldom made clear. As a result, most people grow up believing historians are dealing with 'the truth'— the truth substantiated by decades of painstaking investigation and scholarly research. How powerful interpretations of history become when they are visualized in this way. They take on superhuman powers. As such, they wield an incredible influence over humanity.

Much as it is difficult to live with interpretations of history, it is impossible to live without them. As a result, humanity is always captive in the web of one interpretation of history or another. To illustrate this point, consider the economic interpretation of history, quite possibly the most powerful force in the world today.

The Economic Interpretation of History

If one interpretation of history has dominated human affairs and national and international thinking over the last century, surely it is the economic interpretation of history. As the dominant interpretation of history of the modern era, it has had a profound influence on people and institutions everywhere in the world.

By the middle of the nineteenth century, conditions were ripe for the economic interpretation of history to commence its ascent to the apex of world power. The industrial revolution had given the world a strong economic orientation. Moreover, the scientific revolution had produced a strong backlash against metaphysics, spiritualism, and romanticism, thereby paving the way for a much more pragmatic, empirical and materialistic approach to life. The physical interpretation of history, which subordinated nature to human beings and asserted the primary importance of physical agents in historical evolution, was rapidly gaining ground and winning converts.

Under these circumstances, it did not take Marx and the Marxists long to interpret history and societies in economic terms:

In the social production which men carry on they enter into definite relations that are indispensable and independent of their will; these relations of production correspond to a definite stage of development of their material powers of production. The totality of these relations of production constitutes the economic structure of society—the real foundation, on which legal and political structures arise and to which definite forms of social consciousness correspond. The mode of production of material life determines the general character of the social, political and spiritual processes of life.[2]

Over the last century and a half, the economic interpretation of history has moved from the wings to centre stage on the world scene. Although it has been greatly simplified and popularized to enhance its mass appeal, it still bears the unmistakable stamp of its formulators: the division of human life in general and human needs in particular into economic and non-economic components; the belief that all societies are composed of an economic base and a non-economic superstructure; the assumption that historical change is the product of economic forces; and the conviction that economic activities should take precedence over everything else because they are the *cause* of everything else.

Nothing typifies this causality principle better than the idea of the economic surplus. According to this idea, non-economic activities such as the arts, sciences, religion and education owe their existence to the fact that economic activities generate a surplus over and above consumption. As a result, economic activities are the 'basics' or 'productive forces' in society; all other activities are the 'frills' or 'unproductive forces' in society. The conclusion drawn from this logic is that the frills can only be attended to once the basics have been looked after; they must be cut back the moment the economic surplus is jeopardized.

In its march to the pinnacle of world power, the economic interpretation of history was assisted by two compelling ideas. First, the theory of class conflict, exploitation, revolution and economic equality captured the imagination and attention of people everywhere in the world. Second, the quantitative revolution of the last century or so has reduced life largely to the accumulation, measurement and comparison of material phenomena. As a result, the economic interpretation of history is now so powerful and pervasive that it is taken for granted by many national and international leaders, as well as by many countries in the world. It has become the axiom of the age. Everywhere it is assumed that as economics and economies go, so goes the world.

Verification of this fact is not difficult. In virtually every country, the developmental model that is in use is the quantitative, economic model. This model does not exclude qualitative, non-economic phenomena. Rather, it incorporates qualitative, non-economic phenomena, either by subordinating them to quantitative, economic ends, or by relegating them to a secondary rather than primary role in the developmental process. Susan Hunt comments on the pervasiveness of this ideology:

The economic ideology, the dominant intellectual framework in the world today, has reduced practically every human value to the categories of economics: production and consumption, basic needs and satisfiers, human rights, scarcity, nature, energy, systems, Cartesian time and space, the assumption that all things are measurable and comparable.[3]

It is easy to recognize this economic ideology. The emphasis is on quantity consumption, investment, production, profit and the marketplace, rather than on quality, conservation, and human welfare and well-being. The function of politics and education is often more caught up with generating revenue for governmental and educational coffers than it is with responding to the intellectual and political needs of people. The function of religion, science and the arts is often seen more in terms of maximizing sales, income and economic impact than it is in terms of stimulating and inspiring people. In this way, every element in the system is coloured by the economic container in which it is wrapped.

This ideology dominates the world system at present. Countries are ranked primarily according to the level and rate of their economic growth and technological attainment, despite attempts by the United Nations and other organizations to develop broader forms of measurement which take non-economic factors like education, health and life expectancy into account. Occupations, activities, institutions and people are assessed largely in proportion to the revenue they control or the income, investment, employment and wealth they generate. Planning structures and public and private decision-making processes are geared to the advancement of economic interests. Symbols, myths and advertising inducements are turned over to a celebration of materialistic ends.

The main consequence of this is that economics and economies have become the main focal points and principal preoccupations of developmental activity. People are viewed largely as economic assets or liabilities according to whether they make a net contribution to, or subtract from, the income stream. The concept of 'economic man'—the individual who is concerned first and foremost with maximization of economic interests and consumer satisfaction in the marketplace—becomes the basic personality stereotype. Communities, regions, nations and the world are seen largely in terms of 'economies'—economies where the principal preoccupation is to increase economic growth and consumption in order to fuel more economic growth and development. All roads lead to and from economies, regardless of whether they are economies in a municipal, regional, national or global sense, and concern over economies becomes the central preoccupation of society.

Despite the hold economics and economies have on the world at present, recent developments throughout the world—such as the environmental crisis, deterioration of the globe's fragile ecosystem, exhaustion of renewable and non-renewable resources, rapid increases in world population growth, the dehumanization and impersonalization of life, the breakdown of many traditions and customs, and the failure of the economic model to deliver its promise of material opulence and leisure time—suggest that the economic interpretation of history may be losing its grip. Not only is it too simplistic, deterministic and dangerous to carry forward into the future, but also it provides an inaccurate interpretation of the past.

In conceptual terms, the economic interpretation of history must be rejected for the same reason that all specialized interpretations of history must be rejected: they simplify the process of historical evolution to the point where it is misleading. But considerable care must be exercised with respect to exactly what is misleading here. What is misleading is *not* the belief that fulfillment of economic needs is essential for human survival, or that economic requirements are essential in the total scheme of things. No, what is misleading is the division of societies and human needs into economic and non-economic components for the purpose of asserting the priority of the former over the latter. Such convictions result from a basic fallacy that production is an economic or physical activity, rather than a mental, physical and spiritual activity. In fact, it is the inexorable connection between the mental, the physical and the spiritual which makes it inappropriate to divide societies into economic bases and non-economic superstructures, as well as human needs into economic and non-economic components. Such convictions, however useful in theory, have no foundation in historical fact or in theoretical analysis.

If societies actually developed the way the economic interpretation of history asserts, it would be possible to point to societies that actually developed their economic base first, and only later turned to the development of their artistic, educational, social and spiritual superstructure. Yet, it is impossible to find an example where this appears to have been the case. In each and every case, all these activities have been developed simultaneously rather than sequentially, albeit at different rates depending on the needs and values of particular societies.

By focusing on a part of the whole rather than the whole itself, specialized interpretations of history provide a one-sided, distorted and inaccurate account of the nature of historical evolution and change. In the case of the economic interpretation of history, this has led to a situation where the tail is wagging the dog: economic practices and consumption demands are condoned that are having a devastating effect on the natural environment and people's lives.

If the economic interpretation of history is too inaccurate and simplistic, it is also too deterministic. Human beings clearly have much more control over their affairs than the economic interpretation suggests, inasmuch as they have the power to recreate, redirect and change these affairs in accordance with their individual and collective wills, preferences and priorities. The very fact that human beings are free to make deliberate decisions about their affairs means that human beings are much more the products of free will than determinism. If this were not the case, there would be no point at all discussing the future, since, in deterministic terms, the future will unfold according to some preordained plan or course of action which people are powerless to prevent.

There can be no doubt that the economic interpretation of history has made many valuable contributions to human and world progress. By focusing attention on economics in general and economies, production, distribution and consumption in particular, it has contributed to numerous advances in science, technology, industry, medicine, art, education, communications and the like, thereby expanding the dimensions of human knowledge and making life a richer and fuller affair for many people and countries in the world. Without doubt, many of the gains of the last few centuries would not have been possible without commitment to the economic interpretation of history, since acquiescence to the 'laws of nature', and preoccupation with the super-natural and metaphysical, did little to bring humanity to its present point.

Despite these contributions, sight should not be lost of the fact that continued adherence to the economic interpretation of history could spell disaster for humanity. It could do so by condoning consumption practices and materialistic expectations that are impossible to fulfill, given the size and growth of the world's population, the availability of renewable and non-renewable resources, and the carrying capacity of the earth.

Regardless of its major theoretical flaws and practical shortcomings, there is much to be learned from the economic interpretation of history that is germane to the search for a more accurate and authentic interpretation of history to carry forward into the future.

In the first place, no greater mistake could be made in searching for a new interpretation of history than interpreting the past in terms of the most dominant force or paradigm of the present.[4] It is a mistake that is easy to make. If, as John McHale observed, 'people survive, uniquely, by their capacity to act in the present on the basis of past experience considered in terms of future consequences',[5] then the formulators of the economic interpretation of history were only being true to their age when they used economics to interpret the past and confront the future. After all, they were living at a time when the industrial revolution was in full swing and western society was assuming a strong economic and materialistic orientation. Nevertheless, in retrospect, it is clear that their mistake lay not in concluding that economics was the most dominant force or paradigm of their age, but rather in interpreting history from this perspective and concluding that this must be true for all times and all places. And the mistake of the present, it must be quickly added, lies in not challenging this interpretation of history much sooner.

Another lesson from the impact of the economic interpretation of history lies in recognizing how powerful an interpretation of history can become when it is imbued with ideals that hold out hope for people. Proponents of the economic interpretation of history have been able to do this by claiming that the economic interpretation of history is the most accurate rendering of history possible, as well as by implying that if it is adopted on a universal scale, material well-being and economic affluence will follow. So awesome has been the power of their rhetoric that it proved capable of turning trends into destinies—destinies that are only now being questioned as the shortcomings of the economic interpretation of history are exposed.

With the waning of the economic interpretation of history, the way is cleared for alternative interpretations of history to make their appearance on the scene. To be effective, such interpretations must be capable of providing a more accurate and impartial account of the past, as well as a more viable and equitable foundation for the future. A 'cultural interpretation of history' could provide this, largely by promising less but delivering more. The key to unlocking the secrets of this more comprehensive way of looking at and interpreting history lies in examining history from a holistic rather than specialized perspective.

A Cultural Interpretation of History

Surely what stands out most clearly when an objective and impartial eye is cast back over the past is the fact that people have struggled to build cultures.[6] These cultures have been 'wholes' in the sense that they have been concerned with all human activities and not just economic activities. In effect, they have been concerned with the entire way people visualize and interpret the world, organize themselves, conduct their affairs, elevate and embellish life, and position themselves in the world. History in this sense is a continuous process involving the ebb and flow of different cultures. Spengler called this process 'a picture of endless formations and transformations, of the marvellous waxing and waning of organic forms'.[7]

Whether cultures actually rise and fall or merely pass through periods of greater and lesser creativity and dynamism, who could deny that history has witnessed the successive bursting forth of different cultures—Egyptian, Indian, Chinese, Islamic, Greek, Roman, Mayan, European, African, Asian, Latin American, North American and Middle Eastern? While all of these cultures, and others, have had negative as well as positive aspects, there is hardly a country, society or group of people anywhere in the world that has not experienced this process at one time or another.

It is a process that cuts to the bone of all human and natural experience. It is as applicable to cultures as it is to groups, communities, nations, human beings, and all forms of plant and animal life. What has prevented general acceptance of this insight into the process of historical evolution and change is not its failure to provide an accurate and authentic account of the past, but rather what many see as its undue pessimism, particularly when cultures are past their zenith. Understandably, it is never easy to accept the inevitability of decline when a culture is in the prime of life, just as it is never easy to accept the inevitability of old age when one is caught up in the immortality of youth.

While this conviction that history has been most fundamentally concerned with the creation and development of cultures is not popular at present, it is probably the most accurate and authentic reading of history possible at this juncture in human evolution. For Karl Weintraub, the critical question in any cultural interpretation of history is this: 'how can a civilization or a culture be understood and presented in all its complexity and yet as an intelligible and structured whole'?[8] He goes on to explain the twofold task of the cultural historian:

He studies what a culture is and also how it develops. He must be able to see a culture in the total, relatively static, configuration attained at a given time; but he must trace as well its gradual transformation through time[9]...

He sees a culture not as a mere aggregate of traits but as forming an intricately interrelated pattern. In this delicately fashioned network the arts may have their ties to religion and economic values, morality may affect the constitutional arrangements and in turn be affected by political realities, a mood reflected in literature may also come to the fore in a social custom, and a scientific insight may work back upon a religious belief.[10]

The fact that cultures are wholes composed of an intricate interlacing of interdependent parts is much in evidence throughout the sweep of human history. To illustrate this point, take the hunt culture, one of the earliest cultures known to humankind, although any culture—African, Asian, Latin American, North American, European, agricultural, industrial or post-industrial—could be selected to make the same point.

From everything that is known about the hunt culture, the social, aesthetic, environmental and spiritual aspects of the hunt were as important as the economic aspect. As such, they were as much 'cause' as 'effect'. In other words, the hunt was a *cultural* event *par excellence*. It was a holistic undertaking that incorporated all human needs and requirements into it. In order to hunt successfully, people had to band together in groups; hence there was a social dimension to the hunt. In order to prepare properly for the hunt, people had to mythologize it; hence there was an aesthetic, spiritual and human dimension to the hunt. And in order to eat, people had to catch and consume their prey; hence there was an economic dimension to the hunt. Regardless of whether these activities took place before, during, or after the hunt, they were integral and indispensable components of the hunt itself, as the rock paintings at Ardèche, Altamira, Lascaux and Addaura and the earliest petroglyphs constantly remind us. Clearly this is why all the earliest societies are referred to as 'cultures' rather than 'economies' by archaeologists and anthropologists. Close inspection of all early societies reveals that all human needs were much in evidence from the very outset. Moreover, they were addressed simultaneously rather than sequentially.

What is true of the hunt culture is true of all cultures. It is impossible to point to a culture at any time in the past, or anywhere in the world, that has preoccupied itself initially, or exclusively, with its economic needs and only later turned to the fulfillment of its other needs. No matter how destitute people are or have been, they have never neglected the need for aesthetic and spiritual expression, mythology, social and political organization, recreation, and just plain idling. Clearly, these needs are and have been every bit as conspicuous to people's overall well-being as their economic and material requirements.

Regardless of how important economic needs are or have been—and there is no intention of diminishing their fundamental importance here—the point is that they only constitute one element in the total spectrum of human needs. They do not *cause* other needs, any more than other needs cause them. Human beings have a variety of needs—to breathe, touch, feel, eat, communicate, belong, love and survive—that must be attended to *in concert* if they are to function effectively in society. These needs give rise to a panorama of environmental, social, spiritual, linguistic, aesthetic, economic and technological requirements—requirements that have been very much in evidence in cultures from the outset. General observations of past and present cultures, as well as human nature and conduct, indicate that these needs co-exist at one and the same time and often serve many purposes simultaneously. Consequently, it is impossible to posit a causal relationship between them. In *The Tree of Culture*, Ralph Linton explains why it is impossible to trace a cause and effect relationship between human needs:

A culture as a whole provides answers to all the needs of a society and of the average individual member of it. However, any attempt to establish direct and complete correlations between particular needs and particular cultural elements is foredoomed to failure. Every element of culture appears to have multiple functions, and the same element may bear a significant relation to several different needs. The most that can be said in any case is that the primary function of a particular culture element seems to be related to this social or individual need and its secondary functions are related to such and such other needs.[11]

The study of history confirms the fact that humanity's needs are not as specialized and sequential as scholars like Marx and Engels have contended. Rather, they are multifunctional, simultaneous and interdependent. In visual terms, this means they form a holistic constellation, rather than a pyramid or ladder with the economic needs spread out across the base or lowest rung. Thus, while advocates of the economic interpretation of history believe that cultures follow a rigid linear or sequential path which commences with the development of their economic bases and only later involves the development of their non-economic superstructures, there is no real historical evidence to support this. In fact, all the evidence points in precisely the opposite direction, namely that people have endeavoured to build cultures that embrace all dimensions of life simultaneously.

The simultaneous and indivisible character of human needs sheds light on the holistic nature of cultures as well as the means whereby the totality of human needs are addressed. This fact has significance for the world of the future because it means that adequate provision must be made for all human needs and not just economic, technological and material needs in the formulation and execution of developmental policies, practices, strategies and tactics.

This is not to say that specific cultures have not or cannot be dominated by particular themes, of which economics may be one. Indeed, travelling back along the continuum of time reveals that cultures have been dominated by different themes, just as different ages have been dominated by different ideas. Whereas the dominant theme of one culture or age may be aesthetic or scientific, in another, it may be religious, economic, political or technological. The Dutch cultural historian Johan Huizinga, for example, concluded after his intensive study of the Middle Ages that chivalry was the dominant theme of the late medieval period. A concern for chivalry, more than anything else, governed the actions of individuals, institutions, and society at large.[12]

The view that cultures have been dominated by different themes and not always by the same theme is consistent with accumulated knowledge of the past and much of the archaeological evidence. This means that the developmental patterns of cultures are disharmonic rather than harmonic: highly evolved and sophisticated in some areas and highly simplistic and underdeveloped in other areas. Take the Inca and Mayan cultures as an example:

Turning to more elaborate cultures, we find the Inca in South America reaching an extraordinarily high development in technology, but even more in political organization…

In contrast to this, the Maya, who produced the greatest civilization in Middle America, never developed anything like the Incas' technological skill…In spite of this, they developed an art of amazing beauty and originality, and a writing system, which at the time of conquest, seems to have been on the verge of emerging into a true syllabary. They also made amazing advances in mathematics and astronomy, among other things inventing independently for themselves the use of zero and of notation by position.[13]

If cultures are disharmonic rather than harmonic, interpretations of history must be sufficiently flexible and comprehensive to account for these differences. In order to achieve this, they must be holistic and relative rather than specialized and absolute, varying from time to time and place to place in accordance with changing human needs and environmental circumstances. This is where a cultural interpretation of history proves infinitely more effective than specialized interpretations such as the economic one. Whereas specialized interpretations of history must reconstruct the past in terms of the same theme, paradigm or force, by virtue of its holistic quality and relative character, a cultural interpretation can reconstruct the past in terms of different themes, paradigms and forces. Thus, for example, it makes sense to talk about the medieval *religious* culture, the Renaissance *aesthetic* culture, and even the modern *economic* culture. All have been cultures dominated by distinctly different themes that have played an instrumental role in coalescing around them all sub-themes. Defined in this way, it is clear that a cultural interpretation provides a more effective framework for historical interpretation and analysis than the economic interpretation of history.

There is also another reason why a cultural interpretation of history is valuable. It has to do with the exercise of free will in history. With the exception of cultures dominated by nature or other cultures, cultures have been relatively free to assign priorities and weights to their own needs. It is this process of free selection that explains why cultures are differentiated from each other in terms of needs, values, value systems, forms, structures and worldviews. This process also explains why history has been much more the product of free will than determinism. For rather than viewing the past as an inevitable march along some predetermined path, which human beings are powerless to prevent, a cultural interpretation of history views the past, the present and the future as a much more fluid and flexible affair.

The existence of free will in this sense makes it impossible to 'explain' the past or 'predict' the future. Unlike the economic interpretation of history, which purports to know exactly how the past evolved and the future will unfold, a cultural interpretation of history can lay no claim to such pretense. The best it can do is to uncover trends and correlations in the past which have different degrees of probability and possibility in the future. Thus, while cultures can prepare themselves for certain possibilities, and such possibilities can become actualities, it is not possible to say in advance how cultures will unfold or what direction the future will take. The future is always an open book—an unmarked course to be charted in accordance with humanity's most profound knowledge, wisdom, insight and understanding.

The fact that a cultural interpretation of history is less pretentious than specialized interpretations such as the economic interpretation of history should not be allowed to dampen public or private enthusiasm about its usefulness in providing important clues and insights into the nature of historical change. To uncover these clues and insights, it is necessary to revisit the idea of cultural creativity.

Looked at from the holistic perspective provided by a cultural interpretation of history, it is easy to marvel at the creative element at work in all cultures. As humanity's most precious gift and valuable resource, creativity has rescued humanity time and again from the bleakest conditions and most depressing circumstances. As such, it has produced all the world's greatest ideas and masterpieces, as well as provided the flame necessary to ignite cultures and propel them towards higher and higher levels of accomplishment.

Preoccupation with economic and technological creativity, especially as it manifests itself in the creation of production, distribution and consumption machinery, should not be allowed to obscure the fact that all cultures have been highly creative across the whole spectrum of cultural possibilities and accomplishments. For all cultures—large and small, traditional and modern, temperate and tropical, local and national—have exhibited a high degree of creativity in many if not most dimensions of their cultural life.

Those who doubt this fact need only reflect on the universal character and colossal size of the cultural heritage of humankind. As the true measure of humanity's greatest and most significant achievements from the dawn of recorded time right up to the present day, this living legacy of past and present accomplishments is clearly discernible amidst the rise and decline of individual cultures. It comprises, in addition to countless other things, all the world's greatest cities and historic sites; historical and contemporary civilizations; music, dances, paintings and craft objects; and all the most significant advances that have been recorded in economics, science, medicine, education, social affairs, human thought and technology in all parts of the world.

Preoccupation with the colossal size and universal character of the cultural heritage of humankind should not be allowed to obscure the fact that there is a much more negative and sinister side to cultures that a cultural interpretation of history must take into account. As indicated earlier, this negative side reveals an incredible amount of brutality, bestiality, war, violence, oppression, human rights abuse, suffering, plundering and exploitation.

Like the positive side of cultures, the negative side is also spread liberally over the face of the earth. No group of people or community, region, country or continent has a monopoly on it. It is not only possible to uncover blatant acts of brutality and bestiality in every culture and civilization—as the history of colonialism, imperialism, nazism, fascism, the holocaust and 'cultural revolutions' throughout the world confirms; unbelievable acts of savagery and barbarism may be uncovered in every period of history as well. Recognition of this fact must also be configured into a cultural interpretation of history if a truly accurate and authentic account of human evolution over the centuries is to be achieved.

Recognition of the positive and negative sides of cultural history should help to bring about a rectification of many of the inequalities and injustices existing in historical interpretations. This will not be possible without a reinterpretation of history along more accurate, honest and equitable lines, as these injustices exist everywhere. Take the written history of Africa as an example. Anyone reading it would conclude that it was the Europeans who opened up, settled, and civilized Africa. There are all sorts of books describing how Stanley, Livingstone, Park and others 'discovered Africa', as well as how the Dutch, the British and the Portuguese made it fit for habitation. Yet, how many books document the infinitely greater and more creative contributions by the Africans themselves to the discovery, settlement and civilization of Africa? How many books document the fact that Africans were familiar with the nooks and crannies of Africa long before the Europeans arrived on the scene? More importantly, how many books reveal that there were highly advanced cultures and civilizations in Africa when many parts of Europe were in the throes of barbarism?

These same injustices and inaccuracies appear in the written histories of North and South America, New Zealand and Australia. One reads volumes about the contribution of the French, the British, the Portuguese and the Spanish to their discovery and settlement. Yet, the Incas, Mayas, Aztecs, Indians, Inuit, Aboriginal and Maori were living in these areas for centuries prior to the arrival of Europeans on the scene. Scarcely a hill, valley, lake or river was not known to them. Not only were most of the technologies used by Europeans to penetrate into the interior of these areas native in origin, but as with the Africans, these inventive peoples had evolved many outstanding civilizations prior to the arrival of the Europeans.[14]

As these examples demonstrate only too well, the development of cultures in Africa, North and South America, Australia and New Zealand was not a simple case of European development transplanted on to African, American, Australian or New Zealand soil. In reality the Europeans adopted as many cultural creations, characteristics, artifacts and practices from the indigenous peoples as the indigenous peoples adopted from the Europeans. What is often described as a unilateral process involving cultural transfers from one group to another was actually an interactive process involving cultural transfers between both groups.[15]

Caution must also be exercised here with respect to the meaning of development. To arbitrarily select one or two criteria, such as the rate of economic growth or the level of technological attainment, and measure the degree of progress or retardation of a culture on the basis of these criteria is not only misleading; it is inconsistent with the facts of the matter. If cultures are to be judged at all, they must be judged across the total spectrum of their cultural achievements—that is to say, from a holistic perspective—or they must be judged according to the values, priorities, challenges and worldviews they have established for themselves. Here again, a major reinterpretation of history is required to even up the scales of justice. Many cultures that rank low in terms of economic or technological attainment rank high in other areas of creative achievement, such as artistic, social or spiritual advancement.

There may be no greater need confronting humankind at the present time than the need to rewrite history along more authentic and equitable lines that give credit to the creative ingenuity and achievements of all cultures and all peoples. Clearly, a rewriting of history along these lines is imperative for world progress and global stability in the future. Documentation of the rich contributions to global progress and world affairs made by peoples and cultures from all parts of the world is necessary both to put an end to the myth that global progress and development is the product of a few, economically-developed nations, and to bring about true international understanding and equality.

It would be a mistake to conclude this brief retrospective on the past without commenting on the thorny problem of cultural decline. Unfortunately, little is known about why the flame of cultural creativity burns out, to leave cultures plunging into darkness and decline. Perhaps it is because cultures, like human beings, cannot escape the organic cycle of birth, adolescence, maturity, old age and death, or spring, summer, fall and winter. Or perhaps it is because the challenges confronting cultures get stronger and stronger while the ability to respond gets weaker and weaker, as Toynbee concluded following his massive study of numerous cultures and civilizations.[16] Or perhaps it is because hypertrophy sets in:

In the development of culture also, we have numerous examples of hypertrophy. In our discussion of the organization of cultures we mentioned that each society has certain dominant interests about which it tends to elaborate behaviour. Such interests and elaborations may be carried to the point where they become authentically non-functional and where they even interfere with the successful operation of other and more necessary aspects of the culture. Our own society would be an excellent case in point, since our preoccupation with technological development has led to a neglect of social invention which may well prove catastrophic.[17]

Despite the brevity of this retrospective on the past, flesh has started to appear on the bare bones of a cultural interpretation of history. Deeply rooted in reality and an attempt to conduct an objective reading of the process of historical evolution and change, it is based on a number of interlocking principles: the centrality of cultures in historical development; the holistic nature of culture and cultures; the simultaneous and indivisible character of human needs; the negative and positive nature of cultural life; the creativity of humankind; the unpredictability of cultural forms; the significance of the cultural heritage of humankind; and the inevitability of cultural decline. This interpretation provides a more accurate reading of historical evolution and change than the economic interpretation of history, and also provides a more impartial and equitable account of the past to carry forward into the future.

Uses and Abuses of a Cultural Interpretation of History

If the full potential of a cultural interpretation of history is to be realized, it will be necessary to become its masters rather than its slaves and manipulators. The world has been captive in the web of the economic interpretation of history for too long to fall into the trap a second time. To avoid this, a cultural interpretation of history must act as a flexible framework rather than as cast-iron dogma, and as a source of enlightenment rather than a vehicle for propaganda, exploitation, domination and enslavement. Only when it is used in a positive rather than a negative way will it provide the key to human betterment and planetary progress in the future.

If history can be seen as a process involving the rise and decline of cultures when an objective eye is cast back over the past, exactly the same process can be seen to be at work when an impartial eye is cast around the world at present. The modern world is filled with numerous cultures—group, community, regional and national. These cultures are wholes in the sense that all the ingredients or parts of which they are comprised are combined in very specific combinations and arrangements to produce integrated entities. These entities exude very specific worldviews, values and value systems. This fact explains why different cultures are in different states and stages of evolution: some have reasonably well-developed economic or technological resources while their aesthetic, religious, ethical, social and spiritual resources require improvement; others have reasonably well-developed aesthetic, religious, ethical, social and spiritual resources while their economic and technological resources require improvement. Not only are the particulars of each culture in a constant state of flux, but so are the ways these particulars are brought together to form wholes.

Superimposed on this latticework of group, community, regional and national cultures are even larger cultures—African, Asian, European, North American, Latin American, Middle Eastern and Caribbean, for example.

While the holistic nature, worldviews and values of these larger cultural con-figurations are far less visible and discernible to the naked eye, their bare outlines and contours can be ascertained as soon as the spotlight is shifted to cultural similarities rather than cultural differences. These similarities may be great, as is the case where these cultures share similar traditions, topographi-cal features, religious beliefs, geographical location, outlooks on the world, or some other identifiable characteristic or characteristics. Or the similarities may be few, as is the case where there are substantial variations in the charac-teristics of which they are comprised.

Superimposed on these larger cultures are even larger cultures. These larger cultures—western, eastern, northern, southern and what some even call a 'global culture'—are even less discernible to the naked eye because it is exceedingly difficult to identify the similarities that bind them together. With the possible exception of western culture, about which so much has been written in the modern era, these cultures may be much more a theoretical device than a concrete reality, largely because the differences existing within them far exceed the similarities.

While it is becoming increasingly commonplace to use terms like global culture, western culture, eastern culture, African culture, European culture, Asian culture and the like to refer to larger cultural configurations, three notes of caution should be sounded. First, the larger the cultural configuration, the greater the level of generality and the more likelihood that there will be numerous exceptions to the general rule. Second, considerable care should be exercised with all cultural configurations, and with the larger ones in particular. Lack of clarity and precision may lead to conflict, misunderstand-ing and confrontation. Finally, and perhaps most importantly, much more needs to be known about all cultures, especially the larger ones. While cultural historians and theorists like Spengler, Toynbee and F. S. C. Northrop have paved the way in this regard,[18] far too little is known about cultures in both a specific and general sense at the present time. Much more needs to be known about the similarities, differences, structural arrangements, organizational configurations and details which make it possible to distinguish between different cultures, particularly larger cultures. Moreover, methodological tools, typologies, and techniques will have to be developed to make it possible to classify cultures according to certain criteria and characteristics.

Development of these methodological tools, typologies and techniques, as well as the deeper theoretical and practical insights that stand behind them, is imperative if humanity is to be successful in confronting and dealing with the root causes of injustice, inequality and inequity in the modern world. Many of these causes have their origins in centuries-old relations and conflicts between cultures.

These relations and conflicts result from a variety of factors. In the first place, they result from the fact that all cultures are in a constant state of evolution and change, much as they are today as a result of rapidly-changing economic, social, political, technological and demographic conditions. Secondly, they result from pressures between specific cultures, particularly cultures in close geographical proximity or cultures that have carried on animosities and hostilities for centuries. Thirdly, they result from cultures in a state of ascendancy colliding with those in a state of descendancy. This produces highly explosive situations because cultures in a state of descendancy often have a desire to cling to power while those in a state of ascendancy have a desire to expropriate power. Finally, they result from tensions between dominant and subservient cultures, especially when the conditions for interaction and exchange are far from equal.

While much of the conflict that exists between cultures emanates from these factors, it is particularly evident in the case of conflict between dominant and subservient cultures. Nowhere is this more apparent than in the case of western culture on the one hand and other cultures in the world on the other hand.[19] Much of this conflict results from creation of a system designed largely to promote and disseminate western worldviews, values, value systems and models of development. Not only are these deeply imbedded in the economic interpretation of history with its materialistic orientation, but also they are predicated on the conviction that human beings can control nature and turn the natural environment to their collective advantage.

Given the powerful impact western economies have on international markets and world financial and commercial conditions, African, Asian, Latin American, Caribbean and Middle Eastern countries have been compelled to orchestrate their economies and orient their economic practices accordingly. This has resulted in their specialization in the production of products for which they have little or no real advantage, and in an increase in their dependency on western markets and western consumption requirements. The results have been counter-productive, not only for their economies due to fluctuating prices and economic and technological dependencies, but also for their cultures as a result of the erosion of traditional values, value systems, worldviews and identities. There is hardly an African, Asian, Latin American, Caribbean or Middle Eastern culture which has not been affected by this process. As a result, there are deep feelings of frustration, betrayal and resentment in these parts of the world, largely as a result of excessive economic and technological practices and pressure to conform to values, development models and worldviews that have proven inimical to their interests and needs.

The time is ripe to chart a new course for humanity. This course is best developed not by ignoring the past or lamenting the present, but rather by taking a cultural approach to the past and the present. It is this approach that Takdir Alisjahbana had in mind when he said:

In the great movement of time which we call human history, we must ask ourselves the question, 'Where are we, and where is our road leading to?' in the hope that through an understanding of the growths and declines, of the successes and the failures of cultures, we will acquire some clues that will lead us to the right decisions in our time.[20]

If a cultural interpretation of history is to serve a useful purpose in this regard, it will have to inspire as well as illuminate. In other words, it will have to provide a ray of hope for the future as well as a more accurate and authentic rendering of the past and the present. Fortunately it is capable of satisfying these requirements if it is used in positive and constructive ways rather than negative and destructive ways. The distinction between the inspirational and illuminational aspects of a cultural interpretation of history was made clear by Spengler:

We can differentiate between possible *and* actual Culture, *i.e. Culture as an idea...and Culture as the embodiment of that idea...*Higher history, *intimately related to life and to becoming, is the actualizing of possible Culture.*[21]

If there is one thing that should be actualized in the future, surely it is culture's capacity for transformation. With this capacity, cultures are capable of aspiring to higher and higher levels of accomplishment. Without it, they will quickly atrophy and sink into oblivion.

Given the nature and implications of the environmental, economic, political, social and technological changes taking place in the world, all cultures are going to have to cultivate the capacity for transformation to the greatest extent. Cultures too preoccupied with permanence may find they are unable to create new and more evocative visions of the future. Cultures too preoccupied with modernity may find that they have become unglued or unstuck, largely because their visions of the future are too divorced from historical roots. Thus, the capacity for transformation will have to be achieved by walking the fine line between tradition and modernity, continuity and change, the future and the past.

Viewed from this vantage point, the most important question facing cultures may be whether worldviews, values and value systems can be created that are consistent with the direction in which humanity and the world appear to be headed in the future. Such worldviews, values and value systems will require the participation of all individuals, institutions and countries, as well as a great deal of imagination and forceful action in terms of new directions in the arts, sciences, ethics, economics, politics, technology, education and religion.

In the creation of these new worldviews, values and value systems, there may be no better place to start than with marginalized cultures and peoples, many of which are marginalized not because their worldviews, values and value systems are irrelevant, or because they have little to say about how life should be lived and the world should be visualized, but rather because they do not fit the western model of development. Close inspection of marginalized cultures and peoples and their respective worldviews, values and value systems reveals profound insights into the nature of the universe, relationships between human beings and other species, environmental protection and preservation, the sanctity of human life and the purpose of existence.[22] Aboriginal cultures and peoples, for example, possess finely-tuned and sophisticated beliefs about cosmic unity, environmental harmony, ecological renewal and spiritual awareness. As such, they provide indispensable clues with regard to the direction and substance of the transformation needed for the future.

There is no doubt that the world of the future will be characterized by much more frequent contact between cultures. As a result, intercultural understanding and communication is imperative for global progress and human survival. As indicated earlier, it is through intercultural understanding and communication that people learn to appreciate and accept worldviews and values that are different than their own. While it may never be possible to eradicate the threats and conflicts that emanate from this, many of them might be reduced if a sustained effort was made by people and cultures everywhere in the world to understand cultural differences. Such efforts would not only improve the potential for global harmony and world peace; they would also increase the capacity for cultural co-operation, communication and exchange. As co-operative undertakings between scientists, scholars, athletes, artists and statesmen readily demonstrate, outstanding results can be achieved when humanity shares its knowledge, information, insights, ideas and expertise.

When the prominent cultural statesman Jean d'Ormesson said that 'culture used to look backward in order to try to understand the world; now, all of a sudden, it is looking forward in order to change it',[23] he put his finger on the quintessential role that a cultural interpretation of history can play in the world of the future. A cultural interpretation of history is not only capable of focusing attention on the most essential developments which have engaged humanity in the past—the building of cultures and civilizations and the creation of the cultural heritage of humankind; it is also capable of shining the spotlight on the vital and valuable contributions that *all* cultures and *all* peoples can make to global development and world progress in the future. It is on this undeniable fact that humanity should seek to lay the foundation for a more just, equitable and humane world.

6. The Cultural Personality

He who wills the highest, must will the whole.

Johann Wolfgang von Goethe[1]

Now that a framework has been created for understanding culture and cultures in general and the cultural interpretation of history in particular, it is possible to shift attention to a consideration of the main ingredients which comprise culture and cultures. The starting point for this examination lies in exploring the intimate connection between culture, cultures and the individual. For as James Feibleman said, 'the study of culture properly begins with the study of the cultural elements in the individual'.[2]

This is a propitious moment to be examining the connection between culture, cultures and the individual. Given all the economic, environmental, communications, political, technological, social and spiritual changes that are taking place in the world, how the individual relates to culture and cultures in general, and the natural environment, other people, future generations, other species and the self in particular, is bound to have a crucial impact on the attitudes, actions and lifestyles most needed for the future.

The Context of the Cultural Personality

Clearly more and more people in all parts of the world are having the utmost difficulty coping with the realities of the present and prospects for the future. Why is this? What vortex of forces is at work throughout the world that makes it difficult for people to confront the future with hope, optimism and enthusiasm rather than anxiety and apprehension? It is not difficult to identify some of the forces which are at work. Since many of the forces are external in nature, these forces will be examined first. Following this, it will be possible to consider some of the forces that are more internal in nature.

First of all, there are all the changes taking place in contemporary economic systems mentioned earlier. The changes occurring in employment and income practices, production and distribution methods, taxation measures, capital movements, markets and ideologies are so complex that people everywhere in the world are having the greatest difficulty coping with them. The complexity of these changes is causing concern for people, as are the size, rapidity and pervasiveness of these changes. In today's world, it is difficult to escape the consequences of job loss, unemployment, inflation, increases in the cost of living, decreases in the standard of living, globalization, privatization, the concentration of wealth and power in fewer hands, downsizing and debts. Such concerns are by no means limited to people living in particular parts of the world or working in specific occupations. Indeed, they are shared by people everywhere in the world, as well as people working in every type of profession.

Transformations taking place in economic practices are not the only ones proving difficult to cope with. It is also the fact that technology is transforming every aspect of public and private life. In a world where news about wars, starvation, genocide, military coups, tornadoes and natural catastrophes is transmitted around the world in the flash of a second, it takes an enormous amount of psychic endurance and emotional stability to withstand it. It is one thing to read about the devastation of a hurricane, a drought or a war in a book or newspaper a year or two after it happens; it is quite another thing to see it unfolding before one's very eyes.

If it is difficult to cope with the technological assault on the senses taking place every minute of every day, it is even more difficult to accept the predictions for much more technological change in the future. Rather than being able to look forward to a period of relative calm, tranquillity and a slowing down of technological growth, all the evidence points in the opposite direction. With increased expenditure on computers, communications systems, capital equipment, space exploration, satellites, telecommunications and the like, it could hardly be otherwise. Surely it is going to take a great deal of fortitude on the part of all people to make the transition to an age in which every day feels like the industrial revolution.

If economic and technological change is proving difficult to cope with, so is political and demographic change. Not only are societies becoming increasingly pluralistic and multiracial in character, but also political systems and geographical boundaries are being altered. As a result, more and more people are having to confront the fact that they may be living in an entirely different country in the foreseeable future. Unfortunately, many of the traditional safeguards that have been developed to deal with these uncertainties are undergoing profound transformation as indicated earlier. This is tending to heighten the sense of anxiety and apprehension people feel.

There are also all the changes taking place in the escape mechanisms and outlets that people have created over the centuries to cope with excessive change. Whereas it was once possible to escape from rapid societal and technological change through occasional trips, long weekends and some travel, fewer and fewer people are able to take advantage of these opportunities. The reason for this is not difficult to detect. Either modern economic, technological and political systems are compelling people to be immersed in the system all the time, or people lack the financial resources to take advantage of these opportunities. In either case, it is less and less possible for people to engage in those therapeutic and recuperative measures necessary to enable the mind, the body, the soul, and the spirit to recover from the demands and dictates of a speeded-up existence.

In an age where the family, kinship relationships, neighbourhoods and communities are breaking up, or are in a considerable state of uncertainty and flux, individuals are finding it difficult to turn to these conventional sources of stability and security to counteract the stresses and strains of modern life. While many new social systems and support structures are in formation, particularly among women, the elderly and the disadvantaged, they are in such a formative state of development that it is highly unlikely that they will provide the stability and security that is needed for some time.

Concomitant with these developments is the erosion taking place in traditions and identities. In the past, if transformations at the local, regional, national or international level were proving difficult to deal with, and there were not a lot of safety nets or support mechanisms around to provide assistance, it was always possible to look to traditions and identities for consolation and continuity. Even here, however, it is harder to find solace, stability and relief. Either these traditional touchstones are undergoing dramatic transformations of their own, or they are being altered or changed along with everything else. One only has to look at any African, Asian, Latin American, North American or European culture to realize how difficult it is to maintain individual and collective identities in an age characterized by relentless change.

The combined effect of these developments is that more and more people are feeling disoriented, frustrated and powerless. Whereas it was once possible to look outside the self for help in coping with the consequences of dynamic change, today this no longer seems possible for, perhaps more than ever before, people are being thrown back on their own resources and forced to cope with difficult situations without the benefit of a safety net. This is coming at a time when profound transformations are occurring in the psychological make-up and well-being of people. How could it be otherwise? Given all the revolutionary changes taking place in the external world, is it any wonder that revolutionary changes are also taking place in the internal world?

For one thing, the notion of the individual as a specialist in a particular production function appears to be on the verge of collapse. Not only has specialization made it difficult for people to talk to one another and interact with one another, but also it has produced people who feel fragmented, incomplete and vulnerable. Specialization no longer guarantees a job due to the rapidity and pervasiveness of technological change. It also makes it difficult to fuse mind, body, emotions, soul and spirit together in a meaningful whole.

Underlying all this is the loss of role models and prototypes of the personality on which to base human behaviour. The ability to seek out role models on which people can pattern their behaviour has long been a source of motivation, inspiration and comfort. Unfortunately, there seem to be few role models capable of performing this function. Clearly, when more emphasis is placed on income and profits than on jobs, justice and the needs and rights of others, it is obvious that there are few role models on which to base human behaviour. Moreover, many of the individuals and groups which do provide role models, lack the media attention, social status and public recognition to have an effect on human conduct. Even if they were able to supply the leadership required, many of them are having their own problems coping with the complexities and uncertainties of the modern world.

Contemporary prototypes of the human personality are also of little or no consolation here. Clearly the two personality prototypes which have dominated international thinking over much of the last century—the economic personality and the specialist personality—offer little help. There are difficulties with both these prototypes which make them inappropriate as models on which to predicate human behaviour in the future.

The principal problem with the economic personality—or 'economic man' as it is sometimes called—is that the individual is seen largely as a consumer, a commodity, a profit seeker, and a maximizer of satisfaction in the marketplace. While this may provide a realistic approximation of how people are treated by modern systems, the real difficulty with it is that it relates to one facet of the personality only, albeit an extremely important one. It tends to treat the individual as an object rather than a subject—an object to be subordinated to the interests of the marketplace.

Many of these same objections apply to the specialist personality or 'specialized man' mentioned earlier. Just as economic systems and labour practices are highly specialized in the modern era, so individuals are encouraged to specialize in the development of a narrow range of skills saleable in the marketplace. The problem is that modern economic systems are changing so rapidly that these skills are often redundant soon after they are acquired, thereby leaving the individual at the mercy of powerful producers. Add to this the fact that the specialized personality and the economic personality yield a vision of the individual that is one-dimensional and it becomes clear that it would be foolhardy to predicate human behaviour in the future on either of these two prototypes.

Given this situation, where is the search commenced for a compelling prototype of the human personality? The best place to start is with the historical literature. There exists here a rich mine of insights and information on the nature and character of the human personality, the role of the individual in society, and the specifics of human development. Much of this literature is religious, philosophical and psychological in nature.

In the religious realm, for example, there are the teachings and writings of all the world's religions: Christianity, Islam, Buddhism, Hinduism, Judaism,

Confucianism, and others too numerous to cite here. One only has to look to the Bible, the Talmud, the Koran, the Upanishads, the Analects of Confucius, or any other sacred text to realize how pregnant all the religious teachings and writings are with valuable insights into the human personality in a variety of social situations and cultural circumstances. These insights are multiplied many times over when the focus is shifted to the philosophical literature. From Plato, Confucius, Mencius, Aristotle and Socrates to Heidegger, Sartre, Gandhi, Tagore and the Dalai Lama, a significant portion of the philosophical thought of all cultures has been devoted to an understanding of the individual and his or her role and responsibilities in society. Finally, and perhaps most importantly, a substantial part of the psychological literature has been concerned with the problem of the human personality, not only in an individual but also in a societal sense. While much of this literature seems to raise more questions than it answers at present, there is no doubt that it casts a great deal of light on the way individuals can deal with the demands and dictates of a rapidly-changing world.

While all this literature is enormously helpful in enabling people to cope with the vicissitudes and vagaries of contemporary life, it is not without its problems. In the first place, it is extremely diffuse. It exists in so many diverse locations and places that it is difficult to pin down and pull together in a way that is consistent with reality and contemporary life. Secondly, much of this literature, and particularly the psychological literature, is designed to deal with abnormal rather than normal behaviour, and therefore with personality problems and disorders. As a result, too little attention is focused on the general problem of gleaning a clearer understanding of the role and responsibilities of the individual in the modern world. Thirdly, much of this literature is more appropriate to the past than the present and the future. Many of the most important religious, philosophical, and psychological writings on the human personality, for example, are more in tune with a world that is far different from the world that is rapidly evolving today. In a world characterized by profound secular and sacred change, unprecedented population growth, extraterrestrial discoveries and colossal communications developments, much of the literature that has been written about the human personality seems to be of limited usefulness in coming to grips with the problems people are encountering in everyday life, or may be expected to encounter in the future. In consequence, while a great deal of care must be exercised not to reject this indispensable source of knowledge, wisdom, insight, and understanding, an equal amount of care must be taken to ascertain what is relevant to present day concerns and projected needs.

Although there is much to be learned from the historical and scholarly literature on the human personality, *new* prototypes are needed today. Such prototypes must be capable of coming to grips with the realities of the present and the prospects of the future. Of all the places where helpful fragments can be found for piecing together these prototypes, culture provides more than its share of possibilities. This is because, as indicated earlier, culture has contained in it the depth of understanding and breadth of vision needed to illuminate a path for the future. It is through deeper and deeper forays into the domain of culture, therefore, that it is possible to slowly but surely piece together a portrait of '*the cultural personality*' that possesses many of the attributes needed to confront the complexities of the present and the challenges of the future.

It would be foolhardy to contend that the cultural personality can be fleshed out here in sufficient detail to address the enormity and complexity of this problem. Therefore, what is proposed is the creation of a *general outline* of the cultural personality against which individuals can measure the reality of their own experience. It is an outline based on the conviction that when culture is defined in a holistic sense, it provides a promising avenue for coming to grips with the types of problems individuals are confronted with in the modern world and may be confronted with even more in the future.

The Concept of the Cultural Personality

The cultural personality is a compound term. It derives its meaning from the juxtaposition of two of the most compelling concepts imaginable, namely 'personality' and 'culture'. Since both concepts contain a variety of meanings,[3] it makes sense to examine them separately first, and then connect them to stand face to face with the the cultural personality as a concept.

First, there is the concept of personality. Like the concept of culture, it possesses a long history. It can be traced back to ancient times, to the Greeks and the Romans. In fact, the term 'persona', from which the modern term personality derives, derives from the Romans. In its original form, persona was the term that was employed to denote the masks used in ancient drama. These masks, which were adaptations of the masks of comedy and tragedy and had horns in the mouthpiece to amplify the sound, were used to distinguish the role of the actor. Interestingly, this led to a fundamental distinction between the two basic dimensions of the human personality: the real self, which is more internal in nature; and the role the individual plays in society, which is more external in nature. It is a distinction that has persisted to this day. Whether it is the individual seen in terms of the subjective-objective split, the self and the other, the introvert and the extrovert, the egoist and the altruist, or any other dichotomous view, this basic separation between the internal and external dimensions of the human personality—often in conflict with one another—has been a classic preoccupation of personality theory for centuries.

This split is manifested in the differences that exist between the notions of personality and character. Whereas the former is viewed more as external, socially and environmentally oriented, the latter is viewed more as internal and morally and spiritually oriented. Gordon Allport explains this split in terms of the original Latin and Greek meanings of the terms, as well as their subsequent impact on American and European psychology:

No less fascinating than the term *personality* is the term *character*. The two are often used interchangeably, although the first is of Latin derivation, the second of Greek…It is the mark of a man—his pattern of traits or his life-style…European psychologists, however, seem to have a preference for *character*, while American psychologists favour *personality*. There is an interesting reason for the difference…The former term (personality) suggests appearance, visible behaviour, surface quality; the latter (character) suggests deep (perhaps inborn), fixed, and basic structure.[4]

This same distinction is evident in oriental and occidental philosophy. While there are obviously many exceptions to the rule, generally speaking occidental philosophy has been more externally and environmentally oriented, concerned largely with asserting human and technological control over nature. Oriental philosophy, on the other hand, has been much more internally and spiritually oriented, concerned largely with exploring those deep caverns and vast spaces that exist within human beings.

Over the last two thousand years, both personality and character have acquired a variety of meanings. These meanings are very much in evidence in most disciplines, but particularly philosophy, theology, law, sociology and psychology. In philosophy, for example, personality is often used as a synonym for selfhood, especially as it relates to the idea of perfection and something of supreme value. In theology, both character and personality are conspicuous: character referring to an individual of good moral standing or worth; and personality referring to members of the trinity, that is, the three forms of appearance or persons in the same essence. In law, personality is often used to refer to any individual enjoying legal status, either separately or as a member of a social or community group. In the therapeutic arts and sciences, personality is generally deemed to be the sum total of all inborn or acquired traits and characteristics.

With the advent of modern psychology and psychoanalysis, interest in the notions of personality and character intensified considerably, so much so that Jan Christiaan Smuts recommended the creation of a new discipline called 'Personology' to deal with it:

In Personality will probably be found the answer to some of the hardest and oldest questions that have troubled the heart as well as the head of man. The problem of Personality seems as hard as it is important. Not without reason have thinkers throughout the ages shied off from it. But it holds precious secrets for those who will seriously devote themselves to the new science or discipline of Personology.[5]

With the growing interest in personality has come a renewed interest in the 'essence' of the individual and the individual's 'role' or 'roles' in society.

Concerted attempts have been made to understand how individuals behave in society, as well as how they go about organizing their lives to form an intricate, overall pattern. Psychologists and psychiatrists often liken this process to the peeling of an onion: the removal of successive layers or the 'roles' of the individual until the real self is revealed.

For present purposes, the term personality will be used to embrace both the essence of the individual and the individual's role or roles in society, or the internal and external dimensions of the individual. In other words, character will be viewed as a component, albeit an exceedingly important component, of personality. While this is somewhat inconsistent with some of the scholarly literature, and particularly the historical separation between personality and character, it is consistent with the all-embracing meaning the term personality is acquiring in the modern world. In his fascinating book *The Cultural Background of Personality*, for example, Ralph Linton defines personality as 'the organized aggregate of psychological processes and states pertaining to the individual'.[6] In a similar vein, Gordon Allport defines personality as 'the dynamic organization within the individual of those psychophysical systems that determine his characteristic behaviour and thought'.[7]

The following definition from the Encyclopaedia Britannica serves a useful purpose in this regard, since it brings out many of the fundamental aspects of personality in this combined internal-external sense:

the unique organization of psychophysical traits or characteristics, inherent and acquired, that distinguish each individual and are observable in his relations to the environment and to the social group.[8]

This definition serves a valuable purpose in several ways. First, it emphasizes the psychophysical traits and characteristics that distinguish each individual and are observable in his or her conduct. In so doing, it embraces the mental, emotional, physical, and spiritual dimensions of the personality and places the focus directly on ways of thinking, feeling, acting, behaving, belonging and especially being that are basic to the personality of every individual. Second, it emphasizes the distinctiveness of every individual, since in the final analysis, every individual is 'one of a kind' as manifested by his or her actions, attitudes, beliefs, patterns, values, and ways of perceiving the world and acting in the world. Third, it emphasizes the organization of all the traits and characteristics of the individual, both inherent and exhibited, thereby suggesting that there is some internal process of evaluation and ordering going on as well as some central organizing principle or principles around which individuals orchestrate their behaviour. Finally, it takes into account both the internal and external dimensions of the personality, particularly as these relate to the self as well as to other human beings and the entire realm of nature. Momentarily an opportunity will present itself to probe more deeply into these attributes and characteristics. Here, suffice it to say that they are of utmost importance to the concept of the cultural personality.

If personality is a difficult concept to pin down, so is culture, as was demonstrated earlier. Clearly whatever meaning, definition or concept of culture is employed will have a profound bearing on the personality type associated with it. This is true not only for the philosophical, artistic, educational, historical, psychological and sociological concepts of culture, but also for the anthropological, ecological, biological and holistic concepts of culture.

It is clear that a very specific personality type is buried in each concept of culture. For example, the philosophical concept of culture produces the thinker or intellectual when it is combined with the concept of personality. Here, the emphasis is on the development of the mental, conceptual and analytical abilities of the individual. Similarly, the artistic concept of culture produces the artist. Here, the emphasis is on the development of one's sensorial, perceptual and aesthetic capabilities. Likewise, the historical concept produces the 'cultured person'. In this case, the emphasis is on familiarity with the legacy from the past, and with it, cultivation of the capacity for refined judgment and discriminating taste.

Each of these personality types possesses attributes that are essential to an overall understanding of the cultural personality, largely as a result of their emphasis on the need to think clearly and concisely as well as to react creatively and imaginatively to situations. Nevertheless, each of these personality types, like the concepts of culture underlying them, suffer from a shortcoming. They all represent one-dimensional, partial, or limited solutions to what is essentially a multidimensional, comprehensive and open-ended problem. No one understood this better than T. S. Eliot:

We may be thinking of *learning* and a close acquaintance with the accumulated wisdom of the past: if so, our man of culture is the scholar. We may be thinking of *philosophy* in the widest sense—an interest in, and some ability to manipulate, abstract ideas: if so, we may mean the intellectual...Or we may be thinking of *the arts*: if so, we mean the artist and the amateur or dilettante. But what we seldom have in mind is all of these things at the same time. We do not find, for instance, that an understanding of music or painting figures explicitly in Arnold's description of the cultured man: yet no one will deny that these attainments play a part in culture.[9]

The anthropological concept of culture helps here. By defining culture in a much more expansive and comprehensive way, it broadens the orbit of cultural concern far beyond philosophy, the arts, and the legacy from the past to include every domain and aspect of human life, from eating to sleeping, work to leisure, ideals to ideologies.

When the anthropological concept of culture is fused with the concept of personality, the resulting personality type is 'the whole person'. This has a number of advantages over the personality types derived from the philosophical, artistic and historical concepts of culture, since it focuses attention on the totality of human experience rather than on some limited aspect of it. Here, the individual is seen as the product of all economic, social, political, aesthetic, humanistic and philosophical experiences and encounters and not just certain specialized experiences and encounters.

This personality type has a great deal to recommend it. Placing emphasis on 'the total human being', it represents a much more consolidated way of looking at the human personality. However, like the other concepts considered to date, it also breaks down as a prototype capable of guiding human behaviour in the present and the future. It does so for precisely the same reason that the anthropological concept of culture proves insufficient as a concept for encompassing all aspects and dimensions of culture: it is human-centred and fails to take the external environment and nature sufficiently into account as an integral part of the human personality.

It follows from these examples that there is also a concept of the personality buried in the holistic concept of culture. Clearly this personality is not the philosopher, the artist, the humanist, the 'cultured person', or even 'the whole person'. Nor is it a new age notion or up-dated version of 'renaissance man'. Rather, it is a personality type concerned first and foremost with the way in which all the component parts of the whole are coalesced to form a complete person—a complete person who is integrated internally in the self and integrated externally in the realm of nature. In the final analysis, perhaps this is what personality and character development are about: blending life's infinite ingredients and experiences together in such a way that they form a seamless web that is in tune with both the internal world of the self and the external world of nature.

What is being proposed here is an individual who has a comprehensive and integrated outlook on life and the external world. Just as cultures exude collective worldviews and values based on their unique structure, position and outlook on the world, so individuals exude personal worldviews and values based on very specific conceptions and interpretations of the world as well as actions in the world. These worldviews and values deal with a vast array of issues related to how individuals visualize and interpret the world, organize themselves, conduct their affairs, position themselves in the world, live in the world, live their lives, and prepare for death.

Issues as fundamental as these are surely among the most important of all. Not only are they issues that every individual is compelled to come to grips with and confront regardless of age, station in life, education, gender, social class and geographical location in the world, but they are also issues that lie at the very heart of the human condition. Albert Schweitzer had fundamental issues as these in mind when he talked about the importance of *elemental thinking*. For Schweitzer, not only do individuals manifest personal worldviews and values in the way they choose to live their lives and express themselves in their works and deeds, but also they are compelled to wrestle with a vast range of fundamental questions related to the meaning of life as well as their role and purpose in the world:

Elemental thinking is that which starts from the fundamental questions about the relations of man to the universe, about the meaning of life, and about the nature of goodness. It stands in the most immediate connection with the thinking which impulse stirs in everyone. It enters into that thinking, widening and deepening it.[10]

Issues such as these concern 'the cultural personality' in the holistic sense in which the term is employed here, for while the cultural personality is concerned with addressing all the specific, practical problems to be confronted in life, such as where to live, where to work, who to live with and what to work at, there is an awareness that these problems are fundamentally linked to a deeper and more profound set of philosophical, cosmological and ontological problems related to the individual's outlook on the world as well as being in the world. It is for this reason that the cultural personality is concerned first and foremost with the nature, meaning and purpose of life, as well as with what one sees when one looks inward into the self and outward on the universe.

Despite the importance of this personality type for the present and the future, it is easy to move farther away from it rather than closer to it. The dictates and demands of modern life have become such that they are causing people to get more and more caught up with the details of life than with life's core and those deeper and more profound needs that are the essence of life itself. The farther humanity drifts from the idea of the whole person, worldview and values in this deeper and more profound holistic sense, the more people's lives become fractured and fragmented. It is as if life and people's lives, like people's personalities, were being pulled and stretched in so many different directions that contact is lost with the ability to unify life and give it meaning in the world.

The Characteristics of the Cultural Personality

The time has come to put some flesh on the bare bones of the cultural personality. What is meant by the cultural personality in fact? What are its main characteristics, its fundamental features and attributes? While there are many characteristics, features and attributes that provide the cultural personality with its shape and identity, in the final analysis, the cultural personality is *holistic, centred, authentic, unique, creative, altruistic* and *humane.* Each of these will be examined in turn.

First and foremost, the cultural personality is holistic. By this is meant that the cultural personality is constantly endeavouring to mold all the component parts of being into a coherent and comprehensive whole. To achieve this, according to Jan Christiaan Smuts, is to achieve the highest state of personality development:

Personality then is a new whole, is the highest and completest of all wholes, is the most recent conspicuous mutation in the evolution of Holism…(it is) the supreme embodiment of Holism both in its individual and its universal tendencies. It is the final synthesis of all the operative factors in the universe into unitary wholes, and both in its unity and its complexity it constitutes the great riddle of the universe.[11]

To be holistic in this sense is to be constantly striving to see, feel, experience and comprehend the unity and oneness of all things, or, as Goethe said, to 'will the whole'. It matters little that holism in some ultimate, metaphysical sense may be unattainable; it is always possible to add new information and insights to the ever-expanding dimensions of the whole. What is important, however, is to be relentlessly and systematically struggling to achieve this ideal, and, to this end, consistently acting to fuse the mental, physical, emotional and spiritual aspects of the human personality to form a unitary entity. First and foremost, the cultural personality is about acts of integration and synthesis aimed at melding all the diverse fragments of being together to form a harmonious whole: internal as well as external, subjective as well as objective, material as well as non-material, self as well as other. John Cowper Powys said it best when he said:

The whole purpose and end of culture is a thrilling happiness of a particular sort—of the sort, in fact, that is caused by a response to life made by a harmony of the intellect, the imagination, and the senses.[12]

Just as the cultural personality is engaged in the constant search to discover the inherent wholeness in the self, the world and the universe, so it is constantly endeavouring to recognize the same wholeness in others. For the cultural personality, people are not defined by their colour, age, profession, status, geographical location, or any other single characteristic or set of characteristics. Rather they are defined in terms of their wholeness, taking into account their many attributes, strengths and weaknesses. In other words, they are defined as total human beings and treated accordingly. If judgments are to be made at all, they are made on the basis of the whole person rather than on the basis of one or two selective traits or distinguishing characteristics.

Since holism is in effect the 'tendency in nature to form wholes that are more than the sum of the parts by creative evolution',[13] it is appropriate to ask what it is that makes the whole greater than the sum of its parts in the case of the cultural personality. This 'extra something' has been variously described as a value system, a soul, a spirit, or a philosophy of life. Since it is through this process that the cultural personality becomes centred in the world and the universe as well as in the self, it requires explanation.

As with personality development of any type, the point of departure for the development of the cultural personality is with life's everyday experiences. Initially, these experiences are not only exceedingly diverse, they are also largely undifferentiated. They invade the individual at all times, as well as from all sides. With the passing of time, the cultural personality begins to make associations and connections between and among the myriad experiences which are encountered in everyday life. These associations and connections form the basis of values, since they involve comparisons between one type of experience and another. It is here that assessments are made of life's many encounters and priorities are established among them, thereby making it possible to rank these encounters differently in the total scheme of things. Just how important culture is in this process of value formation was revealed by Mircea Malitza when he said, 'culture is the crucible from which values emerge, where preferences are formed and the hierarchy among them is established'.[14]

What is true in the case of culture and cultures is equally true in the case of the cultural personality. For just as there are values in an expansive, collective sense, so there are values in a specific, personal sense. It is values in this sense which give shape, substance, character and integrity to the cultural personality. Without doubt, these values make it possible for the individual to sort out what is relevant from what is irrelevant, what is meaningful from what is meaningless.

For the cultural personality, there are three aspects to values which require attention. First, there is the conflict between personal and societal values. There are bound to be times when there will be fundamental differences between the personal values of the individual and the collective values of society, particularly in those areas where there are limitations or shortcomings in societal values which the cultural personality must be concerned with addressing. Second, there is the discrepancy between absolute values and relative values—values designed to manifest some universal or immutable truth compared to values that serve a particular function at a specific period of time or in a specific location. Here, the cultural personality is careful to avoid falling into the trap of thinking that values for one person must necessarily be values for another person or all people. Finally, there is the realization that values must be constantly attended to if they are to be cultivated effectively.

In the process of cultivating a viable set of values, the cultural personality becomes aware that values are not only the essential rudiments of a fully-developed personality, but also sources of integrity and inspiration. As a result, they should be savoured and celebrated at every opportunity:

There is a sense in which the whole of human culture is a struggle towards the higher values. Can there be any greater expression of culture than art? Art surely lifts us up, although it would not be likely to exist without us...We were meant to actualize the higher values, and incidental to this task is the privilege of enjoying them.[15]

It is through the process of struggling to formulate, reformulate, and refine values that the cultural personality becomes aware of a deeper development that begins to take root in the fertile soil of the self. It has to do with the formulation of a central organizing principle or set of central organizing principles around which personal values are galvanized and coalesced.

This central organizing principle or set of central organizing principles may be predicated on love, beauty, truth, integrity, creativity, caring, commitment to a cause, or any other worthwhile human attribute or endeavour. Since they are finely honed over long periods of time, they have a seasoned quality, stability, and solidarity about them. Nevertheless, they are not fixed, immutable or unchanging; they are constantly being broadened, deepened, and refined over time in order to remain in tune with the dynamic nature of reality and the internal needs of the self. For just as the world is constantly giving rise to new problems, challenges and opportunities, so the cultural personality is constantly redefining and reformulating its central organizing principle or principles in order to bring them into line with the rapidly-evolving needs of humanity, society and the self.

It is important to emphasize that this central organizing principle or set of principles are what make it possible for the cultural personality to feel rooted in the self as well as flexible, adaptable and responsive to the never-ending changes going on in the world at large. By providing the fundamental focal points around which experiences and values are coalesced, this central organizing principle or set of principles provide coherence, connectedness and continuity in space and time. While they mature and ripen over time depending on individual needs and preferences, they nevertheless remain the benchmarks and touchstones imperative for the effective functioning of the cultural personality.

It is through progressive refinement of what some prefer to call the creation of a viable value system that the cultural personality begins to fashion a very specific philosophy of life. In his book *Cosmic Understanding*, Milton Munitz explains why it is so essential to have such a philosophy:

When acquired, such a philosophy provides a framework of basic principles that helps guide a person's reactions to the crises and opportunities of life, to the universal facts of human existence—being born and dying, being a member of society, being part of a wider universe. To have a set of basic guiding principles, whether accepted from some external source or worked out for oneself, is an inescapable requirement for a human being.[16]

What is significant about this philosophy for the cultural personality is its distinctiveness. Having taken the time and trouble to wrestle with all the diverse elements and ingredients that go into making it, it could scarcely be otherwise:

The art of self-culture begins with a deeper awareness, borne in upon us either by some sharp emotional shock or little by little like an insidious rarefied air, of the marvel of our being alive at all; alive in a world as startling and mysterious, as lovely and horrible, as the one we live in. Self culture without some kind of integrated habitual manner of thinking is apt to fail us just when it is wanted the most. To be a cultured person is to be a person with some kind of original philosophy.[17]

It is through hammering out this philosophy that the cultural personality begins to comprehend what it means to be centred in the self as well as in the world. This is because there is a growing awareness of the fact that a central rudder has been created which provides strength, durability, and a clear sense of direction and purpose as far as the life course is concerned. John Cowper Powys uses a botanical illustration to bring this point home:

Slowly, as life tightens the knot of our inner being, our outer leaves, like those of a floating water-plant, expand in the sunshine and in the rain of pure chance; but we still are aware of the single stalk under the surface, of the single root that gives meaning to all.[18]

It is doubtful whether the cultural personality can ever become fully conscious of the single root that provides centredness in life without becoming 'authentic' or true to itself. It is this requirement that Thomas Carlyle had in mind when he penned his famous *Law of Culture*:

Let each become all that he was created capable of being; expand, if possible, to his full growth; resisting all impediments, casting off all foreign, especially all noxious adhesions; and show himself at length in his own shape and stature, be these what they may.[19]

There are two aspects to this law deserving scrutiny. First, there is the idea of the growth and development of the personality itself, not only in terms of the expenditure of all those energies and efforts required to achieve maturity and full growth, but also in terms of the struggle that must constantly be waged to achieve authenticity. It is cast in the form of a struggle because that is precisely what it is—a struggle that must be continuously waged within the self as well as with the world to 'become what thou art'. To do this effectively is to constantly resist the pressures of imitation and conformity and compel oneself to come to grips with one's real essence and fundamental purpose and beliefs in life. Surely this is what Calvin had in mind when he talked about fulfilling one's destiny or calling, as well as what Joseph Campbell had in mind when he talked about following one's bliss or always striving to achieve one's full potential.

This struggle to realize one's full potential must surely be one of the most difficult challenges of all. It means plumbing the depths of one's being in order to confront the real self and achieve genuine authenticity and identity, rather than giving in to what others might wish or succumbing to the dictates of society. Such a challenge is totally independent of station, profession or geographical circumstances. It relates as much to the farmer in Africa, the scholar in Asia and the landlord in Latin America as it does to the businessman in North America and the housewife in Europe.

There is another aspect of the *Law of Culture* that demands scrutiny. It has to do with 'the limits of authenticity', or where one person's quest for authenticity ends and another person's begins. What happens, for example, when one person's quest for authenticity results in actions which impinge on or interfere with the rights and freedoms of others? For the cultural personality, this always sets in motion the search for an alternative course of action—a course that preserves the right for authenticity without running roughshod over the needs, rights, and privileges of others. It is for this reason that the cultural personality is always careful to examine the bigger picture, as well as look at everything in context rather than in isolation. The quest for authenticity is never used as an excuse or a license for doing whatever one wants in life, or for achieving things at the expense of others.

It is difficult to see how the cultural personality can achieve authenticity without becoming unique or one of a kind. While everyone is said to have a double living somewhere else in the world in a physical sense, this is certainly not true in a cultural sense. In a cultural sense, all individuals are unique. From the moment human beings are born, their lives are filled with a continuous flow of situations, challenges, ordeals and opportunities that are totally different from those of other people. Not only are there enormous variations in the way people interact with friends, family, relatives, strangers and the natural world, but also there are significant differences in the myriad special features and particular circumstances which govern their lives.

In the process of weaving life's infinite elements and experiences together to form an integrated whole, the cultural personality is certain to create a life that is without duplication or parallel. It is a fact that is worthy of reflection. It should be celebrated in good times as well as bad, in moments of pleasure as well as in times of adversity. Not only does it speak volumes about the need that exists in all individuals to be distinctive and different—to have a personal identity and life that is readily differentiated from others—but also it supplies much of the fuel that is required to propel people to higher levels of accomplishment.

It is the ability of the cultural personality to meld life's innumerable fragments and elements together to form a life that is distinctly different from any other person's that makes the cultural personality creative as well as unique.

As profuse and unpredictable as life's events and experiences are, these things in themselves do not make life a creative act. Rather, it is the way they are spun together to form a coherent and comprehensive whole. For in the process of weaving together the infinite strands of life's untold profundities and mysteries, the cultural personality is compelled to exercise an incredible amount of ingenuity and originality deriving from the inalienable right of all individuals to fashion their lives in accordance with the demands and dictates of their own experiences and beliefs. Every individual, regardless of his or her educational background, professional circumstances, social situation, religious persuasion or spiritual inclination has the right to fashion life in such a way that it is creative in its design, development and execution.

It is impossible to overstate the importance of creativity in the life of the individual. For just as creativity is the key to lifting cultures to higher and higher levels of accomplishment, so it is the key to human fulfillment and enrichment. Every individual needs an outlet to express the beauty and worth of human nature, as well as to make constructive contributions to the community and society. It is creativity that provides this outlet, largely by endowing the individual with the means that are needed to express the depth of human feelings and the range of human emotions.

While this type of creativity may never manifest itself in the creation of rare paintings, unusual compositions, fine books, or famous inventions—that is to say in the creation of great works of art, science or scholarship—it is creativity none the less. It involves taking the countless building blocks of life and arranging them in such a way that the result is a life full of value and meaning in the fullest and most complete sense of the term. Viewed in this way, life itself becomes a creative act.

It follows from this that life is a dynamic rather than static affair. It is an affair that is in a constant state of motion and flux, not only in the way in which experiences, values and worldviews are arranged and rearranged, but also in the way in which the central organizing principle or principles and underlying philosophy are enlarged, reformulated, recreated and redesigned. Ralph Linton, writing about the relationship between culture and personality, refers to this dynamic property this way:

Personalities are dynamic continuums, and although it is important to discover their content, organization and performance at a given point in time, it is still more important to discover the processes by which they develop, grow and change...[20]

Each individual is born with a unique configuration of physical and psychological potentialities, and from the moment of birth finds himself in interaction with his environment. The process of personality development is one of continual assimilation and organization of the experiences which he derives from this interaction.[21]

This dynamic property renders to the cultural personality an ability to adjust to a world that is in perpetual motion. While it is important to develop this ability in the short run, it is even more essential to develop it in the long run. Every individual must confront the realization that a kind of 'psychological death' or 'static malaise' can set in at any age in life if the appropriate precautions are not taken to prevent it. Regardless of whether the individual is in the prime of life, mid-career, early retirement, or the final stages of life, there is a constant danger of becoming so mired in reality that it is impossible to extricate oneself and get back on track. If the creative and dynamic capabilities of the personality are not swung fully into play in such situations, the result is a deadening of the personality that slowly but surely sucks every ounce of energy and vitality out of the life process.

The cultural personality is not only fully aware of this but is constantly and methodically taking steps to prevent it. It does so by drawing on its inner reserves and innovative abilities as well as creating new challenges and opportunities. No sooner is one challenge met or opportunity realized than others are put in their place. It is unlikely that the cultural personality will achieve this without acquiring one of the noblest personality characteristics of all. This is altruism, or the ability to give to others and make commitments to causes which are greater than the self.

It was altruism that Matthew Arnold had in mind when he spoke of the need to take education and learning out of the hands of the narrow élite and share it with the whole of humanity. Likewise, it was altruism that Pitirim Sorokin had in mind when he penned the following passage:

If humanity mobilizes all its wisdom, knowledge, beauty, and especially the all-giving and all-forgiving love or reverence for life and if a strenuous and sustaining effort of this kind is made by everyone—an effort deriving its strength from love and reverence for life—then the crisis will certainly be ended and a most magnificent new era in human history ushered in. It is up to mankind itself to decide what it will do with its future life-course.[22]

Throughout history, there have been numerous examples of individuals who have set aside their own personal interests and ambitions in order to devote themselves to the service of others. In the twentieth century, the examples of Mahatma Gandhi, Albert Schweitzer and Mother Theresa spring to mind. Each in his or her own way gave up promising careers and personal aspirations in order to dedicate themselves to serving society and humanity in this larger sense. As impressive as these examples are, they should never be allowed to obscure the fact that there are millions of people working at every level of society and everywhere in the world to promote the interests of society and humanity as a whole.

For the cultural personality, altruism is not seen as an alternative to egoism. Rather, both are seen as dual aspects of the same reality. While the cultural personality is very much interested in the development of the self, this is not seen as an end in itself, but rather as a means to a much broader and more significant end. Why is this so essential? It is essential because, as Samuel Butler observed, the works of all individuals, whether they are in literature, music, architecture or anything else, are always portraits of the self. The more people try to conceal it, the more clearly their characters and personalities appear in their works in spite of it.

While altruism is a fundamental characteristic worthy of a great deal of thought and reflection, it is not sufficient in and of itself to ensure that the cultural personality is humane—the final characteristic of the cultural personality. It is difficult to determine how to address this final characteristic. Perhaps the best place to start is to revisit the idea of the harmonious union of all the characteristics and attributes which in total comprise the cultural personality.

In the process of uniting all these characteristics and attributes, the cultural personality is forced to develop many of the sensitivities and sensibilities that are required to become truly humane. It is here that the heart, the soul and the senses are fused with the mind, the spirit, the body and the intellect; egoism is tempered with altruism; beauty, truth and creativity are brought into line with equality, justice and integrity. The result is an individual who is more settled in the self, as well as more compassionate and respectful of the needs and rights of others.

It is difficult to see how the cultural personality can become humane in this deeper and more profound sense without plunging deeply into questions of ethics and morality. Viewed from this perspective, the current ethical malaise that is sweeping the globe must be seen as a cause for concern. For in the act of asserting human dominance over nature and idolizing technology and material growth, human beings are in danger of losing those basic ethical convictions and moral values that lie at the very heart of the personality.

Perhaps what is needed here more than anything else is a secular ethical code capable of assigning to human beings all the moral and ethical responsibilities and duties that have been traditionally associated with religion. Of what do these responsibilities consist? Surely they consist of accepting responsibility for the sick, the elderly, the disadvantaged and the poor, as well as for lakes, rivers, oceans, forests, streams, flora and fauna, other species and future generations. Such responsibilities, particularly if they are assumed conscientiously and addressed energetically, would compel human beings to develop the sensitivities, sensibilities and capabilities needed to become humane in the fullest and most complete sense of the term. In the process of accepting these responsibilities, human beings, like the cultural personality, would be compelled to develop those deeper and more lasting moral and ethical values, principles, and practices which are needed to become fully committed to the cosmic reality and the human condition.

There is no more fitting way to conclude this section than to quote from Prem Kirpal whose insights into culture and its role in the life of the individual are as relevant as they are timely. Not only does the following poem embody many of the characteristics which are most essential in the cultural personality, but also it strikes at the heart of what the cultural personality is all about:

The abiding quality of life-time
Conferred by God on each alive
Is comprised of care of each other,
Quest of love and peace of mind,
Quietness of spirit, and sheer delight
Of being oneself and belonging to all,
Loving and loved in life-time,
Experiencing bliss and ecstasy
With Serenity and Creativity!
May such Quality of Life
Embellish all in time to come
For a great new world of Humanity![23]

The Cultivation of the Cultural Personality

Of all the possible points of penetration into the cultivation of the cultural
personality, cultivation of 'the art of seeing' provides the most promising possibilities. As indicated earlier, cultivation of this art requires constant
attention and nurturing, since it necessitates the development of a number of
interrelated capabilities: the ability to see things whole; the ability to detect
patterns, themes, and interrelationships among the component parts of
wholes; the ability to broaden and deepen vision and perception in all
directions in order to come into closer and closer contact with the cosmos
and the self; and finally, the ability to make intelligent choices and enlightened
decisions about future courses of action.

It was 'the art of seeing' that preoccupied Ken Wilber in his book *Eye to
Eye*. There, he talks about developing three different eyes of perception as the
key to knowledge and understanding. First, there is the 'eye of the flesh', which
discloses the material world of the senses. Second, there is 'the eye of reason',
which discloses such things as symbols and images. Third, there is 'the eye of
contemplation', which discloses knowledge of spiritual and related realities.[24]

Cultivation of the art of seeing was also uppermost in Goethe's mind
when he said that he learned to comprehend the world more with the eye than
the other sense organs.[25] He was obviously focusing on seeing as a
fundamental prerequisite for coming to grips with the nature of reality and
the self, for how people perceive the world and all that is contained therein is
of singular importance in determining how they assess and evaluate problems
and choose to live their lives.

It is clear from this that the art of seeing should be cultivated to the point
where it acts as a window on the world as well as on the self. In order to do
this, it should be extended in all directions: past, present and future; internal
and external; spatial, temporal and spiritual. Not only should it be finely
tuned to the mysteries of the cosmos, but it should also be clearly focused on

the most mundane details and experiences in life. In other words, it should be concerned with the progressive enlargement of vision, as well as with the perpetual refinement of vision.

The cultural personality seeks to develop and refine the art of seeing not as an end in itself, but rather as the first step towards cultivation of all sensory capabilities, for what is true with respect to the art of seeing is equally true with respect to the art of hearing, touching, smelling, tasting, and sensing. Cultivation and refinement of each of these sensorial abilities requires the same care and attention as cultivation of the art of seeing. For aural acuity, tactile sensitivity, olfactory capability, taste discrimination, and intuitive understanding are equally essential if the object is to expand knowledge and understanding of the external world of reality as well as the internal world of the self. John Cowper Powys expressed this requirement admirably when he said, 'the very essence of culture is the conscious development of our awareness of existence'.[26]

It is difficult to see how the conscious development of awareness of existence can be attended to properly without a comprehensive training in the arts, for education in the arts is essential in opening up one's creative faculties, as well as developing one's sensory capabilities. Through music, there is exposure to sound, rhythm, harmony, counterpoint, and composition. Through dance, there is exposure to touch, balance, movement, muscle control, and physical coordination. Through the visual arts, there is exposure to texture, mass, structure, shape, form, and proportion. Through drama, there is exposure to tragedy, comedy, satire, humour and pathos. Individuals learn more about the self as well as about the world through intensive education in the arts. They also learn to deal creatively and constructively with the countless problems and possibilities encountered in everyday life.

What education in the arts does for the development of the senses and creative abilities, education in physical fitness and health does for the development of the body. Without adequate training in terms of diet, nutrition, disease prevention and proper exercise, the body fails to function properly. Regardless of whether it is through calisthenics, Tai Chi, Yoga, walking, running, swimming, or any other program of physical exercise aimed at loosening the limbs and lubricating the joints, care should be taken to ensure that the body is kept in good physical condition and sound working order.

The cultural personality is careful to attend to the cultivation of its mental capacities every bit as much as its physical capacities. Clearly, development of these capabilities requires the ability to cut through the shell of illusion in order to get at the causes, principles, premises, and assumptions which form the basis of all things. Far too often, too much attention is directed to outward appearances, thereby leaving little time to examine real issues and the fundamental essence of things. As a result, people often end up dealing with secondary symptoms rather than generic causes.

It is through cultivation of the senses, the body, and the intellect that the cultural personality begins its ascent into the more profound and less visible dimensions of the self. In much the same way that the art of seeing opens a window on the other senses, so the senses, the mind and the body open a window on the heart, the soul, the emotions, and the spirit. The development of each of these faculties is attended to with the same vitality and determination as the development of the senses, the body, and the intellect. The goal is always self-improvement, or 'self-actualization' to use Maslow's evocative phrase.

Considerable care should be taken to ensure that the idea of actualization is not confused with the idea of perfectibility. For the cultural personality, perfectibility is something worth striving for even if it is never attainable. For perfectibility demands perfect knowledge and understanding, which stand well beyond the capabilities and potentialities of all individuals. For regardless of how much the cultural personality sees, senses, knows, or feels, there is always much more to be seen, sensed, felt, and known. This is why 'the whole' is always defined in dynamic and open-ended rather than static and circumscribed terms—as a continuously expanding entity rather than a closed system. Moreover, the cultural personality is always aware of its own *imperfectibility*. Thus, while perfectibility is a goal worthy of pursuit, the cultural personality is always conscious of the inherent limitations and shortcomings which stand in the way of ever achieving this.

It is through recognition of the inevitability of imperfectibility that the cultural personality slowly but surely develops the capacity for awe, humility, and wonder which form the basis of cosmic consciousness. For cosmic consciousness is a fundamental concern of the cultural personality. It is external in the sense that it radiates outward from the individual in order to embrace ever-expanding dimensions of reality and the universe. It is internal in the sense that it penetrates inward into the individual in order to embrace all that it is possible to know and understand about the self. As a result, it stretches as far as possible in both directions, even though it is never possible to know what exists at the outer edges of the universe or the inner edges of the self.

Some contend that cosmic consciousness is such a rarefied affair that it can only be experienced by select groups of people. In his book *Cosmic Consciousness: A Study in the Evolution of the Human Mind*, the medical doctor Richard Maurice Bucke distinguishes between three types of consciousness: *simple consciousness* or awareness of one's bodily organs as well as the things that go on in and around one; *self-consciousness* or awareness not only of one's bodily organs and the immediate external environment but also awareness of oneself as a distinct entity apart from all the rest of the universe; and *cosmic consciousness* or awareness of the cosmos as a whole.[27] Having set out these three different types of consciousness, Bucke goes on to describe cosmic consciousness in some detail:

Along with the consciousness of the cosmos there occurs an intellectual enlightenment or illumination which alone would place the individual on a new plane of existence—would make him almost a member of a new species. To this is added a state of moral exaltation, an indescribable feeling of elevation, elation, and joyousness, and a quickening of the moral sense, which is fully as striking and more important both to the individual and to the race than is the enhanced intellectual power.[28]

Using the impersonal rather than personal form to describe an encounter with cosmic consciousness, Bucke then goes on to describe the intensity of this experience:

He was in a state of quiet, almost passive enjoyment. All at once, without warning of any kind, he found himself wrapped around as it were by a flame-coloured cloud...Directly afterwards came upon him a sense of exultation, of immense joyousness accompanied or immediately followed by an intellectual illumination quite impossible to describe. Into his brain streamed one momentary lightning-flash of the Brahmic Splendor which has ever since lightened his life.[29]

According to Bucke, eventually the human species *as a species* may be able to achieve this utopian state of affairs, even though it is limited to a small and select group of people at present. Whether or not this state of affairs is ever actually attainable, are there not grounds for asking if the experience of cosmic consciousness is not far more common than often assumed? While cosmic consciousness may be a highly personal affair which defies scientific quantification or interpersonal comparison, who has not experienced the feeling of Brahmic splendour, bliss or grandeur that Bucke describes at one time or another, where the sense of ecstasy and serenity that comes from some unique encounter with other people or the natural environment is so profound and intense that for the flash of a second there is a feeling of immortality and the entire universe and all of humanity seem united in a cosmic sense? Surely cosmic consciousness in this sense is more commonplace than some people are prepared to admit.

In the process of striving to achieve this ethereal state of affairs, the cultural personality comes face to face with the holistic nature of life in particular and the cosmos in general. For in the process of striving to achieve cosmic consciousness, the cultural personality comes face to face not only with the holistic nature of life and the universe, but also with the means of uniting all the various human faculties and capabilities in a symbiotic and unitary relationship. The senses, the body, the intellect, the mind, the heart, the soul and the spirit become one, so to speak, indispensable ingredients in the total make-up of the individual. Surely this is what Jan Christiaan Smuts meant when he said:

In proportion as a personality really becomes such, it acquires more of the character of wholeness; body and mind, intellect and heart, will and emotions, while not separately repressed but on the contrary fostered and developed, are yet all collectively harmonized and blended into one integral whole;…the wear and tear of internal struggle disappears; the friction and waste which accompany the warfare in the soul are replaced by peace and unity and strength; till at last Personality stands forth in its ideal purity, integrity and wholeness.[30]

It is difficult to see how the cultural personality can 'stand forth in all its ideal purity, integrity, and wholeness' without evolving a comprehensive, coherent and compassionate worldview. In the process of developing this worldview, the cultural personality takes a passionate and consuming interest in everything. Detailed study and exploration of all things is required for this, large and small, esoteric and commonplace, popular and serious. Nothing is rejected, ignored or taken for granted, since everything that is germane to the human situation and cosmic condition is examined in interest and in depth. Whether it is the arts, sciences, religion, politics, philosophy, economics, or the environment, all fields of knowledge and all disciplines are openly and actively probed because they contain valuable clues to the effective formulation and implementation of this highly individual way of looking at life, people, other species, the universe, and the cosmos.

Cultivation of this highly personal cosmology will require the development of educational and learning processes that may be at variance with many of those in vogue today. Whereas most contemporary educational and learning processes are focused on the mastery of a single discipline and acquisition of a set of specialized skills, the educational and learning processes proposed here are predicated on exploration and discovery of many disciplines, as well as acquisition of a very diverse range of skills. Not only is this more in keeping with the nature of education and learning as an open-ended and life-long concern, but also it is more in tune with the newly-emerging global reality.

Development of this significantly broader and more expansive approach to education and learning will be no easy matter. All people are products of their culture to the point where they take many aspects of their culture for granted and accept them without reservation or qualification. To develop an educational and learning system that is finely tuned to the realities of the present and demands of the future does not mean rejecting those aspects of one's own culture that are taken for granted. Rather, it means critically examining every aspect of one's culture to determine what is relevant and what is irrelevant. As indicated earlier, one of the best ways to do this is to juxtapose and compare the values and characteristics of one's culture with the values and characteristics of other cultures. For intercultural comparison—in the spirit of true education and learning—is one of the best means of exposing the strengths and shortcomings of one's own culture and the strengths and shortcomings of other cultures.

However difficult it is to stand on the perimeter of one's culture in order to evaluate it with a critical eye, it is even more difficult to stand on the perimeter of the self in order to view it in a detached and truthful manner. If only it was possible for people to see themselves from the outside rather than the inside. If they could, they would be able to deal with their problems and lives in a far more effective way. Things that are obvious to others are often very clouded and obscured to the self. To see themselves as others see them—their strengths and shortcomings, insecurities and instabilities, problems and possibilities—would be to take a giant step forward in developing a fuller and more complete understanding and sense of self. Perhaps this is why the cultural personality is always searching out the opinions and reactions of others, as well as benefiting from using other people as mirrors for the self. For as difficult as the art of self-assessment is, it is of quintessential importance to personality development.

It is through the ability to see oneself as others see one, as well as through the ability to evaluate oneself with a discerning and critical eye, that the cultural personality comes face to face with the real self. What, in the final analysis, gives the cultural personality its essence, meaning, and sense of identity? In the end, it is the sense of fulfillment that comes from taking the time to develop a comprehensive, compassionate and coherent worldview consistent with the external nature of reality and the internal requirements of the self. By its very nature, this worldview is indigenous rather than imitative. Not only is it hammered out on the anvil of personal experience, but also it is highly original and authentic. In effect, it is fashioned by deciding for oneself what is important in life as well as how one wants to live life and accept responsibility for it.

In the process of hammering out this worldview, the cultural personality slowly but surely masters 'the art of being'. The reason for this is apparent. In the act of dealing with the trials and tribulations of the external world of reality and the internal world of the self, the cultural personality is compelled to cultivate those sensitivities, sensibilities, and capabilities which are needed to live an integrated and harmonious life.

The Conduct of the Cultural Personality

If it is essential to come to grips with the cultivation of the cultural personality, it is equally essential to come to grips with the conduct of the cultural personality. Whereas the former is concerned largely with theory and the realm of ideas, the latter is concerned primarily with practice and the realm of action. While both are essential to an overall understanding of the cultural personality, in the end it is through actions and deeds, rather than theories and ideas, that the cultural personality makes its mark.

If the cultural personality is to take its rightful place alongside other prototypes of the human personality, it will have to flow from the highest forms of human conduct as well as the noblest forms of human action. Providing exemplary conduct and action in this way will be far from easy. In fact, it is probably the most difficult challenge of all, since the problems and temptations of a secular, materialistic and communications-oriented world are so great that exemplary conduct and action may be denied to all but the most committed and courageous.

Strong ethical leadership is the key to exemplary conduct and action. It grows out of the realization that ethical and moral values have the greatest relevance for people as well as societies. As a result, they demand the highest priority and attention. Albert Schweitzer comments on this need:

We may take as the essential element in civilization the ethical perfecting of the individual and of society as well. But at the same time, every spiritual and every material step in advance has a significance for civilization. The will to civilization is then the universal will to progress which is conscious of the ethical as the highest value for all.[31]

For the cultural personality, life is first and foremost an ethical act. It involves recognition of the ethical foundations of social and human behaviour in general and personal behaviour in particular, as well as acceptance of the fact that there are ethical consequences and implications for every human action. Regardless of whether it is confronting oneself, dealing with others, making consumer choices, participating in political causes, or interacting with nature, there are profound ethical consequences and moral overtones to all human actions.

Commitment to the existential belief that in committing themselves, people are committing the whole of humanity provides an ideal starting point for the development of the cultural personality in this sense. Adherence to this conviction causes the cultural personality to think long and hard about the ethical consequences of actions. This necessitates a kind of 'reverential thinking'—a willingness to consider the impact of actions not only for the self, but also for other human beings, future generations, other forms of plant, animal and mineral life, and ultimately the cosmos. Reverential thinking of this type compels the cultural personality to probe deeply into matters of the heart, the soul and the spirit in order to evolve modes of behaviour which do as little damage or injury as possible to everything and everyone that stands outside the self.

For the cultural personality, reverential thinking is not an end in itself, but rather a first step towards reverential action. It is action predicated on a willingness to accept responsibility for actions. If excessive consumption practices are deemed to be disrespectful of the natural environment or wasteful of resources, they are not sanctioned regardless of how they satisfy consumer wants. If success means running roughshod over the rights and privileges of others, it is not pursued regardless of how it advances personal ambitions. If ways of life in one part of the world are practiced at the expense of people living in other parts of the world, they are not condoned regardless of how satisfying they might be. In each of these cases, the cultural personality is always endeavouring to practice a way of life that does not involve exploiting others or the natural environment in order to satisfy the wants, desires and interests of the self.

Albert Schweitzer was one of the greatest proponents of reverential action. To him, all forms of life are precious, and therefore should be protected as much as possible. As a result, he had much to say that is pertinent to the conduct of the cultural personality:

Ethics is nothing else than reverence for life. Reverence for life affords me my fundamental principle of morality, namely, that good consists in maintaining, assisting and enhancing life, and that to destroy, to harm or to hinder life is evil...A man is really ethical only when he obeys the constraint laid on him to help all life which he is able to succor, and when he goes out of his way to avoid injuring anything living. He does not ask how far this or that life deserves sympathy as valuable in itself, nor how far it is capable of feeling. To him life as such is sacred.[32]

It would be foolhardy to contend that the cultural personality can always be a tower of strength in this sense. What the cultural personality is always doing is *striving to achieve* a way of living based on fulfilling personal aspirations without usurping the needs, rights and privileges of others. If this cannot be accomplished with one mode of behaviour, the cultural personality searches for other modes of behaviour capable of achieving it.

In attempting to glean a clearer understanding of the ethical ideals which lie at the root of the cultural personality, it might be helpful to examine two Chinese notions of 'face'. The first is *mien-tzŭ*, and the second is *lien*. Here, Hu Hsien-Chin elaborates on these two notions of face. Their relevance for the cultural personality is readily apparent:

...*mien-tzŭ* (is) a reputation achieved through getting on in life, through success and ostentation. This is prestige that is accumulated by means of personal effort or clever manoeuvring...The other kind of "face", *lien*...is the respect of the group for a man with a good moral reputation: the man who will fulfil his obligations regardless of the hardships involved, who under all circumstances shows himself a decent human being. It represents the confidence of society in the integrity of ego's moral character, the loss of which makes it impossible for him to function properly within the community.[33]

While the cultural personality is obviously an admixture of both *mien-tzŭ* and *lien*, it is clear where the emphasis is. It is on *lien*. While the cultural personality is concerned with personal success and subjective fulfillment as much as anyone else, this is not accomplished at the expense of others. Whatever can be accomplished by maintaining ethical integrity is accomplished; whatever cannot be accomplished by maintaining ethical integrity is rejected.

It is out of commitment to ethical ideals, rather than slavish adherence to the norms of a particular culture, that the cultural personality seeks to fashion its conduct in the world. The goal is always to work out for oneself the type of conduct that is appropriate under the circumstances, rather than following some prescribed rule or preordained course of action. Commitment to this goal causes the cultural personality to transcend the limitations and short-comings of cultures whenever and wherever they are inappropriate. This makes the cultural personality a 'culture-maker' rather than a 'culture-taker', since worldviews, norms, ideological beliefs and value systems which underlie every culture must be constantly analyzed and assessed. Whenever worldviews, norms, ideological beliefs and value systems are based on unac-ceptable assumptions or conflict with the interests of humanity, the cultural personality is prepared to confront them. Whether or not the cultural personality can be successful in this depends on particular circumstances in each case. Despite this, as Goethe observed in a letter to Schiller, 'Your own epoch you cannot change. You can, however, oppose its trends and lay the groundwork for auspicious developments.'[34]

In the process of laying the groundwork for auspicious developments, the cultural personality becomes extremely 'cause oriented'. Rather than calculating everything in terms of how it advances personal ambitions or career aspirations, the cultural personality evaluates everything in terms of how it advances causes. If something does not advance a cause to which the cultural personality is committed, it is not pursued regardless of how it satisfies personal objectives or career aspirations.

What are these causes to which the cultural personality is wedded? In one form or another, they are causes related to the affirmation of moral and ethical values, the conservation of natural resources, respect for the rights and freedoms of others, ecological and economic sustainability, liberty, human dignity, equality and justice.

A seminal step was taken in this direction with the signing of the Universal Declaration of Human Rights in 1948. Included among the many articles aimed at recognizing and ensuring the rights of all people in the world were two articles designed to protect people's cultural rights and increase citizen participation in cultural life:

Article 22

Everyone, as a member of society, has the right to social security and is entitled to realization, through national effort and international co-operation and in accordance with the organization and resources of each State, of the economic, social and cultural rights indispensable for his dignity and the free development of his personality.

Article 27

(1) Everyone has the right to participate in the cultural life of the community, to enjoy the arts and to share in scientific advancement and its benefits.

(2) Everyone has the right to the protection of the moral and material interests resulting from any scientific, literary or artistic production of which he is the author.[35]

It is through sensitivity for the rights and freedoms of others and, more generally, helping people to become full and active participants in cultural life, that the cultural personality seeks to have a lasting effect on the world. Clearly, this involves fighting for justice and equality in its different forms and manifestations. Whereas socialists view this fight largely in terms of economic, social and political justice and equality, the cultural personality views this fight in terms of justice and equality in every conceivable dimension of cultural life. For socialists, the challenge is to eliminate economic, social and political exploitation. For the cultural personality, the challenge is to eliminate all forms of exploitation, regardless of whether it is institutional, legal, bureaucratic, political, social, economic, environmental or spiritual. Any type of exploitation that robs people of their dignity, value, integrity, ideas, achievements and work is of concern to the cultural personality.

In the process of fighting to eliminate all forms of exploitation and injustice, the cultural personality slowly but surely strengthens its commitment to the most quintessential ideals of life. Here again, Schweitzer has something extremely relevant to say:

The ripeness that our development must aim at is one which makes us simpler, more truthful, purer, more peace loving, meeker, kinder, more sympathetic. That is the only way in which we are to sober down with age. That is the process in which the soft iron of youthful idealism hardens into the steel of a full-grown idealism which can never be lost.[36]

Pitirim Sorokin was equally aware of the importance of these ideals and the need to ensure that they are respected and developed in a cosmic context. Speaking of the need for a heightened sense of human consciousness, he observed:

The most urgent need of our time is the man who can control himself and his lusts, who is compassionate to all his fellow men, who can see and seek for the eternal values of culture and society, and who deeply feels his unique responsibility to the universe.[37]

Foremost among this commitment 'to see and seek for the eternal values of culture and society' is commitment to dissemination of the heritage of humankind. The more the cultural personality transcends the limits of specific cultures, the more it gains knowledge and understanding of the importance of the vast reservoir of accumulated wisdom, artifacts, insights and ideas from all cultures and all peoples. In much the same way that the cultural personality is anxious to gain access to this indispensable treasure-trove in order to educate the self, so it is equally anxious to share this precious gift with humanity.

It is here that the cultural personality parts company with cultural purists and imperialists. Whereas the latter personality types are concerned with asserting the superiority of one culture over another, largely for the purpose of imposing the values and norms of one culture on another, the former personality type is concerned with sharing the fruits of all cultures and all peoples with every member of the human family.

It is through co-operation and sharing, rather than competition and hoarding, that this is accomplished. The object is always to create the conditions for a better world—a world characterized by more dignity, equality, justice and freedom for all people. Such a world requires a continuous outpouring of those qualities that are most deeply ingrained in the cultural personality: compassion, caring, sharing, concern for others, and most of all, human love. Without these, the cultural personality is a pale shadow of its self.

It is impossible for the cultural personality to achieve this without considering its position in the world. Presumably this is what Kant had in mind when he said:

If there is any science man really needs, it is the one I teach, of how to occupy properly that place in creation that is assigned to man, and how to learn from it what one must learn in order to be a man.[38]

There is much to be learned about the problem of positioning from people like Gandhi and Mother Theresa, not to mention many others who have had an impact on the human condition and world situation. Whether Gandhi and Mother Theresa set out to change the world is impossible to know. What is known is that they have had an incredible impact on the course of events by positioning themselves in a very specific cultural context, working with local people. They did not travel extensively throughout the world, attempting to make the world a better place for all. Rather, they stayed primarily in one location and hammered away at local problems with deep-seated implications, allowing the force of their personalities and the passion of their convictions to speak for them.

There is much to be learned from these two individuals that is germane to the conduct of the cultural personality. Rather than setting out to influence the course of history or world events, the cultural personality is constantly striving to put into practice those ethical, spiritual and human ideals necessary to inspire others and produce concrete results. The focus is not so much on 'thinking globally and acting locally', although this is obviously an important part of it. Rather it is on 'thinking cosmically and acting personally'. To do so is to discover within the self 'the reflection of the cosmos and its supreme unifying principle'.[39] For the cultural personality, this is what life and living are about.

7. Community Cultural Development

The city is both a physical utility for collective living and a symbol of those collective purposes and unanimities that arise under such favouring circumstance. With language itself, it remains man's greatest work of art.

Lewis Mumford[1]

Communities are fascinating places. Ranging all the way from tiny towns and villages to sprawling cities and megalopolises, they are filled with endless opportunities for experience and delight.

Yet communities everywhere are in trouble. Due to rapid population growth, urbanization, pollution, escalating costs, overcrowding, and unrest there is mounting evidence to suggest that many of the more satisfying and rewarding aspects of community life could easily disappear if forceful steps are not taken to prevent it. Indeed, if consideration is not given to the causes and consequences of urban decay and the need for much more community identity, solidarity, cohesion and belonging, community living could easily become a nightmare.

If human beings are to be successful in making communities havens of happiness and fulfillment rather than sources of unhappiness and misery, much will depend on the capacity to improve community living beyond its present level. This will require the development of four very specific attributes: first, the ability to understand the reasons for the growing importance of communities of all shapes and sizes in the modern world; second, the ability to treat communities as integrated entities or dynamic wholes; third, the ability to develop the tools and techniques which are necessary to engage citizens fully in the process of community development; and fourth, the ability to evolve the administrative structures and institutional mechanisms which are necessary to make culture the principal focus and cornerstone of community life.[2]

The Importance of Communities

During the last few decades, interest in communities has escalated rapidly. Towns, cities, metropolises and megalopolises are assuming greater importance in developmental affairs, and more people are looking to communities to solve their economic, social, political, environmental, aesthetic and spiritual problems.

A concomitant feature of this rapidly escalating interest in communities is the growing commitment to community development. Whereas the focus of much of the post-war period has been on national and international development, now the focus appears to be shifting to communities as the new spawning grounds for innovative activity. It is not difficult to identify some of the reasons for this.

In the first place, approximately half of the world's population is now living in communities: towns, villages, cities, metropolises and megalopolises. Whether this is happening because people are being forced to vacate the countryside as a result of lack of employment opportunities, or because they are enticed by the attractions of big city life, the results are everywhere much the same. Communities are dramatically expanding in actual numbers and physical size. As this happens, more and more pressure is exerted on municipal authorities to provide the economic, social, political, environmental, educational, medical, artistic and spiritual resources which are necessary for a healthy and sustained existence.

In the second place, more and more people are realizing that it is the quality of life in communities which is the decisive factor in life. If communities lack the basic necessities and fundamental prerequisites of life—decent job opportunities, adequate accommodation, fresh water, clean air, recreational outlets, aesthetic ambiance, health facilities, spiritual services and the like—no amount of industrial growth, commercial expansion, technological innovation or national and international development will make up the difference.

In the third place, rapidly changing world conditions are conspiring to make communities one of the most important, if not the most important, forms of cultural configuration. Whether it is the breakup of the nation state, the breakdown of the family, the erosion of social and ethical values and traditions, the quest for identity, the response to economic uncertainty, the call to 'think globally but act locally' or the resurfacing of interest in neighbourhoods, more and more people everywhere in the world are looking to communities to solve their problems.

Finally, as indicated earlier, there is the dialectic reaction to globalization, the creation of large trading blocks, the emergence of superstates, the increased concentration of industrial, financial and commercial wealth and power in fewer hands, and the shrinkage in the psychic size of the world due to phenomenal developments in transportation, communications and technology. This is manifesting itself in a number of countervailing measures aimed at restoring people's sense of personal and collective identity, empowerment, solidarity, and control over the decision-making processes affecting their lives.

It would be a mistake to underestimate the cumulative impact of these developments. While globalization and the emergence of a global village seem inevitable, it is clear that the majority of people are finding this exceedingly difficult to cope with, particularly when it means fewer jobs, more unemployment, loss of personal identity, a great deal more instability and insecurity, and lack of cohesion and solidarity. When this happens, people's instinctive reaction is to put more faith, hope and trust in things that are immediate, concrete, specific and close to home.

It is for reasons such as these that communities are growing steadily in size, stature, and significance. Whether it is due to swelling numbers, growing awareness of the importance of the quality of community life or measures to locate the locus of decision-making closer to individuals and community groups, communities are destined to play a much more powerful role in the future than they have in the past.

How are towns, cities, municipalities and other manifestations of community life responding to this challenge? Not particularly well by many accounts. As more and more people flock to towns and cities in search of work, population densities increase dramatically, causing overcrowding and its attendant problems of congestion, lack of proper accommodation and sanitation and pressure on public utilities. In order to reduce transportation costs and profit from locations close to markets, more and more companies locate in urban surroundings, causing zoning problems and tightening an industrial knot around the core of most communities. More industries mean more traffic on city streets, since more trucks and vans are required to haul produce. The result is an exponential expansion in vehicular traffic, and with it, major traffic tie-ups, soaring maintenance costs, and complex communications problems. Severe pollution problems arise. A layer of soot is added to buildings and a band of smog settles over community skies. Water becomes more and more contaminated and mountains of waste begin to appear. Major pollution, disposal, and processing problems affect the aesthetic state of communities, causing it to deteriorate.

Many of the problems arising from this state of affairs—over-utilization of facilities, inadequate waste disposal, increased water, air and noise pollution, the appearance of ghettos, slums and shanty towns, the loss of safety and security, and the spread of violence—cannot be attended to properly because municipalities lack the financial resources, constitutional powers and institutional mechanisms to deal with them. Whatever the causes, the consequences are clear. More and more resources are siphoned off in an attempt to cope with the rapidly-deteriorating situation. As a result, fewer resources are available to address many of the deeper and more profound cracks and fissures which are opening up in community life.

Many of these cracks and fissures have to do with the plummeting social, psychological, human and aesthetic state of communities. Lewis Mumford expressed it best when he said, 'When the city ceases to be a symbol of art and order, it acts in a negative fashion: it expresses and helps to make more universal the fact of disintegration.³ Many communities are poised close to this precipice at present. Not only are they experiencing difficulties in maintaining the level of public and private amenities and facilities which is necessary for a healthy and meaningful existence, but also they are starting to exude signs of breaking down.

The consequences of this situation are as serious as they are conspicuous. More and more towns and cities are losing their sense of identity and belonging and are becoming impersonal collectivities. As this happens, people withdraw from active participation in community life and search for their identity and sense of belonging in other types of communities. They strike up associations with people in other parts of the world; they become involved in national and international associations, internets and electronic highways related to their profession, employment, area of specialization, or intellectual pursuit; and they commence correspondence with people in different parts of the world. These other notions and manifestations of community and communities, which provide people with a sense of identity and belonging in an entirely different sense, often prove to be a poor substitute for the loss of community identity and belonging in a physical sense. People who feel alienated and unsettled in their own communities are unlikely to find adequate compensation through associations farther afield.

Whenever people lose contact with their communities and withdraw from active participation in community life, the decision-making process is surrendered to people who have other interests, motives and objectives at heart. This tends to result in further community fragmentation and compartmentalization, and with it, an increased loss of cohesion, solidarity, continuity, vision, and purpose. It becomes harder to see where the community has been in the past, where it is at present, and where it should be headed in the future.

Naturally there are many different views about how this state of affairs should be dealt with. For municipal authorities, the solution may be to revamp the tax system and constitutional arrangements so that towns and cities have the financial resources and fiscal vehicles—as well as legislative and constitutional powers—to deal with urban sprawl and the loss of basic necessities and support services. For economists, the solution may be to accelerate the pace and tempo of economic growth, thereby improving investment, expenditure and employment opportunities and expanding the size of markets. For developers, the solution may be to erect skyscrapers, shopping malls and high density developments, thereby making better use of the most valuable land. And for environmentalists, the solution may be to control pollution and improve the capacity for ecological renewal and sound environmental management.

But herein lies exactly the same problem encountered earlier. Each group tends to look at the community from its own perspective and recommends solutions that relate to its own area of interest. Not only are the needs and interests of other groups seldom taken into account, but also few groups look at the needs and interests of the community as a whole. As a result, it is impossible to deal with communities as total, integrated entities because the holistic perspective essential for this is lacking.

Communities as Cultural Wholes

Where is the search commenced for the approach that is needed to deal with communities as total, integrated entities—entities capable of confronting economic, political, environmental, social and aesthetic problems, developing a sense of community identity and belonging, engaging people in the process of community development, and asserting the dignity and value of community life? Of all the places where clues may be found, culture again provides many exciting possibilities. This is because, as indicated earlier, culture possesses the integrative potential which is needed to treat communities as dynamic and organic wholes, as well as the practical means to confront many of the more persistent problems playing havoc with local life.

It should be emphasized that culture is being used here in the holistic sense as worldview in general and values in particular. Looked at in this way, communities are 'cultural wholes' that are concerned with how specific groups of people living in particular parts of the world visualize and interpret the world, organize themselves, conduct their affairs, elevate and embellish life, and position themselves in the world.

Historically, most communities have been seen and treated in partial rather than holistic terms. As a result, community life has usually been dominated by specific activities and institutions, thereby impeding the realization of a more integrated approach to community development.

In medieval Europe, for example, communities were dominated by religion and religious activity. Hence the church became the dominant institution and principal focal point of many communities. Not only did all roads lead to and from the church, but also the church towered over the community in physical size and ideological stature. To live within the sight and sound of the cathedral was to live within the community; to live beyond the sight and sound of the cathedral was to live outside the community.

During the Renaissance, social activity and social institutions replaced religious activity and religious institutions at the core of community life. In a purely physical sense, the square replaced the church. Whereas the church was sacred and religious, the square was social and secular. Not only was the square an important place to meet friends, conduct business, and pass away the time of day, but like the church, it was designed to uplift and inspire.

Through its use as a place to enact rituals and communal celebrations, the square brought people into close physical contact, thereby strengthening the social bonds of the community.

In the modern world, economic activity and economic institutions have replaced social and religious activities and institutions at the core of community life. The objective is to satisfy the economic needs of people as well as the interests of trade, industry and commerce. Even the terms used— industrial zone, residential district, ghetto, worker's tenement, middle-class neighbourhood, and bourgeois area—betray the economic shadow that hovers over all aspects and dimensions of community life. And what has replaced the church, the cathedral and the public square at the very heart of the community? In all likelihood a bank, a mall, a factory, a smoke stack or an insurance company.

Robert Redfield and Milton Singer had this point in mind when they penned the following passage about the changing nature of communities and the historical evolution of the word 'city':

In ancient civilizations the urban centres were usually political-religious or political-intellectual; in the modern world they are economic. The mosque, the temple, the cathedral, the royal palace, the fortress, are the symbolic "centres" of the pre-industrial cities. The "central business district" has become symbolic of the modern urban centre.[4]

It pays to persist with the insights of these two remarkable interpreters of urban life in general and cities in particular:

This symbolism is not of course a completely accurate designation of what goes on in the city for which it stands. The ecclesiastical centres were also in many cases centres of trade and of craftsmen, and the modern "central business district" is very apt to contain libraries, schools, art museums, government offices and churches, in addition to merchandising establishments and business offices.[5]

Recognition of this fact serves to underline the importance of taking an approach to community development which is total, comprehensive and objective rather than piecemeal, partial, and partisan. Such an approach must be capable of knitting together *all* of the various manifestations, factors and forces of community life in such a way that the result is a total, integrated entity or cultural whole that is enriched by the specific activities, people and groups that comprise it.

Why is it so essential to treat communities in this holistic way? It is essential because, as noted earlier, communities are becoming more and more divided, disjointed and compartmentalized, thereby losing their sense of unity, identity, cohesion, order and purpose. As a result, they are less capable of addressing the multifarious needs of their residents for a well-rounded and balanced cultural life.

Rather than putting a church, a mosque, a square, a market, a bank or a municipal office at the centre of community development, would it not make sense to make the community's collective statement of itself the principal focal point and driving force of community development? In this way, everyone could participate in, and accept responsibility for, the statement the community was making to itself and the rest of the world.

This is necessary if communities are to be seen and treated as 'cultural wholes'. They are so in the sense that all the multifarious determinants which define them—economic, social, political, educational, environmental, recreational, artistic, spiritual and the like—are combined to produce collective cultural statements which vary very much from one community to another as well as one part of the world to another. Amos Rapoport comments on the process whereby this comes about:

Culture may be said to be about a group of people who have a set of values and beliefs which embody ideals and are transmitted to members of the group through enculturation. These lead to a world view—the characteristic way of looking at, and, in the case of design, of *shaping* the world. The world is shaped by applying rules which lead to systematic and consistent choices, whether in creating a life-style (i.e. the specific way of allocating temporal, material, and symbolic resources), a building style, or a landscape of a settlement. In all these cases, choices are made from among the possible alternatives.[6]

It is clear from this that culture plays a very different role in community development than economics, politics, industry, the environment, or social affairs. Rather than being another factor or ingredient in community development, culture is the cement that binds all the factors and ingredients together. In effect, it is the sticky substance needed to provide cohesion, continuity, and most of all, context. In so doing, it provides the foundation or cornerstone on which community development is based.

If culture should act as the foundation or cornerstone for community development, it is important to ask how this can be accomplished in fact. Surely it can be accomplished most effectively by developing the methodological tools and techniques which are needed to treat communities as cultural wholes in their own right.

One such tool and technique is the culturescape.[7] As a tool and technique for developing a comprehensive understanding of the community as a dynamic and organic whole, the culturescape provides a useful device for community cultural development and getting people involved in the process.

The Community Culturescape

There is nothing mysterious about a landscape. A landscape is a visual statement of the natural and human-made sights of an environment. It exposes the way the eye surveys an environment, sometimes stopping to focus on distinctive features, often roving rapidly over features it takes for granted, but always taking mental snap shots and making selections as it moves.

Nor is there anything mysterious about a soundscape. A soundscape is the ear's answer to the eye. It is an aural statement of the different sounds of an environment.[8] It reveals the way in which the human ear samples natural, mechanical and human sounds, opening wide to sounds which are pleasant and soothing and closing off sounds which are unsettling and abrasive.

It follows from this that a culturescape is a statement of all the diverse features of an environment: natural, historical, sensorial, social, economic, political, aesthetic, human, and so on. It is an environment assaulted by all human faculties in concert, an explorer's curiosity set loose on the infinite panorama of sights, sounds, smells, textures, tastes, institutions, activities and events encountered in community life.

Landscapes and soundscapes cut down into communities. They are specialized, discrete notions, designed to look at communities in a vertical way. As such, they are structured to explore similar facets of community life. In contrast, culturescapes cut across communities. They are integrative, horizontal notions, designed to reveal the infinite and interrelated nature of many diverse facets of community life. They are structured to bring things together, not set things apart.

One of the most fascinating characteristics of landscapes and soundscapes is the way in which they can differ so much from one person to the next. What may be significant for one person may be quite insignificant for another. Two artists can paint the same landscape and the attention given to layout, detail, colour, shading, and overall composition can be so varied that an observer would swear that two different landscapes have been presented. Two composers can listen to the same sequence of sounds and hear entirely different compositions. In much the same way, two people can be exposed to the same landscape and their eyes will settle on different natural and architectural features. Or they can be exposed to exactly the same sounds—vehicular traffic, human voices, different languages or orchestral compositions—and react very differently to these sounds.

Like landscapes and soundscapes, culturescapes can be personal or collective, simple or complex, conscious or intuitive depending on the amount of detail people absorb. Two people can live in Paris, Mexico City, New York, Toronto, Buenos Aires, Marrakech, Istanbul, Sydney, Calcutta, Beijing, or any other urban environment and their experiences will be totally different. Whereas one person may be highly sensitive to sights and sounds, the other may be highly responsive to smells and tastes. Whereas one person may be extremely sensitive to the historical or architectural features of the community but rather indifferent to its natural features, the other may be wildly enthusiastic about its parks, conservation areas and topographical features but completely bored by its architectural or historical accomplishments.

Such experiences reveal much about the different phases of the cul-turescape process. First, there is the absorptive phase when people soak up a great deal of information about the details and characteristics of the community. Next, there is the imprinting and evaluative phase when people impose their habits, movements, patterns, preferences, likes and dislikes on the community. Finally, there is the action phase when people become involved in the planning and development of the community as 'a cultural resource' or 'work of art'. These phases usually happen simultaneously so that they form a continuous process. But how does the process get started? How does it gather momentum? How does it become an integral part of local life, a tool for community improvement?

The culturescape process commences the moment people start to explore their community. When this happens, every community is a treasure with all sorts of interesting gems hidden just below the surface. But as citizens, how often do people take the time to dig into their communities in order to acquaint themselves with their treasures? How frequently do people take their communities for granted, assuming that they know what experiences, resources, programmes and services are available to enrich local life? Furthermore, how often do people get involved in assessing the aesthetic state of their communities—their captivating and disturbing sights, sounds, smells, textures and tastes? Perhaps too much is assumed and too little is explored and assessed.

For Amos Rapoport, probing a community's sensory and experiential qualities is one of the best ways of commencing the process of community self-discovery and awareness:

In dealing with the urban order, it may be useful to begin with the sensory, experien-tial qualities of cities which are also organized or ordered. Cities, among other things, are physical artifacts, experienced through all the senses by people who are in them. They are experienced sequentially as people follow different paths and use different movement modes through them. Cities look, smell, sound and *feel* different; they have a different character or *ambience*. This is easily felt, but is very difficult to describe.[9]

Given the visual nature of contemporary life, people will probably find when they commit themselves to in-depth exploration of the sensory and experiential qualities of their communities that the visual aspects will predominate. Every community contains an endless panorama of visual images and items—flowers, trees, parks, homes, gardens, factories, stores, office buildings, billboards, halls, malls and shopping centres. In all probability, the eye will immediately fasten on many of the larger visual attractions—homes, buildings and offices. However, this should not be allowed to obscure the many smaller visual delights of the community— lights, benches, flower pots, kiosks, clocks, gables and pieces of sculpture—or the lack of them. At the same time, the eye would be well advised to pay particular attention to the roof and floor of the community—its pebbles, cob-blestones, cut stones, sidewalks, soils, grids and drains, as well as the day-time and night-time silhouette the community etches against the eternal sky.

Visual exploration of the roof, floor, street furnishings and natural features of the community should help train the eye to absorb larger visual patterns and themes: simultaneous movement systems of people and vehicles, city blocks, communal squares, landscaping, and planning arrangements. At the same time, aesthetic faculties should be called into play. Not all of the sights of the community will be pleasing. In fact, many of them will be disturbing and unsettling: traffic congestion, obnoxious signboards, commercial strips, jungles of wires and poles, littered streets, run-down store fronts, shortages of 'people places', and a surfeit of splashy advertising gimmicks.

The strong visual features of the community should not be allowed to obscure other sensory characteristics—textures, smells, tastes and sounds. Satisfaction derived from visual exploration and discovery should help to activate interest in the other sensory dimensions of the community.

At the same time that the community possesses a fascinating admixture of sights, so it also contains an incredible assortment of textures, each one calling out to be caressed. For example, take the building materials of the community. What a vast array of different woods, metals, stones, soils, and bricks abounds everywhere. Some of these materials will be smooth and fine; others will be rough, granular, and full of interesting indentations. Some will be highly finished; others will be left in their natural state. Each one ready to reward the tactile explorer with its intimate secrets.

Are the community's smells and tastes any less important than its sights and textures? Yet, how often do people take the time to examine the different smells of their environment, perhaps because pollution has dulled their sensory faculties. However, it should not prove difficult to piece together an olfactory profile of the community. Such a profile would encompass both pleasant and unpleasant smells—the enchanting scent of flowers in the local park, the intoxicating smells of various perfumes and colognes, the gaseous vapours of exhaust fumes, the revolting odours of certain industries, the distinctive scents of spring saplings and fall leaves, and the beckoning aroma of the local bake shop.

A visit to the bake shop to sample its fresh breads, rolls, cakes and pies should open up the world of tastes. This may be followed up at home by experiments to expand gastronomic awareness of vegetables, fruits, meats, sweets, spices and herbs. Here, the emphasis may not be on what is tradition-ally pleasing to the taste buds, but rather on what needs to be known about the incredible diversity of tastes. Families of spices and herbs—cinnamon, mace, nutmeg, cloves, basil, thyme, marjoram, oregano and tarragon—will be sampled in succession to expand culinary knowledge. New vegetables will be added to salads to enhance the taste. Questions may even be asked at the local supermarket about whether artificially-produced tastes and prepackaged foods are necessary. Requests will be made in restaurants for regional specialties and local delicacies. Slowly, prepackaged, plastic tastes may even yield to indigenous tastes as more and more people express their desire for culinary reform.

The sensory side of the culturescape is also scored for sounds. No less an authority than John Cage contends that music is sound, the sound heard around us whether inside or outside the concert hall. An increasing number of contemporary composers share this conviction.

A group of composers connected with the World Soundscape Project concluded after many years of intensive research that there is a soundscape of natural, human and mechanical sounds that corresponds to the landscape of natural and architectural sights.[10] They argued that the world soundscape is in reality a vast musical composition which has been badly orchestrated in the modern era. There has been an imperialistic spread of many of the most grotesque and taxing sounds imaginable. The hard-edge sounds of modern technology—from power tools, lawnmowers, factories, machines, cars, trucks, planes and motor-cycles to many other mechanical devices—are masking out human and natural sounds in many parts of the world. In non-industrial and rural cultures, natural and human sounds account for the large majority of all sounds, with the sounds of tools and technology accounting for a very small percentage of total sounds. In industrialized and urban cultures, the proportions are virtually reversed. The sounds of modern technology account for the majority of all sounds, and at progressively higher and higher decibel levels. This has brought with it two concomitant developments. In the first place, it has caused increased deafness and impaired hearing. In the second place, it has turned many communities into sonic sewers. By strengthening noise abatement legislation and promoting improvements in aural acuity through 'ear cleaning' and 'ear training' exercises, sound museums and sound walks, the World Soundscape group hopes to inspire a universal movement for a better soundscape. Such a movement is imperative if a soundscape is to be produced in the world which will prove more satisfying to the ear and the mind.

Determined soundscape explorers will not allow their own particular soundscape to pass unnoticed. On the contrary, they will store many memorable sounds away in the bank of acoustical experiences—wind rattling against metal, birds singing at dawn, raindrops on a tin roof, train whistles, fog horns, factory sirens, church bells and the clatter of horses' hooves. Like the composers in the World Soundscape Project, they will discover that many of the most beautiful sounds are disappearing, due to the onslaught of the sounds of modern technology and the lack of effective noise abatement legislation. This too will be added to the expanding sensoryscape of the community.

At the same time that some people may be concerned with the sensory and experiential profile of the community, others may be concerned with other kinds of profiles—environmental, historical, scientific, economic, political, social, human and aesthetic. Each profile will possess its own peculiar features and distinctive characteristics.

Some people may become interested in fashioning an environmental profile of the community and its immediate environs. Here probes will be conducted into the natural features and topographical contours of the community—hills, valleys, rivers, streams, embankments and overall geographical setting. Parks and conservation areas will be studied in depth for their scenic appeal, flora and fauna, fragile botanical systems, and unusual ecological features. Others may be more interested in creating an historical portrait of the community—a portrait that illustrates how and why the community was originally settled, how it grew in response to different types of needs, and when it underwent periods of profound change. To do this effectively, it may prove necessary to draw on museum holdings, archival material, old photographs, library records and newspaper clippings. Through this, an impression will be gleaned of the different layers of culture that have been combined to form the historical portrait of the community. Still others may be interested in preparing a scientific profile of the community. This will entail probes into transportation and communication systems, climatic and meteorological studies, and the activities of educational institutions and research agencies.

Active interest in the economic, political and social dimensions of the community may stimulate frequent visits to different community resources: libraries, welfare agencies, government offices, factories, banks, insurance companies, commercial enterprises, markets, boutiques, community centres, concert halls and sports arenas. Standing behind this complex maze of institutions are the myriad individuals and organisations responsible for the numerous programmes and services which are available to enrich community life. How aware are community residents of these programmes and services? How much knowledge do they have of the functioning of these organizations and institutions? Travelling down this road is essential to the crystallization of a comprehensive community culturescape. Not only is there exposure to the inner workings of the community as a dynamic, organic whole, but also there is much to be learned about the way in which complex decisions are made that have a fundamental bearing on all aspects of community life.

People who are determined to plumb the depths of their communities will be anxious to learn as much as possible about the human profile of the community. Initially, a probe in this area may start when an individual becomes interested in the patterns he or she imprints on the community. Eventually, it may fan out to encompass an interest in the cultural patterns of others.

It is often said that human beings are the products of habit. Plotted over time, these habits form cycles. Some of these cycles, such as eating, sleeping and working, are necessary for survival. Others, such as watching television, enjoying hobbies, reading, attending social functions, or exploring the nooks and crannies of local life, are more optional and recreational in character.

One of the best ways of documenting these cycles is to keep a cultural diary. A cultural diary differs from a general diary in that it is intended to record the various amounts of time and money spent on different cultural activities, rather than on those special events and unique occasions which highlight each day. As such, a cultural diary breaks a given period of time into minutes, hours and weeks as well as different types of cultural activities. Records are then kept of the actual amounts of time and money devoted to these activities. When these recordings are aggregated, they are capable of revealing cycles which expose the extent to which individuals are products of cultural habits and imprint different patterns on their environment.

These cycles, habits and patterns may help to shed light on difficult community development problems. Some of the concerns of community cultural development, such as for more personal and collective fulfillment, a more attractive environment, better conservation of resources, more citizen participation in planning and decision-making and a higher level of community awareness, can only be accomplished by reinforcing or breaking with established patterns of activity. Often new patterns or cycles must be created that bring people closer to real satisfaction in their lives. Creation of these new patterns and cycles may require more income and employment flexibility, reductions in the consumption of goods and services, improvements in recreational and artistic amenities, more effective urban renewal and noise abatement legislation, better control of water and air pollution, greater regulation of business and industry, and more democratic forms of government and decision-making. Such can be the effects of community cultural change.

To achieve a full understanding of the human profile of the community, excursions into the land of personal habits, patterns and cycles should be complemented by probes into the habits, patterns and cycles of others. Although people often betray signs of similarity in an external sense, in an internal sense, they live lives which are exceedingly diverse and unique, reflecting different ethnic background, religious beliefs, upbringing, education, and personal preferences. A little friendly curiosity can bring its own rewards. Often diplomatic probes into this area will reveal significant differences in the way people choose to live life, approach jobs, practise hobbies, celebrate events, cook dishes, celebrate holidays, and utilize leisure time. A rich mine exists here in every community and is ready for the taking.

If the doors start to swing open the moment the human profile is probed, they are thrust open wide the moment the aesthetic profile is explored. Here is where preferences run strong and feelings cut deep. The aesthetic experience is an exceedingly subjective affair. Whereas one person may detest the sound of motorcycles, planes or trucks, another person may revel in such sounds. One person may find billboards offensive, another may find them attractive. Some may feel that the city core needs a face-lift, others may be content to leave it alone. Unfortunately, very little is known at present about the aesthetic preferences of people. Far too often they remain hidden from view due to adverse educational, artistic, or social experiences. However, since they represent one of life's fundamental realities, they should be brought into the open and confronted for what they are: illustrations of the infinite spectrum of opinions and preferences which comprise community life. And herein could lie one of the real strengths of the culturescape process. By allowing many sides of an issue to surface, it is capable of knitting many different and diverse aesthetic preferences into the cultural portrait of the community.

When all these different profiles—sensorial, experiential, environmental, historical, economic, political, social, educational, aesthetic and human—are placed side by side and added up, they produce a comprehensive and compelling statement of the community as an integrated entity or cultural whole. It is this statement which depicts the community's overall worldview and sense of itself because it is predicated on how the community has organized and ordered its affairs and positioned itself in the world. In effect, it reveals how the community has made its cultural imprint on a very specific piece of the world's geography.

A community's culturescape or statement of itself is not only important because it reveals how the community has made a specific cultural imprint. It is also important because it can be organized, orchestrated and choreographed in different ways to produce different results. For example, information on the sensory, environmental, historical, economic, political, social, human and aesthetic profiles of the community can be classified according to the cultural sector it represents, thereby making it possible to prepare different types of inventories. These inventories can then be used for purposes of time, budget and expenditure studies. Or they can be used to undertake opinion polls and attitudinal surveys. Or they can be used to prepare maps, walks, tours, itineraries or exchanges that will prove extremely helpful for administrative, planning, or policy purposes. In one form or another, all this information relates to the supply and demand for community cultural resources, and synchronizing them in a way that meets the needs of citizens and community groups is surely one of the greatest challenges confronting community development.

Given the highly personal and subjective nature of each individual's contribution to the culturescape process, it is highly unlikely that these contributions will contain enough information when they are combined to piece together a comprehensive portrait of the community as a cultural whole. As a result, more systematic measures may have to be adopted to ensure that each sector is represented in depth as well as in breadth. This will necessitate the systematic collection and analysis of comparable data for each cultural sector on the number and nature of organizations, the size and composition of memberships, funding patterns, the use of facilities, and the availability of programmes. Such comprehensive data, which many communities already possess in diverse locations, is a prerequisite to intelligent planning and decision-making since it sheds much light on the supply side of the cultural equation.

Like data on cultural resources, data on the amount of time and money residents spend on different types of cultural activities will not be forthcoming in sufficient detail to provide a composite picture of how the community makes its various temporal and financial allocations and functions as a whole. Where individuals have chosen to keep cultural diaries, these diaries could form the basis of larger community time, budget and expenditure studies. When conducted on a scale large enough to be representative and meaningful, these studies will reveal relative allocations of time and money for the different sectors of cultural activity, thereby providing valuable information on time distributions and financial transactions. Information on the division of time between work and leisure, as well as expenditure on such items as food, clothing, shelter, books, radios, television sets, computer equipment, cinema attendance, admissions to theatres, concerts, galleries, sporting events, and the like, will help to produce a portrait of the demand side of the equation.

Attitudinal surveys and opinion polls can also make extremely valuable contributions to culturescape choreography. In one form or another, both types of inquiries will get people to think about the character of their own lives, as well as exchanging information on the community and how it might be improved in the future. Every individual makes a fundamental commitment to community life by choosing a place to live and work. The factors affecting these commitments vary considerably depending on the nature and location of the community, employment opportunities, proximity to nature, availability of social, artistic and recreational amenities, and shopping facilities. Often surveys and opinion polls that involve discussions of these factors will bring individuals to new levels of awareness with respect to why a particular community was selected or how it might be improved and utilized to better advantage in the future. These discussions can easily lead to discussions in other areas: what residents think of their community; what they like and dislike about it; how they propose making changes in the undesirable aspects of local life; and how they feel governments and political authorities can best serve their interests. This is what makes discussions and non-directive interviews so valuable in detecting people's actual and latent cultural needs.

One of the greatest strengths of the culturescape process is its susceptibility to mapping.[11] Depending on the problem at hand and the symbols used, it is possible to prepare 'culturescape maps' which can be extremely useful for informational, administrative, planning, policy and exploratory purposes. It does not prove difficult to imagine the numerous possibilities here. For example, it is possible to prepare 'inventory maps' that depict the different sectors of cultural activity as well as the location and nature of various types of cultural resources. These maps can be extremely helpful in acquainting residents and visitors with the vast array of resources available to enrich local life.

With slight alterations, inventory maps can be transformed into administrative, planning, or policy maps that can be exceedingly helpful in pinpointing certain types of problems or plotting future directions. For example, by overlaying demographic statistics, transportation grids and density data on inventory maps, it is possible to identify inequalities in the physical distribution of resources, persistent programme deficiencies, limitations on facilities, and transportation and communications problems related to resource availability and accessibility.

Inventory, administrative, policy and planning maps share one thing in common. They all use objective data, such as physical locations, organizational types, user information, time allocations, expenditure patterns or recorded responses as their point of departure. Much of this data will have to be systematically collected and methodically recorded as a means of providing a factual portrait of community cultural life. But there is another equally valid approach to culturescape cartography. It grows out of the subjective side of human nature and takes as its point of departure people's personal impressions and reactions to their community. By using the frequency with which people refer to the things they like and dislike about their community, a portrait of the community can be created which is in reality an aggregation of many subjective impressions and personal preferences.

Suppose residents were asked to list their likes and dislikes with regard to their community. Picture a map on which these likes and dislikes were superimposed, one on top of the other. What begins to emerge is a highly impressionistic map revealing at a glance many of the collective likes and dislikes of community residents. By denoting 'likes' that have been referred to with the greatest frequency by one type of symbol and 'dislikes' by another type of symbol, a collective portrait of the major likes and dislikes of community residents emerges. These 'impressionistic maps', which may reveal such things as favourite restaurants, special haunts, well-travelled streets, noisy intersections, obnoxious odours, traffic irritations, grotesque buildings, and disturbing sights and sounds, may also be extremely valuable for planning and development purposes. In fact, they may be the most salient planning and development vehicles of all, since they do not represent the attitudes of highly-specialized planners and decision-makers, but rather the collective likes and dislikes of residents. To this extent, they may help to explain the strong and often unexpected reactions which often occur when planners or politicians decide to change some aspect of the community which citizens value highly. Getting information about these reactions in advance could help to avoid the needless confrontations which often erupt between citizens, planners, politicians and developers when some cherished community resource is threatened.

Between these objective and subjective extremes, many different types of maps can be created that help to pinpoint important aspects of community cultural life. For example, it is possible to produce maps depicting the different sensory and experiential characteristics of the community, such as its different sights, sounds, smells, textures and tastes. These maps can be extremely useful in prompting people to explore their immediate surroundings, as well as in identifying aggravating sensory irritants. In much the same way, it is possible to prepare maps which expose the different environmental, historical, institutional, human and aesthetic features of community life.

As with landscaping, culturescaping is a process involving selections as well as collections. It draws information together, sifts and sorts it, and selects the information which most satisfies the objectives at hand. Suppose the object is to prepare an exploratory walk or tour of the community. Using the inventory approach, information can be used to identify prominent cultural features and monuments. This information can then be written up in capsule form, symbolized, and plotted on a map of the community. The result is a highly interesting tour or walk that directs people to specific institutions, resources, and landmarks. Most guide books are prepared in this way. Through the collection of a vast array of inventory information, they star or rank selective sights and provide a descriptive itinerary that is broken down according to the varying amounts of time residents and visitors should devote to particular features in a community—galleries, museums, community centres, old buildings, historic sites, festivals, fairs, theatres, distinctive buildings, and recreational and civic facilities.

What is interesting is the fact that a very different type of tour may result when the impressionistic approach is utilized. Much more emphasis may be placed on those 'magnetic cultural attractions' that residents themselves cherish about their community—a dilapidated old building, a pub, a city block of interesting sights and sounds, a favourite restaurant, a special haunt from which to view people, a curiosity shop, or a mural on a building.[12] These attractions reveal a great deal about the intimate character of the community, as well as about the collective preferences of community residents.

Discrepancies between these two approaches may show up most clearly when residents are asked to compare their own preferences with the things they recommend to visitors or friends. Most often, residents' own preferences are highly subjective and impressionistic and often tinged with a certain element of nostalgia. What is recommended to friends and visitors is usually much more objective, systematic and conventional. A curious difference? Perhaps. But how often do people find themselves in a different community longing to know it the way residents do, only to find that they end up following some guidebook of systematically-prepared cultural monuments and historic sites? How often do people find themselves in the position where they recommend things to do and see to visitors and friends which are not even remotely connected with the community experiences which bring joy and happiness to their own lives? Presumably what is needed here is a synthesis of the best features of the inventory and impressionistic approaches to mapping. Here is where science and aesthetics combine to form the art of culturescape choreography.

If communities are to achieve desirable states of development in the future, it is crucial to evolve integrative and participatory methods and techniques that can be used by citizens, professionals and community groups for the collective betterment of the community. Those interested in this side of community development will be struck by two major problems: first, the general lack of effective methods and techniques that can be used by community residents for participatory purposes; and second, the paucity of artistic methods and techniques compared to scientific methods and techniques.

The first problem is understandable. Community cultural development is a comparatively new field of interest and activity. In more established fields, such as economic, social, educational and political development, method-ological methods and techniques are already much more developed and tend to be in far greater supply. Hence the challenge is to apply existing methods and techniques to specific situations and learn from the results. In contrast, the challenge of community development is often to fashion new, innovative methods and techniques capable of integrating many diverse facets of local life and engaging people actively in the process.

As matters stand now, many people are not active participants in the development of the communities in which they are resident. The reasons for this are many and varied. Community development is often seen as a highly specialized and sophisticated affair, and, as such, the preserve of specialists, developers, planners and professionals. As a result, people are often not valued for the constructive contributions they are capable of making to community development. This is largely because citizens are deemed to lack the expertise, knowledge, wisdom, capabilities and understanding necessary to provide valuable input into the process. When this happens, the development process is often dominated or controlled by powerful interest groups that have little or no interest in the abilities citizens do possess to contribute to community development.

The consequences of this situation are clear. Citizens are cut off and set apart from the communities in which they are resident. Rather than feeling that they are vital and valuable members of the community and capable of making substantial contributions to it, they feel they are living independently of the community and are residents and citizens of the community in name only. Having been thwarted from providing any real input into the process, they feel that they are merely sitting on the sidelines. This situation should change. If communities are to become havens of fulfillment and happiness, citizens will have to take their rightful place alongside developers, planners and professionals in plotting and planning community development and change. The name of the game should be involvement, commitment and getting so immersed in community development that there is a sense of being 'in the community' and not 'from the community'. The culturescape process may be capable of contributing much to this requirement. By respecting citizens for the valuable contributions they can make to community development and the creation of the community's collective statement of itself, it prompts people to get involved in the re-creation and revitalization of their communities by contributing their unique insights, ideas, expertise and talents to the short-term and long-term development of community cultural change.

If the lack of effective methods and techniques that citizens, professionals and community groups can use for participatory purposes poses a problem, so does the imbalance that exists between scientific as opposed to artistic methods and techniques. Generally speaking, methods and techniques that have been developed in the scientific domain, such as observational analysis, representative and random sampling, directive and non-directive interviews, time, budget and expenditure studies, attitudinal surveys, opinion polls and public forums are already in a high state of development. Unfortunately, however, many of these methods and techniques tend to be more descriptive than participatory. As a result, they are much better suited to describing situations than getting people involved in the process. Moreover, they tend to be designed for professional use, and as such, preclude all but a very limited number of researchers, experts and specialists from active participation and involvement in the process.

In contrast, methods and techniques that have developed in the artistic domain are still in their infancy. In an historical sense, it is true that many artists have been highly sensitive to the cultural state and characteristics of communities, devoting important segments of their lives and works to the depiction of these aspects and dimensions of community life. In this connection, Brueghel with his lively illustrations of Dutch social celebrations and peasant life, Canaletto and Guardi with their colourful presentations of Venice, Zola with his descriptive portrayals of the vivid colours and pungent aromas of Paris, Turgenev with his incredible descriptions of Russian community life, and Renoir with his captivating street scenes and cityscapes come quickly to mind. The English composer Coates even used a musical composition to immortalize three English communities—Covent Garden, Westminster and Knightsbridge.

Nevertheless, while certain artists have been successful in capturing the cultural character and ambiance of certain communities for posterity, artists generally have not fashioned the artistic methods and techniques that are needed to evaluate the aesthetic state of communities—methods and techniques that might also be used by citizens and professionals to improve the aesthetic and cultural state of communities. Moreover, the arts have not been sufficiently extended into community environments to the point where they can influence and affect the attitudes of people and the decisions of professionals and politicians. Too often, they have remained inside institutional walls, thereby failing to become integral ingredients and effective instruments for community change. As a result, the aesthetic state of many communities is lacking and the prospects for the future are not good.

Unfortunately, these shortcomings are compounded by the adverse experience of many people with the arts. Regrettably, the artistic capabilities and sensitivities of many people remain underdeveloped, despite the fact that all people have artistic tastes and sensibilities and are constantly making aesthetic judgments throughout their lives. The problem here is that these tastes, sensibilities and judgments are often bottled up inside people and hidden from view. What is required here is the development of artistic methods and techniques that can provide outlets for people's aesthetic preferences, tastes and needs, especially for people who have little or no intention of becoming involved in the institutional aspects of the arts. Why is this so essential? It is essential because the aesthetic state of communities will not change until the arts become the business of all citizens, and this will not happen until ways and means are found to permit people to participate actively in the aesthetic transformation of their communities.

Clearly every citizen has something valuable and necessary to contribute to the community culturescape. Some may itemize itineraries of daily or weekly events. Others may record their likes and dislikes. Others still may contribute actual objects: old photographs, artifacts, tapes of oral histories, antiques, maps, historical records, and other memorabilia of community significance.

As the culturescape process starts to take hold and these contributions grow, facilities may be required to house all this activity. This will vary from community to community depending on many factors: the size of the community; the extent of citizen participation; the nature of people's contributions; the availability of space; the level of participation and commitment; the existence of special skills and expertise; the availability of audio-visual equipment; and the unique character of the community.

In some communities, certain aspects of the culturescape process will go on under different names. Museums collecting and classifying local artifacts will be engaged in one aspect of the process. Universities and community colleges taping oral histories of long-time residents will be engaged in another aspect of the process. By undertaking these functions, each of these institutions is making a valuable contribution to culturescape activity. As such, these institutions might make suitable homes for the culturescape process and the community's collective statement of itself.

At the present time, few communities have a central location or source where their culturescape can be assembled. As a result, there may be no single place in the community to which residents can bring their different contributions, from which they can acquire the information they need—this may have to be choreographed to achieve different results—and through which they can become actively involved in the future planning, development and enrichment of their community as a dynamic and integrated whole.

What may be particularly helpful here is the creation of 'culturescape centres' capable of collecting, analyzing, orchestrating and disseminating pertinent information about a community's cultural image or statement of itself. This would make it possible in a single location to: exhibit all sorts of community memorabilia; prepare maps, walks, tours, itineraries and exchanges; and develop models and replicas of the community that illustrate how proposed and actual changes will affect the community's sensory, economic, social, political, aesthetic and human character and profile. Citizens would then have the opportunity to weigh for themselves the relative costs and benefits of different kinds of community action, decisions and change. Moreover, they would have the vehicles to express their concern over certain types of developments, as well as the tools and techniques needed to actively participate in the process. In this way, communities would be shaped less by politicians, planners, developers and professionals and more by citizens, community groups and the community at large.

What facilities, equipment and skills are needed to accommodate these requirements? Presumably they will vary from community to community depending on citizens' needs and particular circumstances. A large, free, comfortable space, capable of hanging billboards and maps, displaying models and replicas, recording feedback, storing memorabilia and artifacts, and dispensing information about walks and tours would be perfect for such purposes. This space should be complemented by people who possess the necessary skills in cartography, photography, documentation, classification, exhibition, and tour preparation. Local artists, craftsmen, librarians, historians, photographers, audio-visual experts, mappers and museum curators would all prove extremely useful in this situation.

Where it is not possible for communities to have a distinct culturescape centre, preferably located at or near the centre of the community, suitable space could be provided in a museum, a library, an arts centre, a sports complex or a community hall. However, given the enormous importance of the community's culturescape or its statement of itself, an independent home is preferable, even if that home is not constructed or created specifically for the purpose. Indeed, a deserted factory, an old warehouse, an abandoned building, a boarded-up shed, or a dilapidated railway station would all make ideal homes for the community's collective culturescape.

Community Cultural Administration

It follows from the foregoing that some fundamental changes will be required in community cultural administration if culture is to form the backbone of community development and the culturescape process is to become a prominent feature of community life. It is impossible to raise issues as crucial as these without raising the related issue of the respective roles and responsibilities of municipal, regional and national authorities for community cultural development. Issues as quintessential as these are best dealt with in context rather than in isolation.

There can be little doubt that determination of the respective roles and responsibilities of the various levels of government for cultural development constitutes one of the most difficult challenges in the political and cultural fields today. Why is this? Surely it is because people have cultural needs at every level of culture that must be attended to: personal, institutional, community, regional, national, and international. As a result, it is not simply a matter of assigning responsibility over culture to a single level of government. Rather it is a matter of determining the most appropriate roles and responsibilities for culture for all levels of government.

While this subject needs a great deal more thought, discussion, research and debate, common sense suggests that each level of government should look after the cultural needs and requirements that are most closely associated with it. This would mean that municipal governments would be responsible for all forms of personal, institutional and community cultural development, or cultural development at the grass roots level. Regional governments would be responsible for all forms of regional cultural activity,[13] including all forms of exchange and co-operation between and among communities. National governments would be responsible for all forms of national and international cultural activity, or the cultural development of countries and cultures as a whole. Presumably this would include all forms of inter-regional cooperation and exchange, as well as all forms of international cultural relations. Despite the fact that this general 'rule of thumb' is far removed from the present situation, it represents a goal worthy of pursuit.

Given the rapidly escalating importance of communities and community cultural needs, it would be foolhardy to underestimate the role that municipal governments should play in the process of community cultural development. However, at a time when cultural development is needed more than ever at the community level, municipal governments appear to be in the worst possible position to respond. Not only do they lack the constitutional powers, taxation powers, and financial and fiscal resources to address the cultural needs of local residents, but also they lack the institutional structures, granting mechanisms and operational procedures that are needed to deal with these requirements effectively.[14]

How should municipal governments respond to this challenge? Firstly, they should dramatically increase their funding for community cultural development, largely by reallocating funds from areas of lesser to greater need. Secondly, they should develop plans, programmes, policies, and practices that broaden and deepen citizen participation in cultural life. Thirdly, they should employ cultural animators, or individuals who are specifically trained to activate community cultural development and are skilled at acting as catalysts for cultural change. Finally, they should commission artists and other types of creative people to become involved in elevating and enriching all aspects of local life.

With these commitments should come corresponding improvements in the institutional structures created to advance the cultural cause. As matters stand now, the overwhelming majority of municipalities either have no administrative structure whatever to advance community cultural development, or they have departments of recreation and community affairs where culture is often regarded as an afterthought. These structures are insufficient to meet the needs of the future. They lack the financial and human resources to do the job properly, and tend to marginalize culture, making it an insignificant ingredient in the total scheme of things.

If municipal governments are to play a forceful role in community development, they should set up administrative structures that are equal to the challenge. In other words, they should set up departments of cultural development, community cultural councils, culturescape centres and the like and endow them with sufficient funds, personnel, and resources to do the job. Only in this way will they send out a clear message to citizens, other levels of government, corporations, foundations, and community groups that they are prepared to play a leadership role in community cultural development.

To say that people's homes are their castles is a commonplace—but in what sense is this true? Surely it is true in the sense that regardless of their wealth or station in life, most people get highly involved in the orchestration of their domestic environments. This involvement takes many forms. For the wealthy, it takes the form of working with designers, architects and decorators in the layout and furnishing of the home. For the less fortunate, it takes the form of arranging and rearranging household possessions, planting a small garden, hanging a picture, using a craft object to enhance a space, employing a carpet to warm a room, or sweeping the floor to keep the home free of insects. In most cases, people take great pride in their homes. By arranging and rearranging the objects in their environment, they find constructive outlets for their creative energies. Their environments respond by becoming places where it is possible to find comfort, security and fulfillment.

What is true for people's homes should be equally true for their communities. Communities should become people's castles. They should be known with the same intimacy and cared for with the same affection and attention to detail as people's homes. It is only in this way that it will be possible to create neighbourhoods, towns, cities, municipalities, metropolises and megalopolises that are suitable and sustainable for an increasing percentage of the globe's population.

This is what makes community cultural development so crucial. It strikes at the very heart and soul of what life and living are all about. At the survival level, it is concerned with the basic necessities of life: food, clothing, shelter, jobs, health, sanitation and security. At the sensory level, it is concerned with preventing excessive amounts of visual, aural, olfactory and tactile pollution. At the social and human level, it is concerned with providing a broad spectrum of services and programmes without which life is intolerable. And at the cultural level, it is concerned with integrating all these activities into a coherent and comprehensive whole.

In the final analysis, what can be said about community cultural development? Perhaps this: without a much higher priority given to community exploration and discovery, cultural planning and decision-making, citizen participation, and especially the development of people's sense of pride of place, communities will not be able to respond to the demands people in all parts of the world are making on them.

8. The Cultural State

Culture is a political question today with serious implications for the humanization of our world.[1]

Felix Wilfred

Of all the challenges that must be addressed in coming to grips with the role of culture in the world of the future, none may be more difficult or demanding than the role of culture as it relates to the state. Indeed, if the mandate visualized for culture and cultures here is to be realized, it will be necessary to fashion a vision of the state that is consistent with this requirement.

Visions of the State

Throughout history, numerous visions of the state have been advanced to entice the imagination and vie for public attention. On the one hand, there have been utopian visions, such as those proposed by Plato, St Augustine, Owen, Marx, Engels and others. On the other hand, there have been practical visions, such as those espoused by Macchiavelli, military strategists, political theorists, economists and the like. These visions have yielded a spectrum of possibilities of the state from which to choose: the philosopher state, the classless state, the military state, the nation state, the growth state, the welfare state, the stationary state, the equilibrium state, the democratic state, and so forth.[2] While the large majority of these visions are theoretical ideals and are never actually attainable in practice, they perform a very valuable function. On the one hand, they provide people with something positive and constructive to aspire to and aim at. On the other hand, they make it possible to play backwards and forwards between real and ideal situations, the state in theory and the state in practice.

Despite the fact that all of the aforementioned visions perform a very valuable function, they all appear to be ill-suited to the world of the future. Take the utopian visions for example. Regardless of whether it is Plato's vision of a state ruled by philosopher-kings, Saint Augustine's vision of the state dominated by religion, morality, Christianity and the church, Robert Owen's vision of a state committed to self-sufficiency, selflessness and co-operation, or Marx's and Engels' vision of a state where governments would eventually wither away and the proletarian class would reign supreme, these visions all seem more suited to a different kind of world than the one that exists today. Either they are too idealistic or discredited to warrant serious attention, or they are inappropriate in a world dominated by colossal developments in communications and profound problems in demography, politics, economics and the environment. While considerable care must be taken not to reject these visions out of hand and every effort should be made to draw on these visions whenever and wherever they are relevant, it is not possible to adopt them as the basis for the state of the future.

What is true for the utopian visions is equally true for the practical visions. Like the utopian visions, the practical visions seem ill-suited to the future. Take the authoritarian or tyrannical vision of the state as an illustration. While Machiavelli may have been right that the state is concerned more with the acquisition and exercise of power than anything else, the unscrupulous, amoral or blatant use of power in this sense is too frightening to contemplate. So also is the vision of a military state, with its commitment to building up an arsenal of armaments and nuclear weapons aimed at crushing other nations.

Closely allied to these visions of the authoritarian, tyrannical and military state is the nation state. Here the objective is to promote allegiance to a very specific state through a variety of nationalistic devices and chauvinistic measures. The problem here is that nationalism is often not possible without recourse to a variety of oppressive and dangerous practices, such as subversion, coercion, and blind adherence to ideological beliefs and convictions. In such cases, the nation state can easily degenerate into a fascist, totalitarian, racist or imperialist state, as history and the experience of the last few centuries readily confirm.

Whereas visions of the authoritarian, tyrannical, military and nation state derive largely from political theory and practice, visions of the growth, welfare and stationary state derive largely from economic theory and practice. In the growth state, maximization of economic growth and technological development is the priority. Economies are encouraged to grow as rapidly as possible, with little or no concern for the consequences. By failing to take the environmental, social and human costs and consequences of economic growth and technological development into account, the growth state has propelled humanity to the brink of an ecological disaster, thereby considerably undermining its usefulness as a vision of the state to be taken seriously.

In many ways, the welfare state is deemed to overcome the shortcomings of the growth state. Since rampant economic growth and technological development reward some and penalize others, the welfare state is designed to compensate people who are not able to cope or compete by providing them with a base of public services and social security benefits which will counteract unemployment, loss of income, and inability to maintain a decent standard of living. While the welfare state is founded on humane principles and compassionate motives, experience in many countries suggests that the welfare state may be far too costly to maintain, particularly if it is implemented on a universal scale. Nevertheless, the sentiments that stand behind it, especially as they relate to care for the poor, the sick, the elderly, the disadvantaged and the unemployed, should never be lost sight of in any vision of the state.

Whereas the welfare state is designed to compensate for the social and human shortcomings of the growth state, the stationary state is designed to eliminate the economic and technological excesses of the growth state. In classical economic theory, the stationary state was inevitable because land, or the natural resource base, was fixed while population was variable. While improvements in technology or 'the state of technique' can outstrip the fixity of land or natural resources and population growth for a time, the stationary state was inevitable in the long-run according to classical theory because technological change cannot postpone the law of diminishing returns indefinitely. When this day arrives, according to the theory, increases in the stock of capital and population through births will be offset by decreases in the stock of capital and deaths, thereby bringing about a stationary state.

Unlike most classical economists, John Stuart Mill saw the stationary state as a magnificent opportunity rather than a diabolical curse:

It is scarcely necessary to remark that a stationary condition of capital and population implies no stationary state of human improvement. There would be as much scope as ever for all kinds of mental culture, and moral and social progress; as much room for improving the Art of Living, and much more likelihood of its being improved.[3]

Mill's perception of the stationary state has received scant attention ever since it was propounded. There are many reasons for this. In the first place, the world has been preoccupied over the last two centuries with economic growth and development much more than 'the art of living'. Second, the dominant conviction has been that technological change and innovation can continuously ward off the law of diminishing returns and the fixity of land and natural resources. Only recently has it been recognized that economic growth and development have been achieved at an incredible environmental and human cost. Not only have they resulted in serious shortages of renewable and non-renewable resources and deterioration of the globe's fragile ecosystem, but also they have been achieved at the expense of many African, Asian, and Latin American nations. As a result, it is now clear that the growth state is far from a self-sufficient state: it demands enormous amounts of natural resources and supplies of cheap labour and consumes them at a phenomenal rate. But the real reason for lack of interest in Mill's vision of the stationary state has much more to do with the fact that it is a positive vision erected on a negative base. Its inability to hold out a ray of hope for improvement in the material circumstances of people's lives, particularly in a highly materialistic world, accounts for the scant attention it has received ever since it was first formulated.

Unlike the stationary state, the equilibrium state holds out a ray of hope and promise to people. Not only can the material conditions of people's lives be improved, albeit at a sustainable rate, but also there is a kind of dynamic fluidity to the equilibrium state, which makes it a much more attractive alternative than the stationary state. Indeed, the very term 'equilibrium' suggests that there is room for growth, development, improvement and change, but also that balance is required between the opposing forces of economics and environment, materialism and humanism. In this case, it is balance between people's material and human needs on the one hand and nature's ability to provide the resources necessary to meet these needs on the other hand. This is what makes the equilibrium state—or the 'sustainable state' as it is often called today—so compelling.[4] Economic growth, techno-logical development, and material advancement are possible, but not at a maximum or unmitigated rate. Rather, well-defined and carefully-controlled limits are set which are linked to the carrying capacity of the earth and the needs of present and future generations.[5]

There is one final vision of the state which should not be allowed to escape scrutiny, since it is exercising such a powerful influence over the con-temporary imagination. This is the democratic state. In many ways, the democratic state is a hybrid of economic and political theory and practice. It is predicated on such political convictions as freedom of expression, free elections and government by the people, as well as on such economic convictions as conservatism, free trade, promotion of the private sector and supremacy of the marketplace. While its political ideals are very laudable and extremely enticing to many nations at present, it sounds dangerously like the growth state dressed up in modern garb. It not only opens the doors to commercial interests, multinational corporations and developers to rule the roost, but also promotes the unbridled movement of people, products, capital and resources in response to economic, commercial, financial, capitalistic and materialistic opportunities.

Like the utopian visions, there are fundamental problems with all the practical visions. The main reason has to do with the fact that they all tend to view the state from a specialized or partisan perspective rather than a holistic and egalitarian one. In so doing, they colour everything that stands in their way: development becomes a one-sided and limited process;[6] life becomes a biased and specialized affair; and progress becomes an obsessive and ques-tionable activity. As soon as the fallacy of the one-dimensional perspective that is inherent in them is exposed, they break down as visions of the state capable of addressing global needs and carrying humanity into the next great epoch in history.

Given this fact, where should attention be directed? One place to start may be with 'the cultural state'. For, as indicated earlier, culture has contained in it many of the qualities and ingredients needed to confront the difficult and demanding problems of the future. If it makes sense to talk about the growth state, the equilibrium state, the sustainable state and the democratic state, surely it makes sense to talk about 'the cultural state'.

While the cultural state is also a theoretical ideal that can never be attained in fact, it still serves a useful purpose by making it possible to move backwards and forewords between real and ideal situations, as well as by providing people with something positive and constructive to aspire to and work towards. It is to the cultural state, then, that attention should be directed for the clues that are necessary to piece together a portrait of the state that is consistent with the direction humanity appears to be headed in the future.

Characteristics of the Cultural State

What is the cultural state? What would it look like? How would it function? Unlike utopian and practical visions of the state which fasten on some particular part of the state, the cultural state focuses on the state *as a whole*. Before examining the component parts of the cultural state, therefore, it is necessary to examine the cultural state as a holistic entity.

First and foremost, the cultural state is *authentic* in that it is true to its origins and roots. While this is easy to say in words, it is amazing how difficult it is to achieve in deeds. It can shake any state to its very foundations. In the modern world, the origins and roots of many states are invisible to the naked eye at present. More often than not, they are concealed by centuries of obstructions and overgrowths. It may take generations, relentless pursuit after truth, and a great deal of pain, conflict, confrontation and suffering to cut away these obstructions and overgrowths and reveal the origins and roots of the state for what they are. During this time, it may prove necessary for the state to withdraw from the world for a time in order to focus exclusively on this process. This may be its only means of identifying those seminal sources that spawned the state and nurtured it through its formative stages of development.

When the origins and roots of the states are exposed, they may prove distasteful to people in positions of power. Many states in existence throughout the world were originally settled by people of a totally different racial stock or skin pigmentation than the people in power today. As a result, people in positions of authority and responsibility may have a vested interest in maintaining a belief about how the state was originally created and nurtured through its formative stages of development—a belief that may be in opposition to the one uncovered by this introspective process. In consequence, there may be considerable political and public pressure to resist any attempt to establish the truth of the matter. Many people may prefer to allow this situation to fester in the side of the state, generation after generation, century after century, than confront it and deal with it. The treatment of the aboriginal peoples provides an illustration of this. Few states have come to grips with the fact that aboriginal peoples played a seminal role in their creation, origins and early development.

In the cultural state, this situation has to be set right regardless of how difficult or painful it is. Not only do truth and justice demand it, but also there can be no 'authentic development' until it has been dealt with effectively. This is why the cultural state is committed to confronting the problem head-on in its constitutional arrangements, historical accounts and political pronouncements. It is also what makes authenticity the most essential characteristic of the cultural state when it is viewed as a whole.

If the cultural state is authentic, it is also *indigenous*. This means it grows naturally and organically from its roots, traditions, origins, experiences and circumstances. It is this process that T. S. Eliot had in mind when he said that the state must be able to go back and learn from its past, as well as absorb and assimilate influences from the outside.[7]

Achieving indigenous development may be as difficult as achieving authentic development. This is due to the fact that many states are as cut off from their historical traditions, experiences and circumstances as they are from their roots and origins. There are two principal reasons for this. In the first place, some states have been out of touch with their past for so long that they have lost contact with it. Slowly and painfully, they must reconstruct and resurrect their past from secondary and tertiary rather than primary sources. Usually there are few historical records in existence, and the ones that do exist are in esoteric locations and disparate places. In this case, historians are compelled to work much like archaeologists and anthropologists, methodically and painstakingly piecing together the scattered fragments and broken remnants of a forgotten civilization. As difficult as this process is, the second reason may be even more difficult to address. Inhabitants of the state may be so preoccupied with imitating the lifestyles, values and worldviews of other states that they fail to recognize the value and importance of their own traditions, experiences, circumstances, values and worldviews. In such case, apathy and indifference can stand in the way of reuniting inhabitants with their past.

In the process of establishing intimate contact with its past, the cultural state is careful not to become so caught up in its own forms, structures, and traditions that it believes these to be superior to others. If this process is carried too far, the result can be chauvinism, nationalism and self-aggrandizement: leaders become convinced that no other state can match their prowess; creative talents are cut off from badly-needed sources of international stimulation and critical scrutiny; and citizens cease to challenge themselves, succumbing to parochialism and provincialism. While the cultural state is careful to maintain close contact with the past, it is equally careful to side-step the dangers inherent in this.

If the cultural state must steer a straight course past the Scylla of nationalism, so it must steer a straight course past the Charybdis of foreign domination. A slip to one side could prove as fatal as a slip to the other side.

In earlier times, foreign domination was accomplished by invasion, military occupation, colonialism and imperialism. Nowadays, it operates in more subtle and invisible ways, such as through the operations of multinational corporations and the universal dissemination of mass media products and activities, particularly those of radio, television, film, video, sound recording, computers and the press. Often, states do not realize they have been influenced by these products and activities until it is too late.

While the operations of multinational corporations pose a serious threat, especially where these operations are accompanied by foreign control over domestic industries and decision-making processes, the universal dissemination of mass media activities and communications products poses an even greater threat for it can destroy the indigenous fabric of the state, not only by obliterating its cherished traditions and ancestral roots, but also by turning the state into a satellite of the superpowers. This is made possible by two powerful developments: technological transfer; and the economics of mass media production.

It is easy to see how successful the superpowers have been in using technological transfers to sell other nations a bill of goods about their superiority and the superiority of their way of life. Many states throughout the world are anxious to adopt the imagery, ideology, behavioural patterns and consumption practices of the superpowers, largely because they are constantly exposed to them through a variety of communications devices. This process is reinforced by the economics of mass media production, where media conglomerates with powerful production and distribution machinery are able to produce and sell media activities and communications products at a fraction of the cost of their competitors. States that fail to develop their own media industries and communications capabilities can easily fall prey to these conglomerates, especially where there is little or no legislation or political machinery to prevent it.

For this reason, the cultural state is careful to develop its own indigenous media capabilities and communications industries. It does so within the context of free movement of products, rather than protectionism. The cultural state is not opposed to the free flow of communications products in particular or information and people in general. It has no intention of blocking out cultural influences from abroad, either by erecting a protective wall around itself or resorting to various forms of censorship. It is quite prepared to allow external influences to penetrate its interior, but is always careful to develop domestic communication industries and media capabilities of its own. Failure to do so results in a serious short-changing of the local population as well as the needs and interests of the state.

Building up powerful domestic communications industries and media capabilities is merely the first step towards creating an effective system of checks and balances in every aspect and dimension of cultural life. For the cultural state, this system allows the state to remain in firm control of its own decision-making processes and destiny. If the cultural state is threatened by too much exposure from one source, it sets in motion countervailing forces aimed at counteracting this exposure by exposure to other sources, both domestic and international. The cultural state is too experienced to get trapped by the rhetoric of the free flow of information and communications by states that espouse it in principle but often do not abide by it in practice.

Nor does the cultural state allow itself to get trapped by the rhetoric of 'free trade'. According to traditional economic theory, states should specialize in the production of products for which they have a comparative advantage. This will result in the creation of an international system where states export products for which they have a comparative advantage and import products for which they have a comparative disadvantage. While this sounds sensible in theory, in practice the reverse is often the case. Proponents of the law of comparative advantage encourage others to specialize in the production of products for which they have a comparative advantage while deliberately diversifying their economies in order to protect themselves from too much dependency on other economies, a handful of products, or unfavourable fluctuations in the terms of trade. As a result, the world is saddled with an international system in which the large majority of states are either subservient to other states, or they are exceedingly vulnerable to changes in economic conditions because their resources are too concentrated in a narrow range of activities.

While the cultural state is committed to free trade as a goal worthy of pursuit, it is equally careful to build up its domestic resource capabilities to the point where they are highly diversified. It does so for two reasons: first, to protect itself from adverse fluctuations in the terms of trade; and second, to place itself in the best possible position to deal with all states as well as its domestic and international problems on the basis of equity, equality and reciprocity.

What is steadily unfolding here is the idea of *self-reliance*, yet another characteristic of the cultural state. Ultimately, it is self-reliance not only in the economic domain, but also across the whole spectrum of cultural achievement. The object is always to create a highly variegated and diversified array of resources in each and every sector of cultural life: social, artistic, scientific, educational, political, environmental, technological and economic. Development of the state's own creative capabilities and resources is the key.

This yields a much richer and wider array of options and opportunities and promotes greater public participation, and utilizes all of its innate potentialities and capabilities as well. It was this process of developing innate potentialities and capabilities that prompted Thomas Carlyle to pen his famous *Law of Culture*. While it was penned primarily for individuals, as indicated earlier, it can be rephrased to express the same sentiment for the state:

Let each [state] become all that it was created capable of being; expand, if possible, to its full growth; resisting all impediments, casting off all foreign, especially all noxious adhesions; and show itself at length in its own shape and stature be these what they may.[8]

Visualized in this way, the cultural state is shaper of its own fate and master of its own destiny. In other words, it is *sovereign* over its own affairs. Herein lies another essential characteristic of the cultural state.

Clearly the cultural state has achieved that level of development where it is prepared to take whatever actions are necessary to ensure sovereignty and deal with the consequences. It has broken the bonds of dependence, colonialism and imperialism and is firmly in charge of its own decision-making processes as well as the forces that originate in it and impinge on it. It is strongly committed to free movement within and across its borders because it knows exactly where it has been in the past, where it is at present, and where it is headed in the future.

It is easy to see how sovereignty constitutes the next logical step in the development of a more equitable system of international relations. On the one hand, sovereignty is needed to give every state a sense of independence, identity, status and stature; without these there is the perpetual problem of dependence, subordination and inferiority. On the other hand, it is needed to give every state the autonomy and authority it needs to deal with other states on the basis of true equality in all areas of cultural life. While much obviously remains to be accomplished in this area, much has already been accomplished throughout the world as a result of the relentless efforts on the part of many states throughout the world as well as the trend towards greater independence and sovereignty in world affairs. This augers well for the realization of a more effective and equitable system of international relations in the future, especially if the forces of neocolonialism, military aggression, imperialism, economic oppression and financial opportunism can be held in check.

If the cultural state is sovereign, it is also *civilized*. This characteristic is exceedingly difficult to achieve because it requires 'the art of living' as John Stuart Mill called it. It is an art capable of yielding greater equality, justice, and dignity for all citizens.

What makes the art of living so necessary to the cultural state? First, it is necessary in order to combine all the different ingredients and diverse elements of the state into an integrated and harmonious whole. Second, it is necessary in order to ensure respect for the rights and freedoms of all citizens and groups, regardless of age, colour, race, creed, ethnic origin, education, income or gender. Finally, it is necessary in order to provide people with a reasonable and balanced array of cultural amenities and opportunities. It is here that 'the art of living' contrasts with 'the standard of living'. Whereas the standard of living focuses largely on the acquisition of possessions and the consumption of material commodities, the art of living focuses primarily on human fulfillment in all its diverse forms and manifestations.

By focusing on the art of living rather than the standard of living, the cultural state endeavours to achieve a better balance between material and non-material forces and quantitative and qualitative needs. It does so by striving to eliminate *excessive* economic and commercial practices, redistributing income and wealth on a more equitable basis, and placing more emphasis on the spiritual, intellectual, emotional and aesthetic side of life. The result is a more realistic distribution of resources and wealth with higher levels of satisfaction and elevated forms of consciousness. On a global scale, this could result in a much more efficient and effective allocation of resources, as well as more fulfillment and satisfaction in life.

If the cultural state is civilized, it is also *creative*. Herein lies the final characteristic of the cultural state when it is viewed as a whole. Doubtless, all states are creative to a degree. However, it is possible to experience a progressive diminution in creativity over time, either because insufficient opportunities are provided for creative stimulation and motivation, or because it proves impossible to break with established ways of doing things. Not so the cultural state. The cultural state is always careful to assert the primacy of creativity, not only in its ideological principles and pragmatic practices, but also in its everyday life. The emphasis is always on promoting more effective and efficient ways of doing things based on innovation, ingenuity and originality rather than imitation, duplication and standardization. In so doing, the cultural state always keeps creativity at the forefront of society.

Esteem for creativity and the creative process places the cultural state in an ideal position to elicit a maximum response from its citizenry by providing citizens with countless opportunities for exploration and discovery. As a result, rather than being organized along rigid, hierarchical lines, the cultural state is organized along fluid, flexible lines. No citizen, regardless of his or her education, income, religion, political persuasion, geographical location or station in life, is precluded from participation in the various plans, policies, priorities, and practices that make up the state. There is ample room for the input of all citizens because there is respect for their output.

This concludes the analysis of the cultural state when looked at as a whole. Viewed from the holistic perspective provided by culture, the cultural state is *authentic, indigenous, self-reliant, sovereign, civilized* and *creative*. These are the fundamental characteristics that give it shape, scope, and most of all substance. Having examined these characteristics, it is possible to turn attention to the component parts of the cultural state.

Components of the Cultural State

Regardless of whether the cultural state is visualized at the group, community, regional or national level, two developments are imperative as far as the component parts are concerned. First, the component parts should be *ordered* effectively to form an integrated and harmonious whole. Second, the component parts should be *formulated* to create a reality that is in keeping with present and future needs.

Of all the component parts of the cultural state—human, ethical, aesthetic, scientific, educational, social, environmental, economic, technological and political—none is more essential, or more pressing, than the human component. What is it about the human component that necessitates its placement at the core of the cultural state? It is concern for human beings—their circumstances, development, relationships with friends, neighbours, foreigners, future generations, the natural environment and other species, and especially their welfare and well-being—that constitutes the essence of all cultural activity.

Failure to give sufficient consideration to the human component of the state accounts for many of the world's most difficult and debilitating problems: the division of the world into two unequal parts; the plight of the vast majority of inhabitants of the earth; the constant threat of nuclear war; the dehumanization of life; unacceptable levels of unemployment and pollution; and loss of personal identity and collective fulfillment. Many of these problems might have been reduced in severity, if not eliminated, if a higher priority had been awarded to the human factor in development.

To rectify this situation, much more attention will have to be accorded to the development of high standards of ethical conduct in the future. The key to this lies in the creation of effective ethical codes. Viewed from this perspective, the current ethical malaise manifesting itself in the world must be viewed as a cause for concern. For the ethical component, like the human component, resides at the core of the cultural state.

Given the profound changes that are taking place at present in religious practices and interpretations of the origins of life, this is a propitious moment for the development of effective ethical codes. Such codes should be based on two considerations: the primacy of ethical values; and the moral integrity of individuals, institutions, cultures and societies.

As far as the primacy of ethical values is concerned, ethical issues and moral problems should be confronted head on rather than perpetually glossed over. For ethical issues and moral problems are buried deep in the womb of the human condition. They are humane in nature, and universal in scope. They are humane in the sense that they deal sensitively and compassionately with people's needs for understanding, equality and trust. And they are universal in the sense that they place the interests of humanity ahead of the interests of particular groups, institutions and nations. As a result, they yield that level of conscience and consciousness needed to open the doors to major redistributions of income, resources and wealth. Ethics, not economics, provides the key to overcoming world poverty, hunger and starvation. The situation will not change until humanity decides to live life on a higher plane of ethical existence.

These ethical codes can be maintained through the moral integrity of individuals, institutions, cultures and societies, for moral integrity is inconceivable without truth, and truth compels people to be honest with themselves and others, as well as to come to grips with the reasons for their own insecurity and limitations. Likewise, truth compels people to confront the causes of injustice and inequality in the world. Without this, it is impossible to claim that the cultural state is an ethical state—a state designed to respond humanely and compassionately to the needs and rights of people and humanity as a whole. In endeavouring to achieve this ideal, it is not the function of the state to dictate ethical values and moral behaviour to the masses. Rather it is the function of the state to set a collective ethical example for others to follow.

If the ethical component deserves a prominent position at the core of the cultural state, so does the aesthetic component. Aesthetic ideals, like ethical ideals, contain many of culture's more compelling and endearing attributes. Without aesthetic ideals, such as the pursuit of excellence and perfection, the quest for creativity, and the love of beauty, humanity would be deprived of much of what is most inspiring and revered in the world. Gone would be the finest music, the most exquisite paintings, the most elegant architecture, the most inspired and expressive language, the most majestic monuments, and the most revered civilizations.

If aesthetic ideals have played an important role in the development of states in the past, they have an even more important role to perform in the future. They must prove capable of opening up those new frontiers of knowledge, wisdom, insight, and understanding needed to propel people to higher and higher levels of accomplishment. To do this, they should be securely fastened to the masthead of society, thereby confirming the seminal importance of artists and arts organizations as 'the antennae of the race'.

This may not be possible without shifting from a philosophy of 'art for the sake of art' to 'art for the sake of people.' This should not be taken to mean 'people's art'—the political glorification of the state and the masses using artists and the arts as the device. On the contrary, it should be taken to mean art that relates to people, societies and humanity as a whole. In other words, it means art that is focused outward on people and nature as well as inward on the individual. The world may not be as far away from this day as might be thought. Already artists and arts organizations seem to exude much more commitment to equality, equity, dedication to a cause and concern for the natural environment than their political and corporate counterparts. As such, they represent ideal models for institutional development and role modelling in the future.

These changes could bring with them fundamental changes in the role of the arts in society. While the arts would still retain their traditional functions of communication, education, inspiration, activation and evaluation, they would assume additional functions as well, particularly in the initiation of social, political and community change and the turning of every activity and occupation into an art in its own right. It would be easy to understand the meaning of the art of science, the art of politics and the art of life in this sense, since science, politics and life would be elevated to the level of art forms and practised accordingly.

Of all the components of the cultural state, none may be more difficult to pin down or come to grips with than the scientific component. The reason for this is clear. In the twentieth century, science has been responsible for some of the greatest gains and most difficult problems humanity has encountered. This has produced an ambivalence about science which makes it extremely difficult to determine how science should be positioned in the future.

Whether one is speaking of explorations in outer space, more effective utilization of land and sea resources, pollution control or the transmission of knowledge, or data and information, it is impossible to visualize the world of the future without a greatly expanded role for science, not to mention the potential it possesses to create the conditions for a better world. Who could deny this potential? Anything that possesses the power to destroy much of the world with a flick of a switch also possesses the power to create an enormous amount of goodness and progress in the world, particularly if it is properly controlled and directed. The challenge is to ensure that the container in which science is situated is a humanistic, ethical and altruistic one.

Viewed from this perspective, the focus of scientific activity in the future should be on ensuring that every member of the human family has sufficient resources and amenities to live a full and secure life. On the one hand, this means adequate food, clothing, shelter, nutrition, accommodation and other requirements of life. Here the emphasis would be on the development of new sources of food production and preservation, solar energy, the purification of water and air, and the creation of durable materials. On the other hand, it means securing greater access to the cultural achievements of humankind. What is needed here is the development of new techniques for knowledge dissemination, technological transfer and audio-visual communication. In recent years, numerous breakthroughs have been recorded in these areas. What is needed now, more than ever, is the will—and the willingness—to share these advances with the whole of humanity.

Major redistributions and redeployments of resources will be necessary if this is to be realized. First, resources will have to be taken out of certain uses, particularly the production of military weapons and nuclear devices, in order to provide scientists with the wherewithal they need to engage in experiments in other fields on a scale to do the job properly. Second, the fruits of scientific achievement will have to be diffused more broadly and equitably throughout the world, notably to African, Asian and Latin American nations. Third, science will have to become much more accessible to people, even if this means robbing it of its mystique. Finally, and perhaps most importantly, pure science will have to gain the upper hand on applied science, so much so that the current technological, economic and commercial domination of science and scientific achievements is broken. In other words, science will have to be redirected to cultural and human rather than commercial, militaristic, imperialistic and technological ends.

Education is also an extremely important component of the cultural state. It should be based on cultivation of the mind and the spirit, stimulating encounters with knowledge and wisdom and exposure to the finest things in life, as well as on storage and retrieval of information and acquisition of specific skills. In other words, it should be based on preparation for a creative and meaningful life, as well as on preparation for a career or profession.

How is this education achieved? Surely it is achieved by carving out a prominent place for culture at the core of educational systems and reformulating pedagogical and curriculum requirements accordingly.[9] As a reservoir filled with many of humanity's most significant accomplishments, culture opens the doors to new types of education and learning, providing avenues and vistas that go far beyond traditional experiences and immediate surroundings, both historically and geographically, and permitting comparisons to be made between different societies, cultures, and civilizations.

As was indicated earlier, comparative cultural education could be extremely helpful here. Through education in different philosophical systems, for example, there is exposure to different concepts of space, time, life and the universe. Through education in different religions, one is exposed to different belief systems and to diverse concepts of behaviour, morals, and spiritual and ethical well-being. Education in different artistic practices and scientific endeavours provides exposure to different perceptions of nature, design, rhythm, balance, proportion and change. As it is with philosophy, religion, science and the arts, so it is with every field of knowledge, be it medicine, social affairs, mathematics or politics. In each and every field, true knowledge and understanding is achieved by juxtaposing and comparing creative accomplishments across the broad spectrum of practices and possibilities.

In the cultural state, the emphasis is on exposure to different cultures and their various strengths and shortcomings, not just on indoctrination into a single culture. In this way, people learn to look at cultures objectively and critically, taking from each culture the ideas, values, insights, worldviews and attributes that are most appropriate to their own circumstances. In so doing, they learn to live their lives in accordance with the pluralistic and multicultural nature of most societies today, and to respond imaginatively, creatively and constructively to complex challenges and situations. This is why education in the cultural state is about learning to react wisely, intelligently and innovatively to life's trials and tribulations.

Of all the yardsticks that might be used to measure the degree of progress in the cultural state, none may prove more effective than the social component. Indeed, if one wants to know how advanced a state is, look at how it deals with its social demands: the sick, the elderly, the needy, and the unemployed in general and workmen's compensation, health care and the creation of a compassionate and caring social environment in particular.

The cultural state never allows the disadvantaged, disabled, minoritized and marginalized to be treated in a disrespectful manner. Regardless of how scarce its resources are, it is always careful to ensure that these groups have the social security benefits and safety nets to function effectively in society. This is achieved by incorporating them into the mainstream of society, rather than locking them away in institutions or pushing them to the margins of society. Disabled, indigenous and minority groups are given a chance to play a full and responsible role in society through gainful employment in a variety of trades and professions. The elderly and the disadvantaged are respected for the unique experiences and unusual insights they possess. In fact, the older people are, and the less in the majority they are, the more they are valued for the rich contribution they are able to make to society. Rather than becoming social outcasts and misfits, they are treated as living treasures and dealt with accordingly.

If one measure of social progress is the treatment of disadvantaged and minority groups, another is the creation of a stimulating social environment. Just as the disadvantaged and minority groups need countless opportunities to participate in the cultural life of the community, numerous opportunities should be available for citizens to engage in meaningful social interaction and exchange.

In the design of communities, the planning of parks and the provision of social services and recreational amenities, the cultural state is perpetually striving to provide people with opportunities to meet, share ideas, engage in conversation, and collaborate in worthwhile undertakings. On the one hand, this leads to a dramatic expansion of institutions which enhance the social fabric of the community: libraries, art galleries, museums, archives, community centres, social organizations and the like. On the other hand, it leads to improvements in the actual sites of community events and neighbourhood activities. Open-air concerts, presentations on city streets and public squares, festivals, fairs and communal celebrations all serve to strengthen the social bonds of the community.

Desire to enhance the social fabric of society should spill over into restoration and renovation measures. Whereas it was once felt that older buildings constitute a blight on the community and should be torn down in order to make way for new developments, there is growing recognition in many countries that older buildings have a pertinent role to play in social life and human affairs. In consequence, more and more old buildings—deserted factories, run-down warehouses, abandoned freight sheds and dilapidated railroad stations—are being spared the wrecker's crane in order to profit from the architect's eye and the artisan's touch. Not only does this strengthen the connection between people and their past, thereby enhancing their sense of community, solidarity and identity, but also it provides many more opportunities for social inspiration, relaxation, recreation and renewal.

Making improvements in the social fabric of the community and society generally should open the doors to improved relations between people and the natural environment. This leads directly to a consideration of the environmental component of the cultural state. There is growing concern everywhere over the state of the environment. In part, this concern emanates from the adverse consequences of modern systems, which, particularly in the highly-industrialized countries, have caused serious environmental damage and forced recognition of the fragile nature of the global ecosystem. In part, it derives from severe population pressures that have made people aware of resource deficiencies and spatial limitations. And in part, it derives from the universal desire to make the environment a healthier and safer place.

If the natural environment is treated with care and respect, it will respond favourably by acting as a source of munificence and fulfillment. However, if it is treated with disrespect and abused, it will strike back in some adverse way, the way polluted environments have by destroying the mood, morale and health of people. This highlights the need for dramatic changes in people's attitudes towards, and assumptions about, the environment. One such assumption is that the environment owes people a living. Another is that nature will eventually surrender its bounty without the need for human struggle. Still another is that nature will ultimately be brought under human domination and control.

None of these assumptions has any foundation in fact. First of all, the natural environment owes human beings nothing. Human beings have always been compelled to earn their living from the environment by the sweat of their brow and the force of their labour, and no amount of soothsaying or myth-making about humanity's technological ingenuity and creative potential will alter this situation. Secondly, while some environments surrender their bounty more readily than others, all environments require a great deal of attention and cultivation. It is always going to take a prodigious amount of human effort and ingenuity to cull a living from the environment. Finally, nature will never be brought under human domination and control. Doubtless, understanding of the laws of nature can help in forging a fruitful accommodation with nature, but no amount of understanding of the laws of nature will increase agricultural yields indefinitely, coax crops from parched soil, thwart hurricanes, floods, tornadoes and earthquakes, or prevent alluvial fields from turning barren when they are exploited. Neither all the machinery in the world, nor the most sophisticated methods and techniques of cultivation, can alter this situation.

Deflation of these myths should pave the way for an environmental awareness that is much more in tune with the rapidly-changing nature of global reality. All of the elements in this awareness—such as never taking more from the environment than is necessary for survival, stamping out needless duplication and waste, developing technologies that conserve rather than consume resources, replenishing and embellishing the environment at every opportunity, and living in harmony and cooperation with nature—are straightforward and based on common sense. Yet, it is surprising how difficult they are to achieve in practice. Much more is often taken from the environment than is necessary for survival, thereby wasting resources at an alarming rate. Also, the environment is seldom given the time and nutrients it needs to return to its abundant state. If these practices are not altered in the future, humanity could end up where all societies and cultures that have pushed the environment beyond its capacity have ended up. This is why it is so imperative to develop a set of environmental policies and practices based on sound methods of conservation, renewal, and resource management. Co-operation, not competition, must be the concern of the future.

In the fashioning of these environmental policies and practices, consideration should be given to two very specific requirements: the development of techniques capable of assessing the actual condition of environments; and the cultivation of lifestyles that make fewer demands on resources. The arts and sciences could be used to advantage to assess the actual condition of environments and the way these environments are being used and abused. Since the arts and sciences broaden and deepen sensory awareness, they tend to expand and heighten awareness of visual, aural and olfactory pollution: jungles of wires and poles; the spread of obnoxious odours and poisonous gases; the use of chemical compounds; the exhaustion of renewable and non-renewable resources; and the lack-lustre character of physical surroundings. But the role of the arts and sciences should not end with environmental assessments and awareness in this sense. It should also be extended to include those improvements which are necessary to enhance the physical, aesthetic, social and human state of environments.

While making improvements in the physical, aesthetic, social and human state of the natural environment is important, it pales by comparison with the need to change consumption practices which make excessive demands on the resources of nature. Whereas some types of consumption practices make maximal demands on the resources of nature and nature's precious legacy, other types make minimal demands on it. Many of culture's most cherished activities consume comparatively few environmental resources. For example, apart from the need for a limited supply of materials—paints for the painter, stone or wood for the carver, clay for the potter, musical instruments for the musician, and books for the scholar—the arts, humanities and education make few demands on the natural environment and nature's precious resource legacy. As such, they do not contribute significantly to the ravages of the countryside, the rapid depletion of renewable and non-renewable resources, and the conspicuous blights that disfigure the natural landscape. As labour-intensive, rather than capital or material-intensive, activities, many artistic, humanistic and educational activities offer ideal models for resource conservation.

Promoting activities that conserve rather than consume resources is an important step in the development of the economic and technological components of the cultural state. The key to fashioning these components lies in the realization that culture is not really an extension of the economy and technology, but rather the economy and technology are an extension of culture.[10]

This realization achieves a dual purpose. On the one hand, it forces recognition of the fact that the lesser and more commercial and financial motives of economic and technological activity—production, consumption, quantity, accumulation and profit—should be subordinated to and constrained by the greater and nobler motives of cultural activity—creativity, quality, excellence, conservation and human fulfillment. On the other hand, it redefines the purpose of economics and technology, largely by making it clear that they have more to do with the skillful management and careful husbanding of scarce material and non-material resources than they do with the creation of excessive material wealth and the promotion of waste and obsolescence. It is a purpose that is more consistent with the original meaning of economics as household management than it is with the current meaning of economics as production, distribution and consumption of material commodities.

Viewed from the perspective of the future, economies and technologies should be seen and treated as gigantic tapestries to be planned and woven in accordance with culture's highest and wisest ideals and principles. On the one hand, much more attention should be paid to the actual crafting of products, from the earliest design stages to the final assembly stages. Here, the production of every product should become a cultural act in its own right, requiring imagination and ingenuity in conception and finesse and daring in execution. On the other hand, much more attention should be paid to the creation of products which are reliable, durable, sustainable, and serviceable. Permanence, not obsolescence, should be the priority. Products should be made which are both appealing to look at, and able to withstand the test of time. There is much to be learned from cultural history here. For cultural history teaches that the higher the quality, the longer the life-span.

If lengthening the life-span of products is one way to conserve resources, reducing the space-scale of products is another. 'Small is beautiful' is the way Schumacher phrased this simple but profound truth, thereby resorting to an aesthetic device to provide a solution to a complex and persistent economic problem,[11] for small is not only beautiful; it is also more economical. Is there anything more beautiful, or more economical, than the finely-crafted pendant, the perfectly-shaped earring, or the Persian miniature? These products are exceedingly beautiful to look at and, also, they conserve rather than consume resources.

There may be nothing more conservation-conscious than the pocket computer. Less than a quarter of the size of the average book and far more portable, it is able to receive, store, retrieve and transmit vast amounts of knowledge and information from every part of the globe and every period of history. Developments like this signal the beginning of a new era in technological and economic activity—an era based on small and highly transportable micro-technology rather than large and cumbersome macro-technology. This new technology, which is largely electronic in nature, will contribute substantially to the realization of new modes of production, distribution and consumption in many areas of the world. In so doing, it will necessitate a whole host of structural changes and adjustments. It may not be out of place to find craftsmen rubbing shoulders with corporate executives, philosophers sitting on the boards of multinational corporations, and artists engaged in environmental and industrial planning, since the emphasis will be on the creative mixing of many diverse skills and professions rather than on the concentration of many specialized skills and professions. The object may no longer be to 'industrialize' culture, but rather to 'culturalize' industry. Quality, craftsmanship, and turning out products that people can be proud of should be the objective rather than piling up profits or increasing consumption.

This could help to break the false dichotomy between work and leisure— a dichotomy that exacerbates the tendency to view work as painful and leisure as pleasurable. All this dichotomy has produced is a world filled with skepticism and suspicion about the value and dignity of work. Since people are unlikely to find fulfillment in their leisure if they are unable to find it in their work, work must become a constructive and purposeful activity filled with stimulating encounters and challenges and a great deal of personal fulfillment and happiness. Eventually the separation between work and leisure may give way to a unified view of life based on the joys of work, industry, effort, creative fulfillment and spiritual satisfaction.

Thus far, attention has been focused on the human, ethical, aesthetic, social, scientific, environmental, economic and technological components of the cultural state. Now, the time has come to consider the political component. Given the pervasive role that politics plays in public and private affairs and everyday life, clearly much more must be known about the complex connection that exists between politics and culture.

People fear political and governmental involvement in culture and cultures for good reason, for, as illustrated earlier, the history of politics and culture confirms the fact that culture and cultures can easily be manipulated and exploited for political ends. This raises a fundamental question. Can the development of culture and cultures in general and the cultural state in particular be achieved without increasing the risk of political and govern-mental manipulation and interference in cultural life? The answer lies, as mentioned earlier, in creating the necessary safeguards and countervailing measures: the democratization of cultural institutions, the decentralization of cultural resources, the creation of specially-designed cultural agencies at arm's length from government and the political process, and especially the development of a viable and vital private sector. With these and other precautions, cultural development should be able to evolve in a manner that best suits and responds to people's needs and circumstances. Without this, there is a need to remain very vigilant with respect to the politics of culture.

Given the necessary precautions, what can be said about the relationship between politics, culture, cultures and the cultural state? Surely this: it is the first and foremost responsibility of politics, politicians and governments to develop culture and cultures. In order to do this, governments and politicians will have to abandon their penchant for thinking about culture and cultures in narrow and often specialized and marginal terms and start thinking about culture and cultures as the very essence and *raison d'être* of their existence.

When culture and cultures are conceived and defined in the holistic sense they are here, there is a very close connection between politics, culture, cultures and the cultural state, for regardless of whether political systems are socialist, autocratic, totalitarian or democratic, they are concerned first and foremost with 'the whole' and ensuring that the whole takes precedence over the 'parts'. Therefore, in principle, political concerns, like cultural concerns, are first and foremost holistic and egalitarian rather than specialized and élitist.

Despite this, the aims of culture, cultures, the cultural state and politics are not the same. Whereas the aims of the former are closely associated with creativity, excellence, diversity, truth, beauty and freedom, the aims of the latter are closely associated with order, security, stability, justice and power. Thus the potential for conflict is always present.

This potential can easily percolate to the surface of society and erupt into deep-seated hostilities. Some people may want to pursue creativity and change at the very time the state wants to promote order and stability. Moreover, some people may feel the need for truth while the state may be preoccupied with security. Whereas the former may feel that freedom of expression is the best means to achieve truth, the state may feel that suppression and censorship are the best means to achieve security. Added to this is the problem of pluralism. Whether political authorities like it or not, most cultures are pluralistic and multicultural in their make-up, possessing numerous languages, dialects, ethnic groups, and modes of behaviour. Official recognition of pluralism can be a difficult process: it can open the doors to many different groups and associations demanding their linguistic, ethnic and behavioural rights under the law. It is questionable how many of these rights can be accorded official political and legal status without causing a great deal of fragmentation. All the same, some measure of official recognition for pluralism is required to recognize the rights of ethnic minorities, the assertion of cultural identities, cultural diversity, and the reality of cultural differences. There are fundamental forces at work here that reach right to the heart of the cultural state.

It would be foolhardy to contend that these problems can be avoided or that they can always be resolved. Not only are they deeply embedded in the human condition and the cultural life of all countries, but also they provide the dynamic and creative tension which is often needed to propel cultures to higher and higher levels of accomplishment. Whenever there are attempts to resolve these difficulties, however, they should be resolved in culture's favour. For the interests of culture should always take precedence over the interests of politics in this area. When this doesn't happen, the doors are immediately opened to the worst abuses of political power.

Since politicians and governments see their responsibilities and *raison d'être* much more in terms of developing economic and political systems than cultural systems, commitment to culture, cultures and the cultural state as the first and foremost responsibility of political and governmental life will be exceedingly difficult to achieve. In fact, it will require a wholesale transformation in political and governmental procedures, structures, policies and practices. Parliaments and cabinets will have to devote much more time to discussing and debating the development of culture and cultures; ministries of cultural development will have to replace ministries of trade, industry and commerce as the key departments in government; cultural models will have to replace economic models as the principal focal points of bureaucratic concern and decision-making; and cultural development and policy will have to be accorded the highest priority in public policy. Ultimately this is what it means to make culture, cultures and the cultural state the principal priority of politics in general and political and governmental activity in particular.

Administration of the Cultural State

It is impossible for governments to play a key role in the evolution of culture, cultures and the cultural state without becoming deeply immersed in the cultural system, for in the process of safeguarding people's rights, formulating and implementing policies, promoting greater citizen participation in decision-making, protecting identity, preserving the heritage of history, and creating a climate conducive to cultural development, governments will get fully immersed in all aspects and dimensions of cultural life. Yet, can they do this without interfering with the natural ebb and flow of cultural activity, restricting the rights and freedoms of citizens and creative people, stifling genuine creativity and freedom of expression, and producing a culture that is oppressive, pedantic, and static? It is impossible to answer this question without posing an even more fundamental question: what constitutes a responsible role for government in the administration of the cultural state?

Every government has a fundamental responsibility to ensure that sufficient options and opportunities are available to satisfy people's cultural needs. These options and opportunities are of two principal types. First, there are options and opportunities that provide people with access to existing resources and institutions. Second, there are those that make it possible for people to create new resources and institutions.

Guaranteeing citizen access to existing resources and institutions will necessitate the removal of as many racial, religious, social, economic, political, educational and geographical barriers as possible. There will be some barriers—particularly racial and religious ones—where governments will have to play a forceful role, since these barriers may contravene codes of ethics and human rights. There will be other barriers, such as economic, social, education and geographical barriers, where governments will have to ensure that no citizen is deprived of access to resources or institutions as a result of lack of status, funds, education, age, gender, income, or geographical location. This is an onerous responsibility, since removal of many of these barriers will not be possible without tenacious actions on the part of governments as well as substantial injections of public funds.

Governments also have a responsibility to ensure that citizens have sufficient possibilities to create alternative resources and institutions for themselves. While such responsibilities are relevant to all countries, they are particularly relevant to countries that have suffered from colonialism and imperialism. Since few existing cultural resources and institutions may satisfy the indigenous needs of the population, the challenge of cultural administration and development in such cases may hinge much more on creating new cultural resources and institutions than it does on ensuring access to existing resources and institutions.

Added to this is the thorny problem of standards. This is bound to be an extremely sensitive area of political and governmental activity. Nevertheless, if cultural progress is to be qualitative as well as quantitative, governments will have to play a forceful role in terms of ensuring that the highest standards are achieved in the creation, enjoyment and appreciation of all cultural resources and institutions.

There are two ways in which governments can fulfill this responsibility. First, they can establish specific codes or standards for the creation, enjoyment and appreciation of cultural resources and institutions and rigorously enforce these codes and standards. Second, they can see to it that all those who are engaged in the creation, enjoyment and appreciation of cultural resources and institutions have the financial, economic, social and educational wherewithal, as well as the political and legal prerequisites, to fashion resources and institutions of the highest levels of excellence. Given the enormous difficulties involved in the articulation and enforcement of codes and standards, the second alternative seems infinitely superior to the first. Indeed, history has proven time and again that when creative talents are given the requisite means to create cultural works, they can create works of the highest quality and utmost professionalism.

When governments entered the public arena in a big way, many were hopeful that there was a chance to deal with societal problems and citizens' needs in a much more concentrated and comprehensive manner that would transcend the interests of private producers and special interest groups. Yet, in many cases, this has not happened. Many governments have been unable to develop the political mechanisms and governmental procedures which are necessary to deal with people's problems and needs in an equitable and objective manner. In the absence of these mechanisms and procedures, private producers and special interest groups have been free to make decisions based on personal preferences, vested interests, commercial and financial considerations, and preservation of the *status quo*. This has often resulted in decisions that run counter to the public interest, thereby reinforcing policies and practices that are highly partisan and at odds with the real interests of people and societies.

How can governments deal with this situation? At all levels of the political process, they can recognize the centrality of culture and cultures and redesign decision-making processes, planning structures, bureaucratic procedures and cultural systems accordingly.

Clearly, cultural systems must be created that are capable of maintaining an open, interactive and symbiotic relationship between citizens and politicians, governments and the public. The objective of these systems should be to evolve the policies, priorities and practices needed both to improve the human condition and people's lives, as well as to help people live in harmony with the natural environment, other people, other species and future generations. Once these policies, priorities and practices have been evolved through this interactive process, it is up to politicians and governments to ensure that they remain a reality.

Ministries of cultural development and specially-designed cultural agencies situated at arm's length from government and the political process have a crucial role to play in this. In order to perform this role, they need to be extremely active inside and outside government. Inside government, they need to act as linking mechanisms and co-ordinating vehicles for all government departments and agencies. They should be constantly involved in winning respect for culture's most elevated principles, values and ideals in all government departments and agencies, and they should also be perpetually engaged in promoting understanding of the way culture and cultures can act as integrating forces and contextual frameworks for public policy and decision-making. Outside government, they need to be actively engaged in sowing the seeds of culture in communities, regions and territories. This they can do by broadening and deepening public awareness and understanding of the vital role that culture and cultures play in community, regional, national, and international affairs, as well as creating a climate conducive to an active and flourishing cultural life. In this way, they can function as cohesive entities capable of uniting all public and private components of the state in the common search for effective ways to improve the human condition for all people.

Clearly it will not be possible for ministries of cultural development and specially-designed arm's length cultural agencies to perform these functions without a strong political commitment to culture. Also, they must have the power, authority and financial resources to execute these responsibilities in a trustworthy, efficient and effective manner. History confirms that these responsibilities are best carried out when they are consistent with the highest principles of excellence, creativity, access, participation, and truth. However, as critics have repeatedly observed, permanent solutions to cultural problems can only be brought about through a strong commitment to freedom, democracy and independence, and the development of a large and forceful private sector capable of creating and implementing programmes, initiating activities, providing funds, acting as a check on political power, and, especially, taking risks. Without these things, cultural development will fail to provide people with the type of cultural system and forms of cultural expression they have the right to expect.

There is no better way to conclude this chapter than to emphasize the holistic, organic and dynamic worldview on which the cultural state is based. This is achieved most effectively through the following passage by John Clauser:

The world is swiftly being revealed...as a totality composed of continuously interrelated and interdependent parts; a holistic and organic system of systems, of which man is an active, functioning component. This view is not only consistent with the developing world view that is increasingly global in scope, but is also in harmony with post-Newtonian science which emphasizes the connectivity of things, their relatedness and their interactions, in a new and strikingly different portrait of the universe.

Within this vision—a far richer, more promising one than the older Newtonian-Industrial view which stressed the divisions and compartments between things—one can sense the emergence of two complementary yet interdependent views of the world, wherein local, cultural life and transcultural global values can co-exist simultaneously.[12]

Nothing expresses the vision on which the cultural state is based better than this. It is a vision that necessitates qualitative and quantitative improvements in all aspects and dimensions of cultural life: human, aesthetic, ethical, social, educational and environmental as well as economic, scientific, technological and political. In endeavouring to realize this vision, the cultural state is in a perpetual state of flux; there is always room for improvements in it as a whole, as well as in the component parts that make up this whole. This is the challenge that lies ahead as the complex problems and limitless opportunities of a new millennium present themselves.

9. International Cultural Relations

> Cultural cooperation…is the way in which the world's peoples can work together, voluntarily, constructively and to mutual advantage, in building a progressive, orderly and more kindly world society…Cultural cooperation is so directly a national interest that it should furnish the fundamental motivating principle in governmental foreign service, replacing or reordering all lesser motives. [1]
>
> Paul J. Braisted

A North American farmer commences the long trek home after a day of back-breaking work in the fields. Planting has been particularly difficult this year. Dry weather has lasted much longer than usual, and the soil is parched and porous from the endless days of scorching sun. Reaching home well after nightfall, he has just enough time to devour a simple meal before it is off to bed to get some badly-needed rest. Dawn comes early for this farmer. Many miles must be traversed before another tedious day can even be commenced.

At first blush, the existence of this North American farmer appears to be humdrum and commonplace. It is an existence not unlike millions of those of other farmers throughout the world. He gets up every day at much the same time, tills the soil until dark, and returns home to a meal of basic foodstuffs. Moreover, he does this without interruption, just as millions of farmers do in all parts of the world. Yet his life is anything but humdrum and commonplace. Take the trouble to dig a little deeper and all sorts of variations and irregularities start to appear. Little variations and irregularities at first. The way he dresses is slightly different from his fellow farmers. His walk is slightly more stooped, especially on the left side. He has his own distinctive style of ploughing, a style he has evolved over many years as a result of his loving intimacy with the land. For this is his land, his soil. He knows it inch by inch, stone by stone, crop by precious crop.

Despite the fact that he is the victim of a difficult set of circumstances, he still has time to think great thoughts and dream original dreams. Occasionally, he dreams of himself and his family, of the day when his toils and the troubles of his family will be less demanding. More often, he dreams of society, of the day when societies will be organized on a different basis. Furthermore, he has his own particular vision of the future, as well as his own way of communicating with God. These give him a cultural identity and spiritual presence all his own.

Elsewhere in the world, an African woman has just returned home from her trip to the local market and is breast feeding her baby. This newest arrival on the scene brings the family to four, including a husband who is a factory worker, and two children. On the outside, her home is indistinguishable from many other homes in Africa. Inside, however, it is different. While there are few decorations and furnishings, each has been arranged in such a way that it conveys the warmth, affection and love of details which are the trademarks of her personality. Even a cursory glance is enough to inform the observer that there is much originality and ingenuity in this abode.

Her favourite pastime is telling stories—interesting stories, stories full of wisdom, insight and understanding. She does not know where these stories came from originally, since they are part of the great African oral tradition stretching back over thousands of years.[2] All she knows is that she learned them as a child, sitting spell-bound at the feet of her mother, eagerly waiting to learn how Mrs Rabbit outsmarted Mr Lion. They were just animal stories then; little did she realize how pregnant they were with meaning and insights into life. Now, she is faithfully recounting them for eager ears, each one told with all the flair and cunning of the storyteller's art. This is one of the many things that give originality, distinctiveness and richness to her life.

On another continent, an Indian businessman has just concluded an afternoon meeting. It was a difficult meeting. Business has been below normal this year and there are many difficult decisions to make—decisions that will affect the company for years. After a long and exhausting day, he is looking forward to returning home and watching some television. Over the years, he has found that watching television is one of the best ways he has of coping with the pressures and tensions of a stress-filled existence. But television serves only for relaxation. For recreation, he turns to his hobby of building model boats. When he first started this hobby, he made model boats from pre-assembled kits. Having tired of this long ago, he now makes them from scratch: he grows and processes his own wood; he makes his own glue and fixtures; he mixes his own paint; and makes his own ornaments. Lately, he has even taken to designing the boats. Today, these highly-prized boats grace many bedrooms throughout the neighbourhood.

In Europe, a craftsman is just putting the final touches on a decorative pot. Life has become difficult for this craftsman; his work has become stale, repetitious and demanding. Try as he will, he cannot seem to locate those internal sources of insight and inspiration which are needed to get a new lease on life. While his work is starting to achieve some real success, he is deeply disturbed by his inability to escape from the plateau he has been on for several years. Despite the fact that his depression is not conspicuous to others, he feels it acutely within himself. Intense personal problems are not his only concern. He is also experiencing real financial difficulties. It is proving more and more difficult to produce and sell his pots. The small market for hand-made products, coupled with the importation of cheap substitutes from abroad, are cutting into his business. To complicate matters, it is proving more and more expensive to acquire the materials he needs to fire and decorate his pots. Despite these difficulties, he persists. The craftsman's life is the only one he has known. Besides, there is a tradition to maintain. His family has been engaged in craft-making for as long as he can remember.

Far to the south, on the other side of the Atlantic, a South American girl is having trouble eking out an existence. Lacking sufficient employment possibilities and educational opportunities, her prospects are not unlike those of the European craftsman. However, unlike the European craftsman, there is no tradition to uphold. In fact, her hopes and dreams are directed towards breaking with tradition and striking out in new directions. Like the others, this South American youth is also highly creative and distinctive. Her distinctiveness and creativity are channelled into finding new ways of doing things and achieving the objectives at hand. For what is at stake here is her ability to open up new approaches to earning a living and living life.

Five people chosen at random from the billions of people who inhabit the earth. Each person is living in a different part of the world and is imbedded in a totally different set of cultural circumstances. Moreover, each is involved in a very different profession or undertaking. Nevertheless, they all share three bonds: the bond of uniqueness; the bond of humanity; and the bond of creativity. These bonds are shared not only with each other, but also with every member of the human family.

The Human Family

The bond of uniqueness, which all people share in common, stems from the fact that every person lives a unique life. Although people are influenced by countless elements in the larger cultural environments in which they are situated, they configure these elements in unique ways and produce a life that is without duplication or parallel elsewhere in the world.

This uniqueness in people's lives is not as apparent as it should be. The reason for this is social stereotyping, the kind of social stereotyping that causes pigeon-holing and categorization of people according to a few simple and specific criteria: age, sex, profession, education, or station in life. Unfortunately, this causes people to get so caught up in similarities that they often miss interesting variations and differences, for people's lives are like snowflakes; while they may appear similar from a distance, closer inspection reveals that they are different in the forms and characteristics they exhibit.

Only when social stereotyping is overcome does it become possible to see that every person lives a unique life. In effect, every person thinks original thoughts, dreams original dreams, lives a distinct life, and does original things. This gift, which is the inalienable right of all people, is a precious gift which should never be taken for granted or assumed, regardless of the circumstances.

People also share the bond of humanity. Whereas the bond of uniqueness provides people with a sense of identity and distinctiveness, the bond of humanity opens up an opportunity to experience solidarity and cohesion. The one is as essential as the other. In a world of escalating problems, difficulties and differences, it is reassuring to know that all human beings share the common bond of humanity, even if there are widely divergent views on how life should be lived and how survival should be addressed and ensured.

It is through recognition of the common bond of humanity that a solid foundation should be laid for international relations. Such a foundation should be based on placing the interests of the human family in general, and human welfare and well-being in particular, at the forefront of relations between people, countries, continents and cultures:

The advancement of peoples and nations requires a radical subordination of profit-seeking motives to humane impulses. The welfare of people must gradually become the primary concern, and the manifold activities of commerce and business, hasty or careless industrialization, competition for natural resources, labor, and markets, must be adjusted accordingly. Too much of the glib talk about the inevitability of war and the evil nature of men is a thin cloak of justification for unprincipled and unbridled exploitation in utter disregard of the fundamental things of human life. Clearly, subordination of economic motives to the humane interests of people is essential to world order, and to preparation for more fruitful cooperation.[3]

It is through co-operation, collaboration, caring, sharing and altruism, rather than through competition, combat, confrontation, exploitation and survival of the fittest, that humanity should seek to build a new system of international relations. Whether this system is based on the realization that co-operation, collaboration, caring, sharing and altruism are imperative in a dynamic, interdependent and indivisible world, or on the religious conviction that people should look after each other and be each other's keepers, the conclusion is much the same. The bond of humanity that unites all people must be strengthened and fortified if the universal problems of poverty, pollution, injustice and prejudice are to be addressed effectively in the future.

It is out of the bond of humanity that the bridges will be built that are needed to usher in a new era in international relations. Such bridges—strong, flexible and enduring—should make it possible for all countries and all people to work together in the common search for satisfactory and sustainable answers to the world's most pressing and persistent questions: Why must so many go hungry when there are sufficient resources to feed all? Why must human beings be condemned to premature death when incredible advances are being made in medical practices and health care systems? Why must individuals and minority groups be persecuted when this seems unnecessary? And why must so many children be exploited and abused? These questions must be placed at the core of the international relations system if the common bond of humanity is to be tightened and strengthened in the future.

Cultivation of the bond of creativity is the key to overcoming the complex problems and challenges confronting humanity, for it is creativity, as indicated earlier, that has rescued humanity time and again from adversity. As a result, it holds the key to human survival and well-being. Regardless of age, gender, education, profession, personal circumstances or location in the world, all human beings are creative to a degree and therefore share the common bond of creativity.

For many people, creativity must be channelled into addressing the most basic problem of all: survival, and eking out an existence under the most debilitating circumstances imaginable. Others are more fortunate. Due to more favourable economic, social, geographical and environmental conditions, they are able to direct their creativity to less taxing pursuits. Nevertheless, this does not alter the fact that all people share the common bond of creativity. It is a fact which manifests itself in every domain of cultural life.

Creativity has given rise to the cultural heritage of humankind. As indicated earlier, this precious heritage is the sum total of the creative accomplishments of all people, countries and cultures. The time has come to put flesh on this precious heritage of hope, particularly as it provides the cornerstone on which to build a new system of international relations.

The Cultural Heritage of Humankind

What stands out most clearly when the cultural heritage of humankind is looked at as a totality is its universal character. It exists everywhere. Not only has it received countless contributions from all cultures, but also there is scarcely a group of people, community, country or region in the world which has not made a strong, vital and enduring contribution to it. Since this living legacy of the past and the present is the product of all people, countries and cultures, it is on this undeniable historical and contemporary fact that humanity should seek to build a more equitable and just system of international relations in the future.

Anyone who doubts the universal character of this heritage need only reflect on its true nature. As the real indicator of humanity's greatest and most significant accomplishments down through the ages, this indispensable treasure-trove of historical and contemporary accomplishments is discernible amidst the rise and fall of different cultures and civilizations. It is comprised of, in addition to countless other accomplishments: the cultural achievements of the Egyptians, the Mayas, the Incas and the Asians; all the world's greatest cities and historical sights—Venice with its enchanting architecture and enticing canals, Isfahan and Istanbul with their exquisite mosques, Kyoto with its ancient temples and Buenos Aires, Marrakech and Savannah with their evocative streets and sumptuous squares; all the greatest music, dances, paintings and craft objects from all parts of the world and every period of history; all the most significant achievements in economics, science, education, social affairs, human thought and technology everywhere in the world from the dawn of time right up to the present day; all the religious teachings and great philosophical writings; eastern as well as western medicine; oriental as well as occidental art; written as well as oral history; and cyclical as well as linear concepts of time. It is all this and much more. It is also the less tangible but equally essential cultural creations of humanity: the pursuit of justice, equality and truth; the thirst for knowledge and wisdom; the love of beauty; and the search for the sublime. Little wonder Jacob Burckhardt called this precious jewel in humanity's crown 'the silent promise' that possesses the potential to transform the entire past and present into 'a spiritual possession'.[4]

Perhaps the best way to convey an impression of the colossal size and universal character of the cultural heritage is to think of all the encyclopedias that exist in the world for artifacts, activities, and other types of creative accomplishments. In an encyclopedia of myths, for example, there are usually myriad myths drawn from different countries and cultures. They are classified according to different categories, such as creators of nature and humankind; heaven and hell; bringers of magic and the arts; animals, monsters and beasts; lovers and bearers of divine seeds; heroes and battles; distant quests and mortal tests; death, rebirth, reincarnation, and so on. Under each category are recorded many myths pertinent to the subject matter. For instance, under lovers and bearers of divine seeds might be found all myths relating to the great mother, the goddesses of life, sacred animals, miraculous conceptions, divine births, fertility gods and goddesses, and divine marriages. Under death, rebirth and reincarnation might be found myths related to the realms of the dead, the journey to the underworld, the messengers of death, the beyond, Hades, the tortures of hell, dwellers in the paradise of heaven, the triumph of death, the last judgment, the journey into heaven, resurrection, returns from the underworld, and the rebirth of light and life.

In an encyclopedia of musical instruments, there are likely to be thousands of different musical devices listed, each organized according to the family it represents as well as the culture with which it is most commonly associated. There may well be flutes, horns, pianos, organs, harps, lyres, violins, chimes, zithers, gongs, bells, and numerous other sonic devices. In the drum category alone, for example, there could be hundreds of different types of drums: water drums, slit drums, cylindrical drums, barrel drums, goblet drums, foot drums, kettle drums, and so forth. Each one serves a different purpose, and is made out of a different substance. As it is for drums, so it is for virtually every other musical instrument.

In an encyclopedia of technological inventions and innovations, there are likely to be thousands of different technological accomplishments recorded. Each one is probably organized according to the category with which it is most commonly associated, such as transportation, communications, energy, food, agriculture, and so on. In the transportation and communications section, for example, there may be inventions like the boat, kite, parachute, train, bus, bicycle, automobile, motorcycle, airplane, helicopter, hovercraft, camera, telegraph, typewriter, telephone, gramophone, radio, film, television and tape-recorder. In the food and agriculture section, there may be inventions like the plough, seed-drill, reaper, lawn-mower, threshing-machine, axe, rolling mill, and hydraulic jack. The list is virtually endless.

These three examples provide only an infinitesimal glimpse into humanity's creativity down through the ages. When one begins to reflect on the fact that there are probably as many different encyclopedias as there are entries in each, one begins to form a visual picture of the colossal size and incredible diversity of the precious treasure-trove of human creativity.

Next to its size, what stands out most about the cultural heritage of humankind is its ubiquity. Select any country in the world and it quickly becomes apparent that every country in the world possesses its own particular cornucopia of creativity—monuments, sacred shrines, rare paintings, religious relics, literary masterpieces, scientific achievements, medical treatments, and commercial and industrial insights.

If the cultural heritage of humankind is universal in character, colossal in size and ubiquitous in nature, it is evolutionary in time. This makes it a living heritage of past and present accomplishments for utilization in the future. Every day, it receives countless contributions from all parts of the world. These contributions not only enhance its universal quality and colossal size, they also make it a dynamic reality that is constantly being created and re-created as new sources of knowledge are uncovered and new facts are brought to light. In this sense, it exists not only in the monuments, manuscripts and artifacts of the past; it also exists in the minds and imaginations of the world's most creative people. This means that it is in constant need of conservation, research, adaptation and change if it is to serve humanity to best advantage.

Since more is always being added to the cultural heritage of humankind than is being subtracted from it, it is highly cumulative in time and space. It is the cumulative nature of this heritage which makes it possible to part company with historians like Spengler. When Spengler said there is no tapeworm industriously adding on to itself one epoch after another,[5] he certainly was not thinking of the cultural heritage of humankind. Had he focused on the way in which humanity has been carefully preserving its most cherished cultural creations for centuries, or on areas where cultures are interdependent and interactive rather than independent and isolated, he would have realized that humankind has been steadily and systematically adding to its legacy of cherished cultural accomplishments from the beginning of time right up to the present day. One only need study the objects in any room to realize how busy the tapeworm of history has been adding to the sum total of its accomplishments day after day, year after year, century after century.

The world's custodial institutions—art galleries, museums, archives, libraries and the like—are filled with evidence of this. From the dawn of recorded time, conservation and preservation of the cultural heritage of humankind has been a constant and conscious preoccupation, despite the fact that many countries still lack the resources necessary to preserve their valuable legacies from the past.

The protection of this profuse legacy of creative achievements has become a highly sophisticated and systematic art in recent years as a result of the increased incidence of theft and pillage and the ravages of nature and time. It is an art which requires a battery of skilled and talented professionals— curators, technicians, conservation experts, and the like. Here, the efforts of Unesco, the International Council of Museums, the International Council on Monuments and Sites, the International Institute for Conservation of Historic and Artistic Works, and others must be singled out for recognition. Not only have these organizations been instrumental in raising global consciousness of the importance of conservation in general and proper conservation methods, measures and techniques in particular, but also they have saved many of the world's most prized possessions from extinction, including the Bamiyan site, Pagan, Angkor Wat and Angkor Thom, Abu Simbel, and many others.

Given the rapid accumulation of monuments, historic sites and artifacts on the one hand and the soaring costs of preservation and conservation on the other hand, new methods and techniques will have to be developed in the future to prevent the slow but steady erosion of humanity's most precious and munificent asset. This is why inventions like microfiche, the computer, CD-ROMS, television, video and satellites, which permit the storage, retrieval and utilization of vast amounts of knowledge, information and ideas, are so essential. They provide a ray of hope in what would otherwise be a bleak and depressing situation.

Many of these inventions enhance the mobility function of the cultural heritage of humankind. Throughout history, this heritage has been highly mobile in space and time whenever this has been possible. Whether mobility has resulted from the plunder of one nation by another, or through the natural curiosity of explorers like Ibn Batuta and Marco Polo, there is hardly an epoch in history that does not bear vivid testimony to the mobility function of the cultural heritage of humankind. Whether it has been by caravan, boat, train, plane, book, scroll, radio, film, photograph or television, there is scarcely a single creation of any significance or size in the world that has not traversed or been transmitted around the globe in response to humanity's insatiable thirst for knowledge and information about its most cherished accomplishments.

Many may ask what it is that makes this heritage so vital to the world of the future. Why, in addition to all its other properties, does the cultural heritage of humankind possess a priceless quality that makes its preservation, perpetuation and diffusion imperative for the future? Perhaps the best way to lift the veil of the priceless value of the cultural heritage of humankind is to reflect on what the world would be like if this heritage did not exist.

Gone would be all knowledge, wisdom and understanding, for these grow out of the accumulated insights and ideas that one generation passes on to the next. Without these, humanity would quickly find itself back in a rudimentary state of existence, confronted by the most treacherous and debilitating circumstances with little or no agricultural, industrial, technical or medical know-how or expertise to combat them. In such a state, people would quickly revert to the most barbaric practices imaginable, pressed cheek by jowl against each other and the ever-present danger of extinction.

Gone would be all communication between human beings, for human communication, undoubtedly the highest form of cultural creation and accomplishment, springs from the ability to make verbal and non-verbal contact with one another. Lacking language and all the other forms of interpersonal communication which have been built up over the centuries, human beings would be limited to grunts, groans and signs, the large part of which would be unintelligible from one person to another.

In addition, there would be no beauty, except that provided by nature. There would be no music to soothe people in times of adversity, no poems, plays or pictures to inspire people in times of depression, and no stories or novels to console people in times of trouble. These would be lost forever, as would all the greatest cities and historical monuments. Everywhere, people would be confronted with a monotonous existence and drab world robbed of the thunder of human passion and the fire of creative imagination.

Lost also would be all hope and memory. For these also form part of humanity's precious heritage. In fact, in many ways, these are the most important part, since without hope to inspire people in times of adversity and memory to enlighten people in times of tragedy, humanity would lack the heart to face the future and would be constantly repeating the mistakes and most unacceptable experiences of the past. As a result, humanity would be suspended in a kind of eternal present, forced to endure the nihilism of despair.

Anyone who still doubts the priceless value of humanity's cultural heritage need only reflect on the things that one nation destroys or expropriates when it subdues or conquers another nation. Does it not immediately expropriate or destroy its most revered books, rarest art objects, most illuminating manuscripts, most revered minds, most effective technology, and most valued treasures? Surely this fact establishes without a doubt the priceless value of humanity's collective cultural legacy.

Given the priceless character and universal nature of this legacy, it is essential to make a clear distinction between the cultural heritage of humankind on the one hand and 'the Western culture' on the other hand. Although it is the product of a long, historical tradition, the Western culture has been shaped largely by economic and technological considerations over the last few centuries. Based primarily on an economic interpretation of history and a highly materialistic outlook on life, it is the product of western countries. Underlying it is a commitment to the belief that the western way of doing things is the most effective way of doing things.

In sharp contrast, there is the cultural heritage of humankind. Although it is equally the product of a long, historical tradition, it is the product of all countries, past and present. Underlying it is the idea of diversity, or the belief that there are many different ways of doing things. As the reservoir of all the world's accomplishments, it is a universal fund which has been created by all cultures, countries and continents for use by all people. It is this fund which should be disseminated, utilized and shared fully by all members of the human family.

This transcendental property in the cultural heritage of humankind sheds a great deal of light on the principal motive behind cultural creation, as well as the real meaning of progress. Why have people laboured so industriously everywhere in the world and in every period of history to build and rebuild cultures? Why, for example, did the Egyptians labour so strenuously to build Egyptian culture? Why did the Polish people struggle so energetically after World War II to rebuild devastated Warsaw and Poland? And why have all the world's greatest creative talents struggled to subdue the nagging ache of creativity?

Ego gratification itself does not supply an explanation. No, a much deeper and more benevolent motive has been at work—a motive so clear in retrospect that it should not be allowed to escape public attention or general recognition. Whether it has been the back-breaking work of the labourer, the meditations of the monk, the abstractions of the artist or the prodding of the scientist or educator, the central motive behind all cultural creation has been to make improvements in all aspects of life for all members of the human family. Who can listen to a Mahler symphony, gaze at an Asian temple, sit spellbound at an African dance, benefit from modern advances in medicine and technology or expand the dimensions of learning and discovery without feeling a sense of communion with this motive? Surely it is impossible to think of a culture, or a creator, anywhere in the world, or at any time in history, that has not engaged in cultural creation with this end in mind.

This central purpose of cultural creation should not be confused with the way in which particular cultural elements—forms, ideas, ideologies and structures—are used, misused and abused. One cultural element can and often is used to exploit or subdue other elements. For example, the arts can be used for political and propaganda purposes, just as technology can be used to enslave and dominate people. This potential for exploitation and manipulation, which is inherent in every single aspect and dimension of cultural life, should not be confused with the deeper motive in all cultural creation to make life a more meaningful and fulfilling experience than it might otherwise be. It is altruism, not egoism, that lies at the heart of all creative cultural activity.

If the cultural heritage of humankind exposes the basic motive behind cultural creation, it also reveals the real meaning of progress. As indicated earlier, progress does not consist in the fashioning of particular works or the building up of specific cultures, although this is obviously very much part of it. Regardless of how important these things are, they are merely the means towards a much more noble and enthralling end: the creation and utilization of a universal storehouse of human achievements by all the globe's inhabitants.

This is what makes the diffusion of the cultural heritage of humankind, in the spirit of true benevolence and common co-operation, the only real hope for humanity, human survival, and human well-being in the future. Arnold Toynbee foresaw this day when he concluded following his intensive study of different cultures that the challenge of the future is for nations and peoples to learn how to coexist and mutually fructify themselves.[6] Waldo G. Leland had the same sentiment in mind when he referred to the ultimate objective of all international relations as:

The advancement of the cultural (and intellectual) life of the participating peoples by the sharing of knowledge and experience. This objective includes the advancement of knowledge in all domains and by all means, through the cooperative activities of scholars and scientists and educators; it includes the enrichment of all aspects of cultural life, through exchanges of knowledge, methods, ideas and experience; it includes, as derivative objectives, the promotion of understanding and spiritual solidarity among peoples and the improvement of the conditions of life.[7]

Armed with this understanding, it is possible to plunge into a consideration of the type of international relations system required to facilitate relations among the diverse peoples, countries and cultures of the world in the future.

A Transformation in International Relations

If the key to international relations lies in co-operation and full utilization of the cultural heritage of humankind, it is appropriate to ask how this can be accomplished in fact. Surely it is best accomplished by creating a system of international relations based on the principles of altruism, sharing, caring, exchange and collaboration.

Humanity is obviously a long way from achieving this ideal. Indeed, reflection on the present system of international relations reveals that nothing short of a major transformation in the way countries, continents, cultures and peoples relate to one another and the world around them will bring this about. For relations between countries, continents, cultures and peoples have become too one-sided, competitive and commercial. They are going to have to be much more open, reciprocal, co-operative and collaborative in the future if humanity is to be deflected down a different path and people in all parts of the world are to gain access to the universal treasure-trove of cultural accomplishments.

The starting point for this transformation lies in the realization that every nation in the world possesses a rich and diversified reservoir of cultural accomplishments. It is on this foundation that a new system of international relations should be erected based on the equality, ingenuity, integrity and dignity of all countries.

Since the arts, humanities and education speak to the greatness, richness and uniqueness of these reservoirs more effectively than anything else, they should be awarded a central position in this new system of international relations. This is in marked contrast to the present system. In the present system, economic, commercial, technological, political and financial interests are awarded central priority. Despite the vast importance of these interests to the world of the present and the future, what must be recognized is that these interests are cold and impersonal, largely because they deal with products rather than people as well as matters of material loss and gain rather than matters of the heart, the soul, the intellect and the spirit. Thus, the potential for conflict, aggression, confrontation and war is always present because the human element is missing. But this is precisely where the arts, humanities and education come in. Human expression is their very nature. Whether it is the sonorous rhythms of the musician, the passionate pleas of the priest, the curiosity of the scholar, or the teaching of the educator, the human element glows through every artistic, humanistic and educational act.

As the true purveyors of a nation's most human and humane expression, music, drama, literature, philosophy, ethics and scholarship expose the real heart and soul of nations. They communicate effectively across geographical frontiers and political boundaries, revealing most clearly what nations and peoples are all about, how they have evolved over time, and what they hold most dear to themselves. Is it not through activities such as these that nations and peoples should be known and judged around the world? Surely countries should interact first and foremost in those areas which give the most profound, compassionate and human expression to their creative achievements.

Bringing countries and peoples into intimate contact in this way is not the only reason for advocating a massive build-up of international relations in the arts, humanities and education. There are other reasons as well. When economic, commercial and military relations are in flux, much as they are today in many parts of the world, relations in these other areas provide a strong stabilizing force. They help to cushion the shocks that can easily result from erratic swings in the pendulums of political, economic, military, commercial and financial power. Thus, a comprehensive program of international exchanges involving composers, writers, theatre and dance companies, symphony orchestras, social workers, scholars, teachers, academics and the like can provide the cement that is needed to keep countries and peoples together when other forces are operating to split them apart. In this way, peace, security, stability and friendship can be more readily achieved and maintained in the world.

Equally important is the fact that exchanges in these areas do more than anything else to eradicate the kind of fear and suspicion that results from the inability to understand the beliefs, convictions, practices, signs and symbols of others. Throughout history, fear and suspicion have often been used as devices to subdue and enslave people. As a result of the communications revolution and the steady emergence of an interdependent world, it is now possible to reduce some of the misunderstandings which result from a lack of understanding of cultural differences. Through the kind of massive build-up of artistic, humanistic and educational exchanges advocated here, which are predicated on in-depth encounters with the creative accomplishments of all countries, continents, cultures and peoples, there exists an opportunity to bring the whole of humanity into intimate, personal contact. It is an opportunity that is too important to be missed.

With artistic, humanistic and academic exchanges acting as the base, it does not prove difficult to visualize a vast panorama of possibilities for co-operative exchanges in science, agriculture, industry, commerce, economics, communications and technology. Such exchanges should be based on mutual flows of people, products and programmes.

Viewed from this perspective, it is clear that the major flaw in international relations at present lies in the fact that the flow of people, products and programmes between the various nations and peoples of the world—north, south, east and west—is often unilateral rather than reciprocal. There are millions of products, people and programmes pouring out of northern and western nations and countries like Japan destined for southern and eastern markets. And what is flowing in return? Comparatively speaking, an enormous pile of raw materials and a trickle of craft objects and semi-manufactured goods.

There must be profound changes in people's attitudes in North America, Europe and Japan with respect to what they are prepared to share with the rest of the world, as well as what the rest of the world has to offer. As long as Europeans, North Americans and the Japanese cling to the belief that Asian, African and Latin American nations have little to contribute to world progress and global development, and as long as they refuse to share their agricultural, industrial and scientific technology, know-how and expertise with the rest of the world, little progress will be made in coming to grips with the problems of the present and the challenges of the future. Nor, incidentally, will the major causes of inequality, conflict and confrontation in the world be overcome. For world equality, peace and security does not revolve around remaking African, Asian and Latin American countries over in the image of North American and European countries. On the contrary, it consists in drawing fully on the cultural assets, resources, talents and abilities that African, Asian and Latin American countries possess in abundance.

If world equality, peace and security is one of the benefits of a transformation in the system of international relations, international co-operation and collaboration is another. Such co-operation and collaboration is imperative in a world characterized by *transnational* problems in urgent need of *transnational* solutions.

It does not take a giant step of imagination to realize the innumerable benefits that could accrue from much more international co-operation and collaboration, particularly if predicated on the principles of caring, sharing, equality, altruism and reciprocity. As mentioned earlier, there are numerous examples in the arts, sciences, media, education, communications, medicine and business where international co-operation and collaboration has produced results that simply could not have been produced in any other way. Such results come from the creative energy and synergy derived from bringing together people and countries that possess vastly different cultural backgrounds and experiences, and therefore very different worldviews, values, perceptions, thought-processes, ideas, ideals and beliefs. This creative energy and synergy now needs to be harnessed and unleashed on a scale hitherto unknown in history. For transnational problems as severe and potentially life threatening as exponential population growth, pollution, environmental degradation, income, gender and resource inequality, shortages of renewable and non-renewable resources, violence, terrorism and human rights abuses will only be solved through genuine co-operation and collaboration among the various peoples, countries and cultures of the world:

Mankind is faced with problems which, if not dealt with, could in a very few years develop into crises world-wide in scope. Interdependence is the reality; world-wide problems the prospect; and world-wide cooperation the only solution.[8]

Many practical benefits could accrue from an international system based on the principles of co-operation, caring, sharing, equality, altruism and reciprocity. Most of these benefits—such as increasing foreign aid and developmental assistance as a percentage of gross national product, improving access to the universal fund of cultural achievements and technological acumen, renegotiating the terms of trade and debt loads on a more equitable basis, drawing more heavily on African, Asian and Latin American skills and abilities, and sharing income, employment and resources more liberally and broadly—require dramatic changes among the rich, powerful and privileged nations and peoples of the world. Until those who possess and control income, investment, employment and resource opportunities commit themselves to co-operation, caring, sharing, equality, altruism and reciprocity—not as a moral duty or theoretical ideal but as a fundamental and practical necessity—the world will be saddled with an international system which is unjust, unfair, and inimical to global harmony and world peace.

In the process of endeavouring to achieve this ideal state of affairs, maximum use should be made of the most recent, advanced and sophisticated means of communication. Fortunately, these means are evolving rapidly. Thanks to the invention of computers, satellites, micro-electronics, the video tape, the microchip, internets, electronic highways, and the like, it is now possible to transmit knowledge, information and expertise from one part of the world to another in the flash of a second. Not only do these developments tend to conserve rather than consume resources, but also they begin to bring the very best global civilization has to offer within the potential reach of every member of the human family. This is yet another link in the long chain of events which is needed to make it possible for all the inhabitants of the globe to live creative, meaningful and fulfilling lives.

An international system devoted to the dissemination of the very best humanity has to offer would be an exciting system indeed, particularly if it was based on the highest principles of culture and cultures. Not only would it open up vast vistas for intellectual inspiration, practical understanding and collective discovery, but also it would contribute to breaking down the geographical, political, linguistic, social, ethnic, racial and psychological barriers that exist between peoples, countries, cultures and continents. In so doing, it would enable people in all parts of the world to make more effective decisions about their future life course, as well as place humanity in the best possible position to make intelligent decisions about future directions in planetary civilization.

A Federation of World Cultures

It is impossible to raise issues as fundamental as transformation of the system of international relations, collective sharing and dissemination of the cultural heritage of humankind and future directions in planetary civilization without raising the related issue of 'world culture' and 'world cultures'. Should humanity be striving to create a single world culture shared by all citizens and all societies? Or should humanity be striving to create many 'world cultures', each with its own distinctive characteristics and sense of identity?

Those who favour a single world culture point to a number of historical and contemporary developments to support their contention that a world culture is inevitable, even though it may be decades away. Those opposed to a world culture counter that there are so many differences in people's worldviews, values, needs and circumstances that a world culture is anything but inevitable. Since the arguments on both sides are compelling, it pays to examine them in detail.

According to those who favour a world culture, there has been a relentless trend throughout history towards the creation of larger and larger cultural units. They cite the progressive movement from small groups to city states to countries to global trading zones, as well as the creation of international institutions like the United Nations, the World Bank and the International Monetary Fund, adoption of English as a kind of international lingua franca and especially the creation of a global financial and commercial system, to confirm their case that a world culture is taking shape. When this trend is pushed to its logical conclusion, it is clear where it ends up. It ends up in the creation of a world language, court, judicial and legal system, police force and possibly government.

Even if this trend does not materialize the way those who favour a world culture predict, advocates of this conviction believe that recent developments in the mass media and modern communications make a world culture inevitable. They point to the universal spread of popular music, the international popularity of American-made films and television programs, improvements in satellite communications, the development of electronic highways and internets, the appearance of a 'global village', the creation of a world without borders and frontiers, and the concentration of media ownership in fewer and fewer hands, as evidence that a world culture is inevitable.

For proponents of this view, a world culture is not only inevitable. It is also desirable. According to the argument, it will open up unlimited opportunities for understanding, co-operation and collaboration because all peoples, countries, continents and cultures will share a common value system and worldview. It will also reduce unrest, fear, conflict, war and violence by eliminating cultural differences, thereby enhancing the potential for peace, stability, harmony and security throughout the world.

Those who oppose a world culture are quick to counter these arguments. They point out that many obstacles and encumbrances stand in the way of ever achieving a world culture. In the first place, they contend that every movement in history towards the creation of larger cultural units has set in motion a dialectical reaction towards the creation of smaller cultural units. In the modern world, this reaction is manifesting itself in the increased emphasis on neighbourhoods, communities, municipalities, metropolitan areas and regions as countervailing forces to globalization. The reason for this dialectical reaction is not difficult to detect. Most people derive their identity and sense of belonging from cultural units which are considerably smaller, more tangible and less abstract than complex notions like global trading zones, superstates, and a world culture. Moreover, the world is already divided into so many different and diverse cultural units that it is highly unlikely these units will disappear, since they are too deeply imbedded in the human condition. Finally, and perhaps most importantly, for every person who favours the creation of a world culture, there appears to be another who is opposed to the idea.

Whereas people who favour a world culture see this as a blessing and the key to a new era in human affairs, people who oppose it see it as a curse. They point to the globalization and homogenization of the world as a development that must be countered at all costs, contending that diversity and variety will be stamped out and apathy, lethargy and alienation will set in if a world culture becomes a reality.

There is a great deal of substance to these arguments. Already certain types of technological developments, media activities and consumer practices have pervaded the world to the point where they have effectively stamped out or obliterated cultural differences. Indeed, it is not difficult to visualize the kind of monotonous existence which could result from the creation of a world culture. Gone would be all originality, variety and diversity, the very things which constitute the spice of life and are imperative for human survival and environmental sustainability.

Is it possible to reconcile these conflicting points of view? Is it possible to derive the benefits which might accrue from creation of a world culture, particularly as they relate to the potential for much more international co-operation and collaboration and enhanced global and human understanding, while simultaneously experiencing the benefits which accrue from many different cultures? The answer would appear to lie in achieving 'unity in diversity' and in creating a federation of 'world cultures'.

Achieving unity in diversity is one of the most formidable challenges confronting humanity, just as it is one of the most formidable challenges confronting multicultural and multiracial societies. On the one hand, there can be no unity without sharing certain similarities, since unity is achieved and maintained by accepting shared values and bonds which link people, countries and cultures together. Likewise, there can be no diversity without preserving certain differences, for too much similarity and sameness can kill the creative spark which makes people, countries and cultures unique. Thus, as indicated earlier, unity in diversity is achieved by walking the thin line between similarities and differences. The key to achieving this unity on a global basis could lie in creating a federation of world cultures. Such a federation could make unity in diversity a living reality rather than a cliché, thereby opening the doors to a new era in international relations.

Since the idea of a federation of world cultures hinges on the dual notion of world cultures and federation, it requires some explanation. As far as the notion of world cultures is concerned, it is clear that all cultures in the world are rapidly becoming world cultures in the sense that they are compelled to cope with all the colossal changes which are going on in contemporary communications and the emergence of a 'global world'. Whereas in previous decades and centuries it was possible for cultures to remain isolated from developments taking place in other parts of the world, today this no longer seems possible. Surely all cultures in the world today, including the smallest, most remote and most inconspicuous, are 'world cultures' by virtue of the fact that they are constantly being bombarded by all the latest developments in contemporary communications and international affairs.

As far as the notion of a federation is concerned, it implies a coming together of all cultures of the world to improve the environmental situation, human condition and quality of life for all members of the human family. Realization of this noble and worthwhile state of affairs will not be possible without a great deal more intercultural interaction, cross-cultural fertilization, understanding, and exchange among all the various cultures and peoples of the world.[9] It is through the development of these interactive and interdependent capabilities, or what the French call 'the dialogue of cultures', that the foundations will be laid for the realization of a more humane and compassionate world system in the future.

Viewed from this perspective, it is clear that the major challenge in international relations in the years ahead lies in creating an international system capable of enabling all countries, cultures and peoples to maintain their distinctive identities while simultaneously working together in a spirit of true equality and common co-operation. Such a system demands the highest possible priority because it possesses the potential to usher in a whole new era in global understanding and world affairs.

10. The Art of Cultural Development and Policy

> Development is not merely an economic and political concept; it is more fundamentally a process of culture and civilization.[1]
>
> *Report of the Scheveningen Symposium*

If culture and cultures are to become the centrepiece of the world system of the future and this system is to be designed and developed in accordance with culture's highest, wisest and most enduring principles rather than basest and crudest practices, a powerful force will be needed. This force must be so compelling that it proves capable of harnessing the creativity of all countries, capitalizing on humanity's finest accomplishments, and bridging the destructive gap between theory and practice.

Such a force is cultural development. As one of the most evocative and ebullient rays of hope to appear on the global horizon in decades, cultural development is undoubtedly a force to be reckoned with as far as the world system of the future is concerned.

The Nature of Cultural Development

If cultural development is to fulfill the mandate visualized for it here, there must be no mistaking what is meant by this term.[2] Lack of precision here could have adverse consequences for the future. Like economic development, political development, social development or any other type of development, cultural development is a compound term. It derives its meaning from the juxtaposition of two of the most complex and controversial terms imaginable; namely, 'culture' and 'development'. It is necessary to determine what is meant by these terms when they are used separately, and also to determine what is meant when they are used in combination.

Since culture has already been dealt with at length, the task here is to evolve a suitable understanding of development. This is not as easy a task as it might appear, since development, like culture, is the cause of a great deal of confusion, ambiguity, misunderstanding and controversy throughout the world. The reason for this stems largely from the way development has been perceived, defined and practised in the twentieth century. According to Wolfgang Sachs, who has spent an enormous amount of time researching the experience with development in the twentieth century,[3] interest in development can be traced back to Truman's belief, as set out in his inaugural speech to Congress in 1949, that development is the key to increased production, productivity, material wealth, higher standards of living and world peace in the future.[4] According to Truman, this would be realized initially by returning Europe to pre-war levels of prosperity after the Second World War and eventually, albeit with much greater difficulty, through the development of Africa, Asia and Latin America, and the waging of an all-out campaign against the causes and consequences of underdevelopment.

Throughout the nineteen fifties, sixties, seventies and eighties, development was conceived and defined largely in terms of economic growth and technological progress. Nations everywhere committed themselves to development in this sense in general and to models of development in particular, while international organizations like the United Nations promoted development everywhere in the world through a series of 'decades of development'. This quickly gave development a global significance and legitimacy it never had before.

It was not long before the entire world was divided in terms of development. Western nations were deemed to be 'developed' because they had achieved high levels of economic and technological progress and a high standard of living. African, Asian and Latin American nations were deemed to be 'underdeveloped' or 'developing' because they had not achieved these goals. Thus the developmental challenge facing the world was seen largely in terms of extending development to African, Asian and Latin American nations.

There has been a strong reaction to this view in recent years. Ecologists and environmentalists claim that development in the economic and techno-logical sense fails to take the needs and interests of the natural environment and other species into account. African, Asian and Latin American nations claim that development is a political tool used by western nations to subdue, dominate, control and enslave them. And people everywhere in the world are claiming that development results in maldevelopment: spiritual poverty in the midst of plenty.

This reaction has spawned demands for a less prejudicial and more broadly based understanding of development. It was this process that led par-ticipants at the second World Conference on Cultural Policies at Mexico City in 1982 to define development as 'a complex, comprehensive and multidi-mensional process which extends beyond mere economic growth to incorporate all dimensions of life and all the energies of a community, all of whose members are called upon to make a contribution and expect to share in the benefits'.[5] Visualized and defined in this way, development is spiritual, intellectual and emotional as well as material and physical; theoretical as well as practical; an art as well as a science; being as well as becoming. In other words, development is cultural in the holistic sense in which the term is used here. As such, it is not just a case of developing the economic and technological resources of society. More fundamentally, it is a case of developing all the resources of society.

It is clear from this that there is an intimate connection between culture and development. In fact, in many ways, they are dual aspects of the same reality. They are qualitative as well as quantitative, and they are processes as well as products. Ultimately they are concerned with improvements in all aspects and dimensions of life for all members of the human family.

This intimate connection between culture and development means that the two separate concepts of culture and development can be fused together to form the concept of cultural development. What is most distinctive about this concept is its holistic and egalitarian nature. On the one hand, it is concerned with all sectors of society: the arts, sciences, education, social affairs, religious and spiritual endeavours and the environment as well as economics, politics and technology. On the other hand, it is concerned with all people: the poor, the disadvantaged, the marginalized and the elderly as well as the rich, the affluent, the educated and the powerful.

This makes cultural development a very different kind of activity from economic, technological, social, political or educational development. Whereas the latter are sectoral in character and specialized in nature—parts of the whole so to speak—the former is comprehensive in character and holistic in nature. It is concerned, like culture and cultures, with the whole. Visualized and defined in this way, there is no difference whatsoever between cultural development and general development. In fact, they are dual aspects of the same reality or synonyms for one another.

If it is important to emphasize the holistic and egalitarian nature of cultural development, it is equally important to emphasize its spatial and temporal nature, for cultural development does not take place in a vacuum. It takes place in very specific spatial and temporal settings, regardless of whether it is the cultural development of the individual, the institution, the group, the community, the region, the nation, or the world. As a result, the natural, historical and global environment plays an active, dynamic and indispensable role in cultural development because it impacts on every aspect and dimension of cultural life.

While cultural development is concerned with all aspects and manifestations of cultural life and the human condition, it hinges on six concerns which are of quintessential importance to the future. These six concerns are: culture as a whole; the component parts of culture; the relationships between the component parts of culture; the relationships between the component parts of culture and culture as a whole; the relationship between the quantitative and qualitative dimensions of culture; and etched on a much larger canvas, the relationship between culture and the natural, historical and global environment. Since these six concerns hold the key to unlocking the secrets of cultural development in the future, it pays to examine them in detail.

As far as culture as a whole is concerned, the ultimate objective of cultural development is to develop culture in a comprehensive, holistic sense. In order to achieve this, it is necessary not only to build up the component parts of culture—the arts, social affairs, political processes, economic systems, educational endeavours, technological resources, ethnic groups, subcultures, scientific, educational and spiritual endeavours, and the like—but to achieve a harmonious and synergistic relationship between them as well. Only in this way can a dynamic and organic whole be created which is capable of meeting the complex challenges and demands made on it. This task is immediately apparent as soon as attention is shifted from culture to cultures. It is necessary to develop all the resources of a culture, regardless of whether it is African, Asian, Latin American, North American or European, and it is also necessary to achieve an interactive and reciprocal relationship between them.

While the ultimate objective of cultural development is to develop culture as a whole and cultures as wholes, this will not be possible without recognition of the fact that culture and cultures are made up of many component parts, all possessing an importance, identity and integrity in their own right, as well as in relation to the larger culture and cultures of which they form an indispensable part. A fundamental part of cultural development, therefore, involves developing these component parts as entities in their own right. Not only must they be developed in terms of their own form and structure, but also they must be developed in terms of the excellence, creativity, and ingenuity of which they are comprised. Given the highly specialized nature of the contemporary world, a great deal is already known about these component parts of culture and cultures, even if the financial, capital and human resources are not always available to develop them properly.

While a great deal is known about the component parts of culture, much less is known about the complex relationships that exist between and among them. As a result, an understanding of the complex relationships that exist between the component parts of culture—the economy and ethics, science and religion, technology and the arts, different ethnic and racial groups, education and politics, and the like—is looming larger and larger in the total matrix of cultural development concerns. What, for example, is the relationship between the economy and ethics? This is especially important in an age where economic affluence and the pressure of economic performance are having a profound effect on ethical practices and moral and religious values everywhere in the world. Or, to cite another example selected from many, what is the relationship between the arts and technology? Specifically, how do developments in publishing, radio, television, film, recording, computers, graphics and video impact on and affect the performing, exhibiting and creative arts? Or to cite a final example, and quite possibly the most important example of all in view of the fact that countries and cultures are becoming more and more multicultural and multiracial in character, what is the relationship between different ethnic and racial groups in an age when these groups are anxious to assert their identities and protect their cherished ways of life? As these three examples illustrate, there is a vast and complex array of relationships which must be understood and dealt with if cultural development is to be mastered in a holistic and egalitarian sense.

Just as cultural development is concerned with the myriad relationships existing between the component parts of culture, so it is concerned with the myriad relationships existing between the component parts of culture and culture as a whole. Viewed from this perspective, culture provides the *context* or *container* within which the component parts of culture are situated. This makes it imperative to focus attention on the dynamic interplay that is constantly going on between culture and the component parts of culture. How are changes occurring in culture as a whole impacting on the economy, the arts, the sciences, politics, education, social and ethnic affairs, recreation, religion and the like? Conversely, how are changes occurring in the economy, the arts, the sciences, politics, education, social and ethnic affairs, recreation, religion and the like impacting on culture as a whole? Unfortunately, far too little is known about these relationships at present. Here again, the shortcomings of specialization are apparent: so much time and energy have gone into developing and dealing with the component parts of culture that little time and attention have been devoted to examining and dealing with the complex relationships that exist between and among the component parts of culture and culture as a whole.

It is equally necessary to broaden and deepen collective understanding of the complex relationship existing between the quantitative and qualitative dimensions of culture. Of the two, it is the qualitative dimension that presents the greatest challenge because it cannot be seen, touched, handled or exchanged, and is therefore virtually impossible to measure and define.

Subdividing culture into quantitative and qualitative dimensions makes it possible to shine the spotlight on one of the most crucial relationships in cultural development of all, namely the relationship between the material and non-material aspects of culture. How large should the quantitative dimension of culture be compared to the qualitative dimension? What should the relationship be between them? It is apparent that the larger the quantitative dimension or material aspect of culture, the more pressure is exerted outward on the qualitative or non-material dimension of culture and the natural environment. Conversely, the smaller the quantitative dimension or material aspect of culture, the less pressure is exerted outward on the qualitative or non-material aspect of culture and the natural environment.

This way of depicting the problem is brought home with startling clarity when attention is shifted from culture to cultures. It is clear that highly materialistic cultures consume excessive amounts of renewable and non-renewable resources, thereby exerting enormous pressures on the qualitative aspect of culture and the natural environment as a result of their need to produce and consume material resources. However, the more time and energy that is devoted to the production, distribution, consumption and promotion of material resources, the less time and energy is available for the appreciation and enjoyment of the qualitative dimensions of culture. Too little time and energy is available for the arts, social interaction, spiritual renewal, religion, recreation, friendship, human love, and all those things which tend to make life a fuller, richer, deeper and more fulfilling affair, while activities are promoted that make more and more demands on the resources of nature.

This leads directly to the most important relationship in cultural development of all, namely the relationship between culture and the natural, historical and global environment. Just as culture provides the context or container within which the component parts of culture and the maze of relationships existing between and among them are located, so the natural, historical and global environment provides the context or container for culture as a whole. Careful scrutiny of this relationship is imperative if human survival, global stability and ecological well-being are to be assured in the future.

It is impossible to come to grips with the development of cultures without understanding the spatial container within which this development is situated. As indicated earlier, the natural and global environment in general, and geography, climate, flora, fauna, landscape, other countries and other cultures in particular, have a profound bearing on each and every aspect of cultural life—economic, social, political, aesthetic, scientific, ethical, educational, technological and spiritual. Also, the natural and global environment provides the sustenance and resources essential to ensure the survival of cultures. As the history of cultural development and the rise and decline of cultures and civilizations illustrates only too well, cultures failing to give sufficient consideration to the crucial relationship that exists between culture and the natural and global environment run the risk of over-extending themselves and collapsing entirely.

If the natural and global environment plays a crucial role in shaping cultures, so does the historical environment. For cultures are situated in time as well as in space. Temporal factors, such as the legacy of objects and artifacts, the heritage of history, and especially the cultural baggage that people carry from one generation to the next and one century to the next, exercise a profound impact on cultures. Once the pattern of a culture is set, it is difficult to change it. It tends to perpetuate itself generation after generation and century after century without interruption or transformation in its most fundamental features and basic characteristics.

These six fundamental concerns help to shed light on the essence of cultural development. What is cultural development when it is stripped to its essence? Surely it is concerned with two matters. As illustrated earlier, the first is worldview, or the general outlook on the world, which underlies culture, cultures and cultural development. The second is values, or the specific weights and priorities assigned to the component parts of culture, cultures and cultural development. In effect, worldview and values are the codes or maps required to 'read' culture, cultures and cultural development and unlock their secrets.

Without a vastly improved understanding of the worldviews underlying culture and cultures in general and cultural development in particular, humanity may not be able to cope with the debilitating problems of the present and the severe challenges of the future. This could result in significantly higher levels of environmental degradation, resource shortages, pollution, violence, terrorism, racial unrest and cultural conflict and confrontation. It is a frightening prospect in view of the high levels of these atrocities and adversities today, but one that is inevitable if much more consideration is not given to the worldviews which people use to determine every aspect and dimension of their cultural life.

Much more attention will also have to be given to values. How much emphasis should be placed on the economic component compared to the environmental component? How much emphasis should be placed on the artistic, ethical or spiritual component compared to the scientific and technological component? And what about the political component? Where does it fit in?

These questions all have to do with values because they are all concerned with the weights or priorities assigned to the component parts of cultural development. How these values are determined in specific situations will depend on the circumstances and needs of cultural development in each case. Whereas one culture may prefer to put more emphasis on the religious component of cultural development compared to the economic component, another may prefer to put more emphasis on the economic component compared to the religious component. It all depends on the values which prevail, as well as how people decide to order and orchestrate their cultural life.

Zeroing in on the essence of cultural development in this way helps to clarify the nature of cultural development because it indicates that all cultural development depends on the worldviews underlying it as well as the values of which it is comprised. It also clarifies the need for cultural development to be awarded a priority that it has never achieved before—a priority that makes it of utmost importance to the present and the future.

The Mechanics of Cultural Policy

A forceful tool is needed if cultural development is to become a reality. This tool is cultural policy. Its aim is to translate the goals, objectives, ideals and principles of cultural development into workable strategies, tactics, procedures, programmes and practices.

Like cultural development, cultural policy is a compound term. It derives its meaning from the juxtaposition of culture and policy. Whereas there is an intimate connection between culture and development because they represent dual aspects of the same reality, culture and policy are packed with dynamic tension because they represent different ways of looking at reality.

At the mention of the term culture, many people conjure up a process that is organic, unpredictable, spontaneous and natural. It is a process that grows naturally and organically and seems to defy quantification and predictability. In fact, it is the organic and unpredictable nature of culture that makes it a largely grass roots and spontaneous affair. The idea of culture being deliberately imposed from the top down or systematically planned to produce a preconceived result proves repulsive to many, as many communist countries discovered when they attempted to plan culture and impose it on the masses. As an idea that stems more from the arts, sociology, anthropology, biology, ecology and philosophy, culture implies something that is natural and not contrived; that is spontaneous and not predetermined.

The same cannot be said for policy. In fact, most people would be appalled at the idea that a policy might be organic, unpredictable, spontaneous and natural. As a term that derives more from business, government, politics, science and economics, policy tends to connote a process that is systematic, rigorous, methodical, and deliberate. There is nothing distasteful about the idea of a policy being designed to achieve some set of predetermined goals and objectives, or being deliberately imposed from the top down. Indeed, it is deemed prudent and necessary to do so.

This is what makes cultural policy such a potentially explosive process. By pressing together two disparate and seemingly incompatible concepts, cultural policy becomes the arena in which individualism encounters institutionalism, freedom challenges authority, creativity confronts conformity, truth wages war with propaganda, and citizens counter the state. Can there be any doubt that cultural policy is packed with dynamic tension?

Yet, much depends on the vantage point from which cultural policy is viewed. From the perspective of the past and the present, culture and policy may seem irreconcilable. In this case, cultural policy is a divisive concept, which perhaps helps to explain why some people view cultural policy with suspicion. However, from the perspective of the future, cultural policy can be seen as an exciting and dynamic process capable of uniting many disparate values and ways of seeing and confronting reality which have long proved to be destructive when kept apart. When cultural policy is viewed from this perspective, it holds out great promise for human fulfillment and global progress in the future.

Much of the tension that is packed into the term cultural policy results from the implication that the state should play an active role in cultural life. Indeed, cultural policy is defined by some as 'a body of operational principles, administrative and budgetary practices and procedures which provide a basis for cultural action by the state'.[6] To be consistent, such a definition should include lack of action by the state, since this is often a conscious and deliberate part of cultural policy. Either way, however, the state obviously has a major role to play in the cultural life of the nation when cultural policy is defined in this way.

In the execution of its cultural responsibilities, the state has recourse to many different types of vehicles—grants, subsidies, taxation, legislation, regulation, research, intervention and the like—which are designed to ensure that there is a sufficient stock of resources and opportunities to meet citizens' needs. This plunges the state deeply into the cultural affairs of society, since the state must act to ensure that these resources and opportunities are of the highest possible calibre and citizens have access to them, regardless of race, creed, education, socio-economic status, or geographical location. Whether or not it is able to do this without resorting to techniques that harden existing cultural arteries, interfere with the free flow of information, people and products, restrict the rights and freedoms of citizens and cultural creators, stifle genuine creativity and create a culture which is rigid, pedantic, and official is a moot point.

There will be some, particularly those prizing personal liberty and individual freedom, who will sense danger in the intrusion of the state into the affairs of society. For such people, culture, cultures and cultural development are largely private affairs. Once they are dragged into the political arena, they run the risk of being subjected to the worst abuses of bureaucracy, subversion, propaganda, manipulation and censorship. Since each step along the path to cultural development plunges a country deeper and deeper into the politics of culture, there is a need to be aware of the actual and potential political, governmental and bureaucratic uses of cultural development and policy, as well as to establish an effective system of checks and balances to ensure that the state does not get too involved in the cultural affairs of society and the lives of people.

Cultural policy can also be defined in terms of the need to ensure the most efficient and effective allocation of scarce public and private resources. At a seminal meeting of experts on cultural policy convened in Monaco in 1967, cultural policy was defined not in terms of involvement by the state, but rather as 'the sum total of the conscious and deliberate usages, action or lack of action in a society, aimed at meeting certain cultural needs through the optimum utilization of all the physical resources available to that society at a given time'.[7] This definition has the advantage of broadening and deepening understanding of cultural policy and the policy process because it defines cultural policy and the policy process in terms of optimal utilization of resources, regardless of who actually owns or controls these resources. The advantages of such a definition are obvious. Not only does it focus attention on the need to conserve resources at a time when people everywhere in the world are becoming increasingly conscious of the scarcity of resources and the fragile nature of global ecosystems, but also it highlights the fact that there are alternative uses to which public and private resources can be put.

One final way of conceptualizing and defining cultural policy, which is relevant here, has to do with policy as 'a comprehensive statement of the ideals, principles, objectives, priorities, procedures and strategies of cultural development'.[8] It is obvious from this definition that cultural policy is comprehensive in the sense that it runs the entire gamut of possibilities, from lofty ideals to specific strategies. It commences with a vision of cultural development, continues with the relentless refinement of this vision over time, and concludes with the practical implementation of the results. Each step in the process is important, and is slightly more tangible, pragmatic and specific than the step immediately preceding it, thereby yielding a process that moves progressively from initial inspiration to concrete action. The creation of ideals compels countries to develop a vision of how they would like their culture to develop, and holds particular importance at present when so many countries are being forced to rethink their directions and goals as a result of the rapidity of community, regional, national and international change. The identification of principles compels countries to examine those deeper landmarks, touchstones and traditions that have shaped their cultural development, as well as the historical forces and factors that have given rise to them. As the prominent French authority Augustin Girard contends, the articulation of objectives compels countries to establish the long-term and short-term goals and targets essential to the achievement of effective cultural development.[9] The establishment of priorities necessitates bringing the hopes and dreams of cultural development into line with available resources, and is the most essential part of the policy process as the spotlight is focused directly on the expenditure of public and private funds and the values and value systems which underlie them. The determination of procedures determines what individuals and institutions do and why by working out all the various relationships and responsibilities to be shared among the various players in cultural development. Finally, the creation of strategies focuses on the need to develop the action plans and specific initiatives needed to achieve concrete results. Without this, it is impossible for cultural development and policy to achieve the ideals and aspirations set for them.

In the process of broadening and deepening knowledge of the requirements and complexities of cultural policy, it may prove helpful to visualize cultural development as a garden and cultural policy as the process whereby the garden is cultivated. Just as the secret of successful gardening is to apply a subtle hand to the wonders of nature, so the secret of cultural policy is to apply a masterful hand to the requirements of cultural development. Application of this hand will vary from situation to situation depending on many factors. Whereas in some situations, little more may be required than some periodic arrangement of flowers and shrubs or some basic weeding, in other situations a great deal of transplanting, weeding and rearrangement will be necessary. Some gardeners prefer to embellish as little as possible, believing it is better to leave a garden as close to nature as possible. Others may prefer to arrange every plant, branch, leaf, stone and petal to achieve some preconceived plan or desired effect. However, the ultimate test is always the same. Has the intervention produced the best result? Has a harmonious whole been created which achieves a symbiotic relationship between the parts? These are crucial questions, not only for gardening, but also for cultural development and policy.

This analogy contributes much to the understanding of the art of cultural development and policy. The art of gardening involves the effective application of tools and techniques to the wonders of nature. The art of cultural development and policy involves the effective application of tools and techniques to culture and cultures. In gardening, it is always wise to have an overall plan or strategy in mind, even if it is altered many times during execution. In cultural development and policy, it is equally advisable to have an overall plan or strategy, since cultural policy is concerned with the orchestration of all aspects and manifestations of cultural life. However, just as care must be taken in gardening to ensure that tools or techniques are employed with creativity, imagination and flair, so care must also be taken in cultural development and policy to ensure that tools and techniques are applied with a sensitive and skilful hand—the kind of hand which raises cultural development and policy to the level of an art form.

It is clear from this that cultural development and policy are processes as well as products. On the one hand, they give rise to specific cultures and civilizations. On the other hand, they are in continuous states of change. While the product role is extremely important, given the highly dynamic nature of contemporary society and prospects for the future, it may well be that the process role is even more important. This is because the emphasis is placed on the transformational role of cultural development and policy.

The Cultural Development and Policy Tradition

Unfortunately, pressure to activate cultural development and formulate and implement cultural policies has been so intense over the last few decades that little time has been available to examine the tradition on which cultural development and policy are based. This produces a very dangerous state of affairs. On the one hand, it makes cultural development and policy vulnerable to external pressures and forces, particularly economic opportunism, techno-logical manipulation and political exploitation. On the other hand, it makes it difficult to see clearly how cultural development and policy have evolved in the past, where they stand at present, and where they should be headed in the future. This makes elucidating the intellectual and practical foundations of the cultural development and policy tradition one of the most pressing priorities in the cultural field today. The longer it is neglected, the more adverse the consequences will be.

In an historical sense, cultural development and policy are as old as civi-lization. Wherever there have been attempts to improve the human condition and elevate life—whether they be in the aesthetic endeavours of artists, the diplomatic maneuvers of politicians, the scholarly endeavours of scientists and economists or the social activities of humanists—cultural development and policy are to be found. They are to be found in the remnants of all the oldest cultures and civilizations, such as the pots and utensils of prehistoric man, the rock formations of Stonehenge and Carnac, and the Sumerian and Hittite settlements at Ur, Catal Huyuk and Alaca Huyuk.

Egypt was probably the first civilization to manifest awareness of the fact that the fruits of culture can be multiplied many times with a coherent approach to cultural development and policy. One does not have to travel to Egypt to confirm this. There is ample evidence of it in the many programmes and books on Egyptian culture, as well as in the many Egyptian exhibitions which have been touring the globe in recent years. One only need marvel at the throne of Sitamon, the funeral mask of Tutankhamen, the Giza pyramids, the Sphinx, Thebes, Luxor, Abu Simbel or the tombs of the pharaohs to appreciate the lofty heights to which cultural development and policy can be raised when they are perceived and practised as art forms.

These art forms were perpetuated in brilliant style by the Greeks and the Persians. In Greece, cultural development and policy reached their zenith in Athens, Mycenae, Delphi and Corinth, thanks to the inspired policies of a succession of visionary leaders and the triumph of the city state. As in Egypt, a real cultural renaissance flourished there during this period—a renaissance known worldwide for its aesthetic, intellectual, political and economic achievements. In Persia, where it also culminated in a brilliant civilization, it is best known for its elegant and highly decorative buildings—such as those at the imperial cities of Susa, Persepolis and Pasargadae—as well as its fantastic metalwork and spectacular stone reliefs.

There is hardly a place on earth or epoch in history that has not benefited from cultural development and policy when they have been practised and elevated in this manner, even if the terms have not been used as such. Whether it is the Incan, Mayan, and Aztec civilizations of the Americas; the Ashanti and Benin civilizations of Africa; the Tang, Sung or Ming dynasties of China; the Heian and Ashikaga periods of Japan; the Gupta and Moghul civilizations of

India; or the Medician and Elizabethan eras in Europe, there is scarcely a geographical region anywhere in the world which has not profited from cultural development and policy when they have been devised with imagination and executed with flair.

It would be a mistake to conclude that the fruits of cultural development and policy are limited to vast civilizations. They are also much in evidence in towns and cities throughout the world. Only the scale is different; the consequences are the same. Places like Kyoto, Beijing, Vienna, Buenos Aires, Isfahan, Marrakech, Bangkok and Jerusalem are inconceivable without inspired cultural development and policy. In each case, and others too numerous to mention here, cogent cultural development strategies and policies have been necessary to turn these places into cultural treasures. Today, they all have lives of their own, marching to the tunes of the drummers who conceived them and brought them to fruition.

Stretching back to the very origins of human life, it is clear that the practical side of the cultural development and policy tradition has been steadily gathering momentum and accumulating energy for centuries, giving rise to the wealth of cultural treasures humanity knows and loves today. These treasures range all the way from haunting civilizations and captivating towns and cities to libraries, art galleries, archives, museums, educational institutions, foundations, medical and health facilities, business and political organizations and scientific endeavours.

If an inspiring cultural development and policy tradition exists in practice, an equally inspiring one exists in theory, even if it is less visible and conspicuous. Full progress will not be made in the cultural field, however, until the theoretical side of this tradition has become much more familiar and utilized.

In retrospect, it is easy to see that cultural development and policy has been on the minds of scholars, artists, scientists, politicians, statesmen and religious leaders for centuries, even if they did not use the terms cultural development and cultural policy as such. However, it was not really until the nineteenth century, when scholars like Arnold, Burckhardt, Klemm, Tylor and Spengler arrived on the scene, that more specific theoretical foundations were laid for cultural development and policy. It was only when scholars like these appeared that interest in the development of culture and cultures was taken up in earnest.

The pioneering work of these scholars did much to pave the way for successive generations of scholars concerned first and foremost with the intricacies and complexities of culture and cultures in general and cultural development and policy in particular. Included among these scholars are anthropologists, sociologists, historians, philosophers, artists, writers and thinkers.[10] It is on their insights, ideas and research findings that humanity should seek to build the theoretical side of the cultural development and policy tradition of the years and decades ahead.

While each cultural scholar has his or her own specific theories and pet preoccupations, nevertheless, many cultural scholars share a number of common convictions that make it possible to unite them as a group. While this is a risky business and subject to numerous generations and qualifications, there would appear to be common understanding among many if not all cultural scholars on the following: the centrality of culture; the holistic character of cultures; the primacy of cultural values; the importance of 'cultural striving'; the incredible amount of time, effort and hard work it takes to build cultures; the equality and non-comparability of cultures; the key role played by identity, diversity and pluralism in cultural life; and the necessity of cultural change. Time spent studying these areas of common understanding is rewarding because it provides many of the clues which are necessary to flesh out the theoretical side of the cultural development and policy tradition.

Foremost among these areas of common understanding is the centrality of culture. As the cement which binds cultures, civilizations, societies, communities and people together, culture is the basis of human existence for most if not all cultural scholars. As Edward Hall explains:

Culture is man's medium; there is not one aspect of human life that is not touched and altered by culture. This means personality, how people express themselves (including shows of emotion), the way they think, how they move, how problems are solved, how their cities are planned and laid out, how transportation systems function and are organized, as well as how economic and government systems are put together and function.[11]

If cultural scholars appear to share a common understanding with respect to the centrality of culture, they also appear to share a common understanding with respect to the holistic character of cultures. Recognition of this is helpful for a number of reasons. First, it focuses attention on 'the big picture', and with it, the ability to deal with cultures as integrated and comprehensive wholes. Second, it provides the potential for unity, oneness and togetherness, which is especially important in a world characterized by division, discord, conflict and confrontation. Third, it helps to combat fragmentation and compartmentalization, which is essential in a world where everything is broken into smaller and smaller units. Finally, it helps to counteract polarization and the tendency to divide all things into opposites. Little wonder more and more scholars and world leaders are calling for a 'holistic revolution' to deal with the host of interrelated and interconnected problems which has appeared on the global horizon. For as Rajni Kothari observed, 'there is need to restore the comprehensive and holistic perspective that was there and still survives in many cultures but is at the moment submerged'.[12]

It is impossible to deal with matters as fundamental as these without dealing with the primacy of cultural values, yet another area where there appears to be common understanding among many if not all cultural scholars. As indicated earlier, it is important to make a distinction between absolute and relative cultural values. Whereas relative cultural values depend on the time and circumstances in which they are formulated, absolute cultural values are universal and immutable. While cultural scholars have been in the vanguard of the movement to establish respect for relative cultural values,[13] they have likewise recognized the crucial importance of absolute cultural values. Perhaps this explains why Takdir Alisjahbana believes that culture represents the aspiration to realize the highest form of life.[14]

The best way to lift the veil of absolute cultural values is to recall the notion that culture is all that remains long after everything else is forgotten. While this is a much more restrictive notion of culture than the one utilized in this text, it has the advantage of focusing attention on those cultural creations and accomplishments which have withstood the test of time and been accorded humanity's highest accolades down through the ages. What are these absolute cultural values? As set out at some length earlier, they include, in addition to others: the thirst for knowledge, wisdom, beauty and truth; the pursuit of perfection, excellence and creativity; the importance of justice, equality, access and participation; the need for order, stability, diversity, caring and sharing; respect for the rights and traditions of others; and the search for the sublime. While these are not the only absolute cultural values with which culture is concerned, adherence to them should help illuminate the path for the future because they tend to take the needs of human beings, other species, the natural environment and future generations into account.

There are two aspects to absolute values which should not be allowed to escape attention. First, they tend to place a great deal of emphasis on the arts, sciences, scholarship, education, spirituality and human affairs, thereby providing a counterpoise to economics, technology and materialism. Second, they highlight the importance of 'cultural striving', or the need to aspire to the very best humanity has to offer.

If cultural scholars share a common understanding concerning the importance of absolute cultural values, they also share a common understanding concerning the incredible amount of time, effort and hard work it takes to build cultures. Cultures are simply not built in one or two generations, or with minimal amounts of labour. Perhaps this is why Spengler and Toynbee measured the life span of cultures in hundreds and even thousands of years. During these long time periods, a prodigious amount of effort and ingenuity was required to build cultures to any significant level of accomplishment.

Voltaire and Burckhardt understood this better than other cultural scholars. Take pleasure in worthwhile things and labour intensively was Burckhardt's prescription for building cultures and achieving human fulfillment and well-being. And Voltaire's? Plant. Build. Cultivate. For cultivation is not only the best antidote against boredom and vice according to Voltaire, it is also the best guarantee of civility and refinement. Here, hard work is not advocated for some religious reason, such as redemption of the soul, eternal salvation, or entry into the kingdom of heaven. Rather, it is advocated for a very practical reason: it is essential for human survival and imperative for progress. Furthermore, it is needed on all fronts—environmental as well as economic, ethical as well as political, artistic as well as technological and spiritual as well as social—if it is to rescue humankind from chaos and barbarism.

Yet another area of apparent common understanding among many if not all cultural scholars lies in the equality and non-comparability of cultures. Anthropologists like Frobenius, Malinowski, Mead, Benedict, Boas and others were in the forefront here. Through their studies in many parts of the world and particularly in Africa, Asia, the Pacific and west coast of North America, these and other anthropologists revealed how every culture has a dignity, integrity and value in its own right, as well as how meaningless it is to compare cultures or rank them in terms of superiority or inferiority.

Cultures exist to satisfy a variety of human needs. These needs vary greatly from one culture and one part of the world to the next. In some cultures, a great deal of energy, effort and ingenuity must be channelled into activities relating to people's physical needs. In other cultures, less human energy, effort and ingenuity is required in this area. However, this should not lead to the conclusion that one culture is superior to another. Nor, as Frobenius noted, should cultures based on reason and intellect be assumed to be superior to cultures based on emotion and the soul. This means simply that different dimensions of the human collectivity have been used to anchor cultural development in each case.

It follows from this that the most that can be said about cultures is that they differ from one another because they emphasize different aspects of the human condition. Even statements about their simplicity or sophistication must be couched in caution. Cultures which appear 'simple' or 'primitive' from the outside, or to the untrained observer, are often highly complex and sophisticated when they are examined up close and analysed by the professional. Such cultures usually betray extremely complicated and sophisticated patterns of sensory perception and expression, social and economic organization, kinship relations, environmental awareness and verbal and non-verbal communication. This fact makes cultures equal and non-comparable by their very nature.

This conviction is rapidly gaining currency throughout the world as a result of efforts by cultural scholars and the passing of declarations like the Declaration of the Principles of International Cultural Co-operation which assert the dignity and value of every culture.[15] Fortunately the equality of cultures is no longer confined to a small and select group of individuals and institutions but is winning its way into the hearts, minds and beliefs of people everywhere in the world.

If anthropologists have done much to broaden and deepen understanding of the equality and non-comparability of cultures, they have also done much to broaden and deepen the understanding of the key role played by cultural diversity and pluralism. No sooner did anthropologists begin to undertake field work in a significant way than they discovered that every culture possesses an incredible mixture of people, customs, languages, traditions, ethnic groups, races, signs, symbols, artifacts and beliefs. In so doing, they established beyond a doubt that cultural diversity and pluralism are a reality that all nations and governments are compelled to deal with fully and effectively in their planning and decision-making. This knowledge and understanding has been enriched considerably by sociologists in recent years as a result of their intensive studies of race, gender, class, ethnicity, subcultures and the assertion of cultural identities.

The contributions of anthropologists and sociologists do not end here. By exposing the two faces of cultural diversity and pluralism—the dangers that are inherent in it as well as the benefits that can be derived from it—anthropologists and sociologists have contributed a great deal to the knowledge and appreciation of cultures in general and cultural development in particular. On the one hand, they have made people more aware of the role pluralism and diversity play in broadening, deepening and enriching cultural life by expanding the range of options and opportunities available to people. On the other hand, they have made people more conscious of the fact that pluralism and diversity can degenerate into violence, conflict, confrontation and racism, particularly if precautions like cultural education and the establishment of race relations committees and interracial councils are not taken to prevent it. This serves to underline the necessity of developing policies, programmes and practices aimed at improving cross-cultural communication, dialogue and exchange.

Cultural scholars also appear to share a common understanding of the importance and necessity of cultural change. However, very few cultural scholars are optimistic about the possibility of transforming cultures from the inside. This means that if cultural change is to occur at all, it must often be initiated from the outside. This makes international cultural relations extremely important. Not only do they help to expose the strengths and shortcomings of cultures, but also they set in motion forces which can produce constructive or destructive cultural change.

Landmarks in Cultural Development and Policy

If it is important to shed light on the theoretical and practical sides of the cultural development and policy tradition, it is equally important to shed light on some of the landmarks that have been realized in cultural development and policy over the last three or four decades. For these also form part of the foundation on which cultural development and policy should be based in the future.

One such landmark was the Universal Declaration of Human Rights, which was passed by the General Assembly of the United Nations in 1948.[16] While it was designed to deal with the articulation and assertion of human rights rather than cultural rights, as indicated earlier, it recognized the importance of cultural rights, the need for active participation in cultural life, and the need to protect the moral and material interests of creators. No sooner where these matters recognized in principle than pressure started to build to realize them in practice. As a result, over the last few decades, public and private authorities in many countries have been working diligently to gain acceptance for these ideals in constitutional arrangements and legal affairs.

Spurred on by the passage of the Universal Declaration of Human Rights and growing recognition of cultural matters and concerns, governments everywhere in the world started to intensify their efforts in cultural development and policy in the 1950s and 1960s. Had governments not grown rapidly during this period, it is unlikely that cultural development and policy issues would have generated much attention. However this was a period in which governments were being pressured to undertake development and introduce policies in a variety of fields. In an era when people were clamoring for economic, social, environmental, educational and political development and policies, it was inevitable that sooner or later pressure would build to execute cultural development and policies.

At the international level, this pressure was felt most acutely by Unesco. In many ways, Unesco had been established to give concrete shape and material substance to cultural development in general and cultural policy in particular. Having generated a great deal of public and professional interest in cultural development in the 1950s and 1960s, Unesco turned its attention to cultural policy in the late 1960s by organizing a seminal seminar on cultural policies in Monaco. This proved to be a valuable precursor to the first World Conference on Cultural Policies, held in Venice in 1970.

Long recognized as one of the jewels of cultural development, Venice proved to be the ideal setting for this unique event. For the first time in history, representatives with authority over culture from over one hundred nations, including about forty Ministers of Culture, Education or Foreign Affairs, assembled in this historic place to discuss the complexities and intricacies of cultural development and policy. Although there was far from unanimous agreement on all points, there was one point on which all representatives agreed: every nation should have a cultural policy. Cultural policy, as a field aimed at giving concrete shape and material form to cultural development, had arrived.

While delegates recognized the fact that cultural policy possesses the capacity to be a unifying force, a democratizing influence and an expression of personal and collective identity, they also demonstrated an uncanny awareness of the potential dangers involved in formulating and implementing cultural policies. Given the tension between politics and culture, many questioned how much state intervention in cultural affairs is possible without severe encroachments on creative freedom. Other potential dangers signalled as causes for concern were: the tension between democratization, decentralization and standards; the political manipulation of cultural development and policy by governments and politicians; and the conflict between traditional and contemporary forms of cultural expression.[17] Many delegates openly expressed the fear that too much democratization and decentralization, like too much governmental involvement in cultural development and policy and too much emphasis on history and tradition, could dilute standards and stifle genuine cultural expression. Then there was the thorny problem of defining culture. It was such a contentious issue that it was not discussed at any length. In retrospect, this may have been a wise decision. For culture was such a fragile field at the time that it may not have withstood the kind of stormy semantic debate the problem of defining culture can elicit.

Spurred on by the success of the Venice Conference, Unesco plunged into cultural policy and cultural development in earnest. Throughout the 1970s, it instituted many activities and programmes aimed at promoting greater interest in culture, cultures, cultural development and cultural policy. For example, numerous studies were undertaken and seminars organized on the training of arts administrators and animators, cultural planning, cultural statistics and indicators, diversity and pluralism, the role of the artist in society, and the development of the cultural industries. In addition, a series of Studies and Documents on Cultural Policies for Member States was commenced in the early 1970s.[18] These activities complemented several intensive intergovernmental conferences at the regional level, including the European Conference on Cultural Policies in Helsinki in 1972, the Asian Conference on Cultural Policies in Yogyakarta in 1973, the African Conference on Cultural Policies in Accra in 1975, and the Latin American and Caribbean Conference on Cultural Policies in Bogota in 1978.[19] These conferences were convened to consolidate thinking on a variety of cultural development and policy issues in the major geographical areas of the world, as well as to provide the basis for the second World Conference on Cultural Policies in Mexico City in 1982.[20]

Combined with earlier conferences and other developments, the second World Conference helped to set the stage for the establishment of the World Decade for Cultural Development. Affirmed by the United Nations and Unesco and designed to broaden and deepen commitment to cultural development and policy over the ten-year period from 1988 to 1997, the Decade had four main objectives: 'to ensure that the cultural dimension is taken into account in all economic development planning; to assist in the preservation and enrichment of cultural identity, including promotion of the arts and safeguarding of the national heritage; to broaden participation in cultural activity; and to foster international cultural co-operation'.[21] These objectives recognized the steadily-growing importance of cultural development and policy in community, regional, national and international affairs in all parts of the world.

This fact helped to account for the establishment of the World Commission on Culture and Development by the United Nations and Unesco in 1992. Generally viewed as a follow-up to the World Commission on Environment and Development (the Brundtland Commission), the principal task of the World Commission on Culture and Development was to broaden and deepen knowledge and understanding of the concept of culture as well as the intricate relationship between culture and development. This was confirmed in the terms of reference established for the Commission, where it was proposed that the Commission focus attention on identifying, describing and analysing basic questions, concerns, and challenges related to: 'the cultural and socio-cultural factors that affect development; the impact of social and economic development on culture; the interrelatedness of culture and models of development; the ways in which cultural development, and not only economic conditions, influence individual and collective well-being; and the cultural sector as such and as an important area for development and for international co-operation'.[22]

Why all the sudden interest in culture, cultures, cultural development and cultural policy? There are many explanations. First of all, culture and cultures are becoming increasingly important forces in global development and world affairs. Second, there is a sinking feeling that the development dream has turned sour and cultural development and policy may possess the potential to set things right. Third, much more knowledge and understanding of culture, cultures, cultural development and cultural policy is needed if increased violence, oppression and unrest are to be prevented. Finally, and perhaps most importantly, many believe that it is through assertion of cultural values in general, and the creation of new cultural values in particular, that it will be possible to ensure environmental sustainability, human survival and global progress in the future.

Future Directions in Cultural Development and Policy

The time has come to put the cultural development and policy tradition to work. This is achieved by asking what lessons can be learned and insights gleaned from the cultural development and policy tradition that are helpful in confronting the complex challenges and limitless opportunities of the new millennium.

Although there is no guaranteed formula for success, the prerequisites for successful cultural development and policy appear to be everywhere much the same: a coterie of enlightened rulers; a community of creative talents; a society of dedicated citizens; a commitment to making improvements in all aspects and dimensions of the human condition; and a high priority for culture in the total scheme of things.

Whether it was Pericles in Greece, Cyrus in Persia, the shoguns in Japan, the paramount chiefs in Africa or the Medici in Italy, enlightened rulers have been a prerequisite for effective cultural development and policy since the dawn of recorded time. Such leaders have always had visions of the societies, communities, institutions and cultures they want to create, even if they are not always clear about the requirements, initiatives and directions that are most needed to achieve this. But this is precisely where their enlightenment comes in. Invariably they have had the wisdom to gather around them communities of creative talents capable of fashioning the artistic, architectural, scientific, social, spiritual, economic, technological and educational works which are needed to execute these visions. Without such leadership, creative people would never have the opportunities to translate noble visions into concrete realities.

Once the opportunities are provided, it is up to creative people to make the most of them, regardless of whether they be architects designing buildings, planners laying out communities, corporate officials responding to commercial opportunities, public servants planning social services, or artists and educators fashioning artistic and educational works.

History proves that such possibilities come along all too infrequently not to make the most of them. It proves something else as well. It proves that countries that ignore their creative talents—artists, architects, scientists, educators, inventors, designers, businessmen, bureaucrats, blue collar workers and the like—do so at their peril. If creative people are not provided with the physical, financial and administrative resources they need to do the job properly, creativity will quickly atrophy and societies will lose their dynamic and innovative quality.

If the creative capabilities that all countries possess in abundance are to be utilized effectively, creative people must have the freedom to follow their instincts and ideas wherever they take them. Moreover, they must have the right to fail as well as to succeed. When it comes to cultural creation, there are no proven recipes for success. For every Taj Mahal, Sistine Chapel, *Divine Comedy* or Theory of Relativity there is, there are millions of other cultural creations which never achieved immortality, and billions of others which never materialized at all. All that can be done is to provide creative people with the resources and safeguards they need and hope for the best.

While every creator and creative work must find its own place, the task of creative people is lessened considerably with a dedicated citizenry to appreciate their efforts. For an intimate bond exists between creators and citizens. Creative people and creative works need a response, and the more informed and knowledgeable the response, the more inspiration there will be for creative people to create works of the highest possible calibre.

When attention is shifted from individual creators and creative works to creation in general, it is easy to see that cultural development and policy are not to be rarefied or created in isolation. On the contrary, they are created in very specific settings through the efforts and interactions of all people and all classes. As such, they are as much the products of labourers as executives, farmers as artists, peasants as philosophers, tiny towns as sprawling cities, rural areas as mighty nations.

Since cultural development and policy are collective undertakings in this sense, every citizen has certain cultural responsibilities to execute as well as certain cultural rights to expect in return. Of what do citizens' cultural responsibilities consist? Surely they consist, in addition to many other things, of the following: the acquisition of the skills, abilities, knowledge, experience and expertise necessary to function effectively in a culture and make a constructive contribution to cultural life; participation in the cultural life of the community as a citizen, consumer, expediter, creator and audience member; respect for the rights, freedoms, values and beliefs of others; respect for the natural environment and the fragile nature of local, regional, national and international eco-systems; and respect for the needs and interests of other species and future generations. In return, citizens must be assured certain cultural rights. These rights include the right to life, to work, to social security, to education, to recreation, to renewal and to resources, regardless of colour, creed, language, race, social status, economic situation and geographical location.

What is steadily unfolding here is an approach to cultural development and policy which is deeply rooted in citizenship and society. It is an approach which sees cultural development and policy as an interactive process involving three distinct communities or groups of participants: the creators of cultural activities, or the creative community; the regulators of cultural activities, or the political community; and the appreciators of cultural activities, or the public community. This makes it possible to shine the spotlight on the various ways in which creators, governments, and citizens interact over time to evolve specific cultural development policies and practices.

The needs of these three communities seldom coincide. In fact, usually they are at variance. This necessitates the determination of very specific goals and objectives, as well as the need for compromises and concessions. Depending on how these goals and objectives are set and compromises and concessions concluded, cultural development and policy can lead to an effective utilization of material, capital and human resources and real fulfillment in cultural life, or it can lead to wastage of material, capital and human resources and the stagnation of that life. In the final analysis, whether cultures exude vitality or lethargy depends on how effectively these three communities have interacted and executed their respective responsibilities.

If cultural development and policy require a coterie of enlightened rulers, a community of creative talents and a society of dedicated citizens, they also require a commitment to making improvements in all aspects and dimensions of human life. This requires an objective, comprehensive and systematic approach to cultural development and policy rather than a piecemeal, partial and partisan approach to them. Such an approach places the emphasis squarely on the need to develop all the resources of society, as well as achieve an effective blending of these resources.

It is impossible to realize this without assigning a high priority to culture and cultures in general and cultural development and policy in particular. Surely this is the most effective way to ensure that culture is every citizen's business, and that the new vistas and avenues that are needed for the future are opened up today.

11. Towards a Cultural Age

Culture in the future is the crux of the future.[1]

Eleonora Barbieri Masini

Like economics, politics, technology and religion, culture is an extremely powerful force. There is not a single aspect of the world situation that is not affected, and affected deeply, by it. Given this fact, how is the escalating interest in culture, which is manifesting itself throughout the world, to be interpreted? Is it to be interpreted as the inevitable consequence of earlier preoccupations with economics, politics, religion and technology? Is it to be interpreted as an early warning signal that all is not right in the world as it is presently known? Or is it to be interpreted as a sign that humanity may be standing on the threshold of a new age which may derive its inspiration more from culture than anything else?

It is impossible to answer these questions without directing attention to the momentous shift that has occurred in world thinking over the last few decades. Three or four decades ago, a significant part of the world was filled with expectations of an imminent nirvana. How was this nirvana to be achieved? Through the application of self-regulating technologies to economic processes, it was assumed that humanity could be relieved of its traditional dependence on the work ethic, so that more and more people could get on with the real business of life and living. It was hardly possible to pick up a book or read an article without encountering the belief that the Western world was passing over the threshold to a post-industrial society characterized by material abundance and leisure time for all. Once achieved, it was assumed that this society could be extended, albeit with far greater difficulty, to the rest of the world so that people in all parts of the world could live a life of affluence and leisure.

Four decades later, the entire world seems poised on the brink of a crisis about to assume major proportions. Almost without warning, the post-industrial enthusiasm of the sixties and seventies has given way to the post-modern anxiety of the nineties and the new millennium, as economic and political optimism give way to social, environmental and human pessimism.

Many contend that this is a sign that humanity needs to cross over the threshold to a new age. For as John McHale so convincingly argued:

Ours is possibly one of the most critical periods in human experience. Poised in the transition between one kind of world and another, we are literally on the hinge of a great transformation in the whole human condition.[2]

If humanity is to pass over the threshold to a new age, much will depend on the ability to size up and evaluate the strengths and shortcomings of the present age. Without this, it is difficult to see how humanity will be able to make informed choices and intelligent decisions about future courses in planetary civilization.

While many forces have shaped the present age, clearly economics, economies, specialization, technology, development, science and the marketplace have played the dominant role. Relations between individuals, groups, institutions, governments, countries, continents, the human species, other species, and nature are conducted largely in terms of these forces, which also play the pivotal role in keeping the world system functioning and intact.[3]

This system has produced, and continues to produce, countless benefits for humanity. To confirm this, one need only reflect on the incredible advances recorded in agriculture, industry, commerce, medicine, health, land, sea, air and extraterrestrial travel, communications, the arts, education and social affairs as a result of the dominant forces of the present age. While these advances are by no means universal in scope and are accorded to some but denied to most, anyone who doubts the innumerable benefits that have accrued as a result of the dominance of the driving forces of the present age need only reflect on what life was like in earlier periods of history. Not only was it exceedingly strenuous and demanding—much as it still is for most people in the world today—but also it was very risky and uncertain.

Incredible advances in productive capacity account for the numerous benefits that have been realized through the dominant forces of the present age. Not only is humankind capable of producing more of virtually everything than at any other time in history, but also the capacity for production appears to be increasing rapidly and threatening to escalate out of control. According to many experts, humanity now possesses enough productive capacity to satisfy the basic human needs of people everywhere in the world. The problem is one of distribution, not production.

It would be a mistake to allow preoccupation with the strengths of the present age to obscure the shortcomings. For as more and more questions are raised about the viability of the world system on which the present age is based, it is clear that it may not be possible to sustain this system for much longer. The costs, consequences and dangers may be too great.

First of all, there is the very real possibility that the entire global eco-system will collapse as a result of the colossal demands and expectations which are being placed on it. Preoccupation with economics, economies and the other dominant forces of the present age has produced consumer demands and expectations that are impossible to fulfill in view of the size and growth of the world's population and the carrying capacity of the earth. As a result, there could be chronic shortages of renewable and non-renewable resources in the near future if humankind does not control its material appetites and bring its consumption demands under control.[4] Surely wars over resources, famine, plague, pestilence and the breakdown of the entire global eco-system are inevitable if humanity persists in this practice.

Secondly, it is becoming increasingly apparent that the major inequalities that exist in the world will not be overcome by the world system as it is presently constituted. If anything, they will be exacerbated and enlarged. As commercial, industrial and financial power is concentrated in fewer hands and there is more emphasis on globalization, free trade, capitalism and the marketplace, it is likely that the gap between rich and poor countries and rich and poor people will widen considerably in the years and decades ahead if steps are not taken to prevent it.

Thirdly, the world is rapidly becoming a fragmented, disorganized and divided place. Substantial gains in economic, technological and scientific capacity have not been matched by corresponding gains in social and human cohesion, education, the arts, spiritual fulfillment, and individual and collective well-being. While it would be a mistake to blame the existing system entirely for this, there can be little doubt that it has been a major contributor to it. It has failed to create the bonds of humanity, solidarity and friendship necessary to keep people, ethnic groups, races, countries and continents together when other forces are operating to split them apart.

Finally, and perhaps most importantly, the world is becoming a more dehumanized and impersonal place. It is being denuded of much of its humanity and compassion as relationships between people, countries, and continents turn cold and measured in terms of profit and loss and matters of commercial interest and gain. Could it be otherwise in a world where commodities have triumphed over people and commercialization and the marketplace have taken precedence over human beings?

If a way is to be found out of this conundrum, a world system must be created which is capable of confronting these problems and making serious inroads on them. To date, little consideration has been given to the role that culture is capable of playing in this. This is surprising in view of the fact that culture is concerned with human needs and the world is going through a period of pronounced cultural transformation and change. Viewed from this perspective, any perception of the world system of the future which fails to take culture fully and forcefully into account may be doomed to failure from the outset.

If a viable world system is to be created in the future, it will have to be erected on proper foundations. Viewed from the cultural perspective proposed here, these foundations include: recognition of the centrality and holistic nature of culture and cultures; utilization of culture's long and distinguished intellectual tradition; adoption of a cultural interpretation of history; establishment of culture as a distinct discipline; affirmation of culture's highest, wisest and most enduring values and principles; and last but far from least, carving out a prominent place for cultural development and policy in the major pentagons of power and individual, institutional, community, regional, national and international affairs.[5] Since these foundations provide the keys that are necessary to cross over the threshold to a new age, it remains to reiterate their importance here.

Recognition of the centrality of culture and cultures is important because it shines the spotlight squarely on worldviews, values and value systems, and therefore on the way people visualize and interpret the world, organize themselves, conduct their affairs, elevate and embellish life, and position themselves in the world. This helps focus attention directly on how people relate to themselves, each other, the world around them, other species, future generations, the world system, and the natural environment. This broader and deeper way of looking at reality and the human condition is imperative if people are to live in harmony with each other and the natural environment and make sensible decisions about the future courses of life on earth.

Acceptance of the holistic nature of culture and cultures is important because the parts of the whole must be situated effectively in the whole if excesses and imbalances are to be prevented. Nowhere is this more essential than with respect to economics, economies and technology. Although these forces will always occupy a prominent position in the total scheme of things because they are concerned with people's material needs, sources of livelihood and the ever-recurrent problem of survival, situating them effectively in culture and cultures will make it possible to bring the more specific goals of economics, economies and technology into line with the broader and deeper goals of culture and cultures. Moreover, it will make it possible to reduce the demands that these forces make on the natural environment and peoples lives because more emphasis will be placed on the qualitative side of development, and hence on activities which tend to conserve rather than consume resources.

Utilization of culture's long and distinguished intellectual tradition is important because cultural scholars have had a great deal to say which is relevant to the design, development and functioning of the world system, including the organization and orchestration of cultural life, the role of the state, the relationship between human beings and the natural environment, the nature and purpose of life, the place of the individual in society, and the character of personal, community, regional, national and international development. Sohail Inayatullah captured this best when he said, 'now considered the last unified discourse, culture is believed to be the voice of community, of a coherent set of meanings and relationships, the core of the Good Society, and of humanity itself...Culture, is then, the voice of the past and the hope of the future'.[6]

Adoption of a cultural interpretation of history is important because a major reinterpretation of the past is needed to even up the scales of historical justice and confirm the fact that all groups, peoples, countries and continents have made and continue to make a valuable contribution to global development and the cultural heritage of humankind. While reinterpretations of history are a difficult, demanding and dangerous business, they simply must be undertaken if groups, peoples, countries and cultures in all parts of the world are to live in harmony and the world is to be characterized by equality, dignity, freedom and independence rather than inequality, subversion, coercion and dependence.

Establishment of culture as a distinct discipline is important because much more will have to be known about culture as a concept and a reality if humanity is to go fruitfully into the future. In the realization of this objective, maximum attention should be paid to the multidisciplinary character of culture and cultures, as well as to the fact that culture and cultures can be used in positive and negative ways. This makes it imperative to be ever watchful and mindful of the uses and abuses of culture and cultures, as well as to establish the proper mechanisms and safeguards to ensure that they are used in constructive rather than destructive ways.

Affirmation of culture's highest, wisest and most enduring values and principles is important because people need something to aspire to if they are to realize higher and higher levels of accomplishment. Without this, the world system and people's lives will slowly deteriorate, particularly given the rapid rate of population growth and the strain on renewable and non-renewable resources.

Carving out a prominent place for cultural development and policy in the major pentagons of power and individual, institutional, community, regional, national and international affairs is important because governments, international organizations, educational institutions, corporations, towns, cities, regions and countries have a crucial role to play in cultural life. Neglect of this role could cause significant hardships for people everywhere in the world in the future.

With these foundations in place, it is possible to discern the pale outlines of a 'cultural age'. The most distinctive aspects of this age could be its emphasis on culture and cultures, as well as its emphasis on holism, creativity, unity, diversity, caring, sharing, and co-operation. Pressing qualities like these to the forefront at this time could go a long way towards carrying humanity forward into the next great epoch in human history.

It is here that culture's capacity for 'links' becomes crucial, for cultural links are imperative if people, ethnic groups, countries and continents are to live in peace and harmony rather than conflict and confrontation. Peter Brook recognized quintessential importance of this when he said:

For the third culture [after the culture of the individual and the culture of the state] is the culture of links. It is the force that can counterbalance the fragmentation of our world. It is to do with the discovery of relationships where such relationships have become submerged and lost—between man and society, between one race and another, between the microcosm and the macrocosm, between humanity and machinery, between the visible and the invisible, between categories, languages and genres. What are these relationships? Only cultural acts can explore and reveal these vital truths.[7]

In thinking about the kind of age that is most needed for the future, no greater mistake could be made than that of falling into the trap of polarization. Regardless of what types of problems are encountered as a result of excessive preoccupation with the dominant forces of the present age, rejecting these forces out of hand will result in the same kind of over-loaded and imbalanced system with which the world is saddled at present.

Culture's capacity for synthesis provides a way out of this dilemma, for when culture is conceived and defined in holistic terms, it possesses the potential to combine all the parts of the whole in a more coherent, compelling and harmonious rendering of the whole. Here the challenge is not to downplay or disregard the powerful forces of the present age, but rather to blend these forces with other forces in the creation of a more integrated and humane approach to the human condition. The cultural historian, Johan Huizinga, gave us an inkling of what this might be like when he contended that 'the realities of economic life, of power, of technology, of everything conducive to man's material well-being, must be balanced by strongly developed spiritual, intellectual, moral and aesthetic values'.[8] Ultimately this is what crossing over the threshold to a cultural age and viewing culture as a beacon of the future is all about.

Notes

Chapter 1

1. Bernard Ostry, *The Cultural Connection* (Toronto: McClelland and Stewart, 1978), p. 1.

2. Fritjof Capra, *Uncommon Wisdom: Conversations with Remarkable People* (New York: Simon and Schuster, 1988), p. 232.

3. R. King (ed.), *Goethe on Human Creativeness and Other Goethe Essays* (Athens: University of Georgia Press, 1950), p. 236.

4. Alexander King, 'Technological Determinants and Educational Needs of Society in Transition', *Razvoj Development International* 5(2) (Zagreb: Institute for Development and International Relations, 1990), p. 199.

5. D. Paul Schafer, *The Cosmological Conception of Culture: Canadian Culture Used as a Case Study for Illustrative Purposes* (Markham: World Culture Project, 1992); see also D. Paul Schafer, *The Character of Culture* (Scarborough: World Culture Project, 1989).

6. Biserka Cvjetičanin, 'Editorial' and 'Cultural Change: Global Challenge and Regional Response', *Razvoj Development International* 6(2–3) (Zagreb: Institute for Development and International Relations, 1991), pp. 193–4, 319–29.

7. Paul J. Braisted, *Cultural Cooperation: Keynote of the Coming Age* (New Haven: The Edward W. Hazen Foundation, 1945), p. 5.

Chapter 2

1. Edward T. Hall, *The Silent Language* (Garden City, NY: Anchor Press/Doubleday, 1973), p. 20.

2. Alfred Kroeber and Clyde Kluckhohn, *Culture: A Critical Review of Concepts and Definitions* (New York: Vintage Books, 1963).

3. Member States of Unesco, *Studies and Documents on Cultural Policies for Member States* (Paris: Unesco, 1970–1996).

4. Pekka Gronow, 'The Definition of the Sphere of Cultural Development', in *Planning for Cultural Development; Methods and Objectives* (Documents of the Expert Meeting at Hanasaari, Espoo, Finland, 17–19 March 1976), Cultural Development: Documentary Dossier 9–10 (Paris: Unesco, 1978).

5. Kroeber and Kluckhohn, *Culture*.

6. D. Paul Schafer, *Arguments for the Arts* (Scarborough: Arts Scarborough, 1982).

7. Matthew Arnold, *Culture and Anarchy* (Cambridge: Cambridge University Press, 1960), pp. 6, 69.

8. Ibid., p. 70 (Arnold's italics).

9. Kroeber and Kluckhohn, *Culture*, p. 83 (emphasis mine).

10. Raymond Williams, *Culture and Society 1780–1950* (London: Penguin, 1966), p. 16.

11. Edward Burnett Tylor, *The Origins of Culture* (New York: Harper and Row, 1958), p. 1 (emphasis mine).

12. Kroeber and Kluckhohn, *Culture*, pp. 81–4 (emphasis mine).

13. Melville J. Herskovits, *Cultural Relativism: Perspectives in Cultural Pluralism*, edited by Frances Herskovits (New York: Random House, 1972).

14. Braisted, *Cultural Cooperation*, p. 6.

15. Eike Haberland (ed.), *Leo Frobenius: 1873–1973* (Wiesbaden: Franz Steiner Verlag GmbH, 1973).

16. Thomas Sterns Eliot, *Notes towards the Definition of Culture* (London: Faber and Faber, 1963), p. 31.

17. Kroeber and Kluckhohn, *Culture*, p. 57.

18. Unesco, *Mexico City Declaration on Cultural Policies* (Paris: Unesco, 1982).

19. Unesco, *A Practical Guide to the World Decade on Cultural Development, 1988–1997* (Paris: Unesco, 1987), p. 16.

20. Carmen Blacker and Michael Loewe (ed.), *Ancient Cosmologies* (London: George Allen and Unwin Ltd., 1975).

21. Robert Redfield, *The Primitive World and Its Transformations* (Ithaca, NY: Great Seal Books, 1963).

22. Milton K. Munitz, *Cosmic Understanding: Philosophy and Science of the Universe* (Princeton, NJ: Princeton University Press, 1986), pp. 4–5.

23. Edward R. Harrison, *Cosmology: The Science of the Universe* (Cambridge: Cambridge University Press, 1981), pp. 10–12.

24. Robert J. Wagoner and Donald W. Goldsmith, *Cosmic Horizons: Understanding the Universe* (San Francisco: W. H. Freeman and Company, 1982), p. 1.

25. Raimon Panikkar, 'The Religion of the Future', *Interculture* 23 (2 and 3) (Montreal: Intercultural Institute of Montreal, 1990), pp. 3–24, 25–78.

26. H. P. Rickman, *Wilhelm Dilthey: Pioneer of the Human Studies* (London: University of California Press, 1979), p. 10.

27. See, for example, Munitz, *Cosmic Understanding*; Wagoner and Goldsmith, *Cosmic Horizons*; Harrison, *Cosmology*; The New Encyclopaedia Britannica, *Macropaedia*, vol. 16 (London: Encyclopaedia Britannica, 1986), pp. 762–95.

28. Mary E. Clark, *Ariadne's Thread: The Search for New Modes of Thinking* (New York: St. Martin's Press, 1989), pp. 156, 184.

29. Robert Redfield in Anthony F. C. Wallace, *Culture and Personality*, (New York: Random House, 1967), p. 99.

30. Munitz, *Cosmic Understanding*, p. 6.

31. Pierre Pascallon, 'The Cultural Dimension of Development', *Intereconomics*, Jan.–Feb. 1986, p. 7 (insert mine).

32. Clark, *Ariadne's Thread*, p. 156.

33. Ruth Benedict, *Patterns of Culture* (London: Routledge and Kegan Paul, 1963), pp. 33, 36.

34. Eliot, *Notes towards the Definition of Culture*, p. 120 (emphasis mine).

35. Jerzy A. Wojciechowski, 'Cultural Pluralism and National Identity', *Cultures* 4(4) (Cultural Trends VI) (Paris: The Unesco Press and la Baconnière, 1977), p. 54.

36. Ibid., p. 54.

37. Redfield, *The Primitive World*, pp. 85–6 (emphasis mine).

38. Albert Schweitzer, *Civilization and Ethics* (London: A. & C. Black, 1923) pp. vii, viii.

39. Fritjof Capra, 'A New Vision of Reality', *New Age*, Feb. 1982 (Watertown: New Age Publishing Co., 1982), pp. 29–30.

40. Gustavo Esteva, 'A New Source of Hope: The Margins', *Interculture* 26(2) (Montreal: Intercultural Institute of Montreal, 1993).

41. Wole Soyinka, 'Culture, Memory, and Development', International Conference on Culture and Development in Africa, 2–3 April 1992 (Washington: The World Bank, 1992), p. 21.

42. Blacker and Loewe (ed.), *Ancient Cosmologies*, p. 220 (insert mine).

43. Schafer, *The Cosmological Conception of Culture*; see also Schafer, *The Character of Culture*.

44. This metaphor was set out in a letter to the author from Dr Min Jiayin of the Institute of Philosophy, Chinese Academy of Social Sciences, Beijing, China. It provides a very useful way of visualizing and thinking about culture as a concept.

Chapter 3

1. Margaret Mead, *Letters from the Field: 1925–1975* (New York: Harper and Row, 1977), p. 16.

2. Giles Gunn, *The Culture of Criticism and the Criticism of Culture* (New York: Oxford University Press, 1987), p. 95.

3. Nada Švob-Đokić, 'Culture as a System: Identity, Development, and Communication,' *Razvoj Development International* 6(2–3) (Zagreb: Institute for Development and International Relations, 1991), pp. 299–315; see also, Clark, *Ariadne's Thread*.

4. S. Takdir Alisjahbana, *Values as Integrating Forces in Personality, Society and Culture* (Kuala Lumpur: University of Malaya Press, 1966).

5. Kroeber and Kluckhohn, *Culture*, p. 340 (emphasis mine).

6. Prem Kirpal, 'Culture and Development–The Incipient Crisis', *Cultures* 3(4) (Paris: The Unesco Press and la Baconnière, 1976), p. 86.

7. Kroeber and Kluckhohn, *Culture*, pp. 345 (emphasis mine).

8. Cvjetičanin, 'Cultural Change', pp. 319–29.

9. Benedict, *Patterns of Culture*, p. 179.

10. See, for example, Edward T. Hall, *The Silent Language*, *The Hidden Dimension* and *Beyond Culture* (Garden City, NY: Doubleday and Company, 1959, 1966 and 1976 respectively).

11. Clark, *Ariadne's Thread*, p. 158.

12. Thomas Robert Malthus, *An Essay on the Principle of Population* (Ann Arbor: University of Michigan Press, 1959).

13. Arnold Toynbee, *A Study of History* (New York: Weathervane Books, 1972).

14. Herman Hesse, *Magister Ludi* (New York: Bantam Books, 1969), p. 255.

15. Alisjahbana, *Values as Integrating Forces*, p. 228.

Chapter 4

1. Soedjatmoko, 'Culture and Development: A Seamless Web', International Conference on Interactions of Development and Culture: From Dilemmas to Opportunities, 30 June 1987 (Koningswinter: Friedrich Naumann Foundation and the International University Foundation, 1987), p. 1.

2. St. Loretta Pastva, SND, with Stephan Nagel and Carl Koch, *Great Religions of the World* (Winona, Minnesota: Saint Mary's Press, Christian Brothers Publications, 1986). See especially the Introduction on The Great Religions and Your Worldview.

3. S. Takdir Alisjahbana, *Indonesia: Social and Cultural Revolution* (Kuala Lampur/London/Melbourne: Oxford University Press, 1966), p. 3. The entire chapter on 'The Growth of a Culture' is germane to the discussion.

4. Pastva *et al.*, *Great Religions of the World.*

5. Joseph Campbell with Bill Moyers, *The Power of Myth* (New York: Doubleday, 1988); see also *Interculture* 28(2) (Montreal: Intercultural Institute of Montreal, 1995).

6. Ronald Wright, *Stolen Continents: The "New World" Through Indian Eyes Since 1492* (New York: Viking, 1992), p. 5.

7. Alisjahbana, *Values as Integrating Forces*, pp. 206–7.

8. Jan Christiaan Smuts, *Holism and Evolution* (New York: Viking Press, 1961), p. 104.

9. Hall, *Beyond Culture*, p. 195.

10. Pitirim Sorokin, *Social and Cultural Dynamics: A Study of Change in Major Systems of Art, Truth, Ethics, Law and Social Relationships* (Boston: Extending Horizons Books. Porter Sargent Publications, 1957). See Part I on the ideational, sensate, idealistic and mixed systems of culture.

11. Ibid., p. 2.

12. James Feibleman, *The Theory of Human Culture* (New York: Humanities Press, 1968), p. 75.

13. Oswald Spengler, *The Decline of the West* (New York: Alfred A. Knopf, 1962).

14. Harold Innis, *The Bias of Communication*; see also *Empire and Communications* and *The Strategy of Culture* (Toronto: University of Toronto Press, 1951, 1972 and 1972 respectively).

15. Innis, *The Bias of Communication*, p. xii.

16. Robert Redfield, *The Little Community: Viewpoints for the Study of a Human Whole* (Chicago: The University of Chicago Press, 1973), pp. 158–9.

17. Ibid., p. 161.

18. Max Weber, *The Protestant Ethic and the Spirit of Capitalism* (New York: Charles Scribner's Sons, 1956).

19. Eliot, *Notes towards the Definition of Culture.*

20. Mircea Malitza, 'Culture and the New World Order: A Pattern of Integration', *Cultures* 3(4) (Paris: The Unesco Press and La Baconnière, 1976), p. 102.

21. Antonio Alonso Concheiro, 'The Futures of Culture in Latin America', in E. Masini (co-ordinator), *The Futures of Culture*, Vol. II: *The Prospects for Africa and Latin America* (Paris: Unesco, Future-oriented Studies Programme, 1992), p. 65.

Chapter 5

1. E. H. Gombrich, *Ideals and Idols* (Oxford: Phaidon, 1979), p. 56.

2. P. Gardiner (ed.), *Theories of History* (Glencoe: Free Press, 1959), p. 131.

3. Susan Hunt, 'The Alternative Economics Movement', *Interculture*. 22(1) (Montreal: Monchanin Cross-Cultural Centre, 1989), p. 3.

4. Thomas Kuhn, *The Structure of Scientific Revolutions* (Chicago: The University of Chicago Press, 1970).

5. John McHale, *The Future of the Future* (New York: George Braziller, 1969), p. 3.

6. Karl J. Weintraub, *Visions of Culture: Voltaire, Guizot, Burckhardt, Lamprecht, Huizinga, Ortega y Gasset* (Chicago: University of Chicago Press, 1966); see also Spengler, *The Decline of the West* and Toynbee, *A Study of History*.

7. Spengler, *The Decline of the West*, p. 18.

8. Weintraub, *Visions of Culture*, p. 1.

9. Ibid., p. 3.

10. Ibid., p. 2.

11. Linton, *The Tree of Culture* (New York: Alfred A. Knopf, 1955) p. 35.

12. Johan Huizinga, 'The Task of Cultural History', in *Men and Ideas: History, the Middle Ages, the Renaissance* (London: Eyre and Spottiswoode, 1960).

13. Linton, *The Tree of Culture*, p. 58–9.

14. Unesco, *The Futures of Culture*, Vol. I: *Meeting of the Working Group on the Futures of Culture, Paris, 9-10 January 1990; The Futures of Culture: Vol. II: The Prospects for Africa and Latin America*, co-ordinated by E Masini (Paris: Unesco. Future-oriented Studies Programme, 1992). See also Eleonora Barbieri Masini and Yogesh Atal (eds.), *The Futures of Asian Cultures: Perspectives on Asia's Futures III* (Bangkok: Unesco Principal Regional Office for Asia and the Pacific, 1993); and Unesco, *The Futures of Cultures* (Paris: Unesco Publishing, 1994).

15. Unesco, *The Futures of Culture*, Vol. II.

16. Toynbee, *A Study of History*.

17. Linton, *The Tree of Culture*, p. 52.

18. See, for example, F. S. C. Northrop, *The Meeting of East and West : An Inquiry Concerning World Understanding* (New York: The Macmillan Company, 1946).

19. Eleonora Barbieri Masini, 'The Futures of Culture: an overview with specific reference to Western Culture', in Unesco, *The Futures of Culture*, Vol. II, pp. 5–18.

20. S. Takdir Alisjahbana, *Socio-Cultural Creativity in the Converging and Restructuring Process of the New Emerging World* (Pulo Gadung, Jakarta: Penerbit Dian Rakyat, 1983), pp. 12–13.

21. Spengler, *The Decline of the West*, p. 42 (emphasis Spengler's).

22. Gustavo Esteva, 'A New Source of Hope: The Margins', pp. 5–62.

23. Council of Europe, *Cultural Policy Dossier No. 2–3/81* (Strasbourg: Council of Europe, 1981), p. 3.

Chapter 6

1. King (ed.), *Goethe on Human Creativeness and Other Goethe Essays*, p. xiii.

2. Feibleman, *The Theory of Human Culture*, p. 5.

3. Gordon Allport, *Pattern and Growth in Personality* (New York: Holt, Rinehardt and Winston, 1963); see also Kroeber and Kluckhohn, *Culture*.

4. Allport, *Pattern and Growth in Personality*, pp. 30–2.

5. Smuts, *Holism and Evolution*, p. 289.

6. Ralph Linton, *The Cultural Background of Personality* (New York: Appelton-Century Crofts, 1945), p. 84.

7. Allport, *Pattern and Growth in Personality*, p. 28.

8. Encyclopaedia Britannica, *The New Encyclopaedia Britannica*, Volume 9, Micropaedia (Chicago: Encyclopaedia Britannica Inc., 1989), p. 311.

9. Eliot, *Notes towards the Definition of Culture*, pp. 22–3.

10. Charles R. Roy (ed.), *Albert Schweitzer: An Anthology* (Boston: The Beacon Press, 1947), p. 4.

11. Smuts, *Holism and Evolution*, pp. 263 (insert mine).

12. John Cowper Powys, *The Meaning of Culture* (New York: W. W. Norton and Company, 1929), p. 77.

13. E. McIntosh (ed.), *The Concise Oxford Dictionary* (Oxford: Clarendon Press, 1965), p. 581.

14. Mircea Malitza, 'Culture and the New Order: A Pattern of Integration', *Cultures* 3(4), p. 98.

15. Feibleman, *The Theory of Human Culture*, pp. 326–7.

16. Munitz, *Cosmic Understanding*, p. 260

17. Powys, *The Meaning of Culture*, pp. 8, 23.

18. Ibid., p. 11.

19. Thomas Carlyle, *Home Book of Quotations* (New York: Dodd and Mead and Company, 1967), p. 348.

20. Linton, *The Cultural Background of Personality*, p. 3.

21. Francis L. K. Hsu (ed.), *Aspects of Culture and Personality: A Symposium* (New York: Abelard-Schuman, 1954), p. 202.

22. Pitirim Sorokin, *Modern Historical and Social Philosophies* (New York: Dover Publications, 1963), p. 319.

23. From a personal card sent to the author by Prem Kirpal and printed in India by Kamal Sales Publishers Put., Ltd.

24. Ken Wilber, *Eye to Eye: the quest for the new paradigm* (Boston: Shambhala, 1990) as discussed in R. Ralston, *Teaching the Stones to Speak* (Kelowna: Vision Action Conference, Assembly of B. C. Arts Councils, 1990).

25. King, *Goethe*, p. 236.

26. Powys, *The Meaning of Culture*, p. 18.

27. Richard Maurice Bucke, *Cosmic Consciousness: A Study in the Evolution of the Human Mind* (New York: E. P. Dutton and Company, 1969), pp. 1–2.

28. Ibid., p. 3.

29. Ibid., p. 9–10.

30. Smuts, *Holism and Evolution*, p. 298.

31. Albert Schweitzer, *Out of My Life and Thought: An Autobiography* (New York: Holt, Reinhardt and Winston, 1964), pp. 149–50.

32. Joy, *Albert Schweitzer*, pp. 259–60, 273.

33. Hu Hsien-Chin, 'The Chinese Concepts of Face', in Douglas G Haring (ed.), *Personal Character and Cultural Milieu* (Syracuse: Syracuse University Press, 1964), p. 447.

34. King, *Goethe*, p. ix.

35. Unesco, *Cultural Rights as Human Rights* (Paris: Unesco, 1970), pp. 117–22.

36. Joy, *Albert Schweitzer*, p. 131.

37. Sorokin, *Social and Cultural Dynamics*, p. 628.

38. E. Becker, *The Denial of Death* (London: Free Press, 1972), p. 255.

39. Symposium on Science and Culture for the 21st Century: Agenda for Survival, 'Survival in the 21st Century: The Vancouver Declaration', in *International Foundation for Development Alternatives, ifda dossier* 77 (Nyon: International Foundation for Development Alternatives, 1990).

Chapter 7

1. Lewis Mumford, *The Culture of Cities* (New York: Harcourt, Brace and World, 1938), p. 5.

2. A significant part of the material for this chapter is taken from D. Paul Schafer, 'The Culturescape: Self Awareness of Communities', *Cultures* 5(1) (Culture and Community) (Paris: The Unesco Press and la Baconnière, 1978), pp. 33–61.

3. Mumford, *The Culture of Cities*, p. 6.

4. Robert Redfield and Milton Singer, 'The Cultural Role of Cities' in Richard Sennett (ed.), *Classic Essays on the Culture of Cities* (Englewood Cliffs, NJ: Prentice-Hall, 1969), pp. 208–9.

5. Ibid., pp. 209.

6. Amos Rapoport, 'Culture and the Urban Order', in John A. Agnew, John Mercer and David E. Sopher (ed.), *The City in Cultural Context* (Boston: Allen and Unwin, 1984), p. 51.

7. The culturescape methodology was developed for the Ministry of Culture and Recreation in Ontario in 1975 and 1976. It was designed to take a cultural approach to community development and involved intensive probes into four communities in Ontario. Lack of funds prevented application of this methodology to a specific community. For a more detailed description of the culturescape process, see D. Paul Schafer, *Explorations in Culturescapes* (Toronto: Ministry of Culture and Recreation, Government of Ontario, 1974).

8. For a comprehensive statement on soundscapes and soundscape methodology, see R. Murray Schafer, *The Tuning of the World* (New York and Toronto: Alfred A. Knopf and McClelland and Stewart, 1977).

9. Rapoport, 'Culture and the Urban Order', p. 54.

10. The World Soundscape Project was headquartered in the Department of Communications Studies, Simon Fraser University, Burnaby, British Columbia in the late 1970s and early 1980s and pioneered a great deal of soundscape research. Its immediate concern was the Canadian soundscape—past, present, and future—but it also included studies of soundscapes in other countries. A number of documents were published in *The Music of the Environment* series, including *The Music of the Environment, The Vancouver Soundscape, European Sound Diary, Five Village Soundscapes,* and *A Dictionary of Acoustic Ecology.*

11. France and the former Yugoslavia are examples of two countries that have used maps very effectively for cultural development purposes. See, for example, Secrétariat d'Etat à la Culture, *Atlas Culturel.* (France: Secrétariat d'Etat à la Culture, 1975); Steven Majstorović, 'A Note on the Cultural Atlas of the Socialist Republic of Serbia', *Cultures* 2(1) (Paris: The Unesco Press and la Baconnière, 1975). While these and other types of cultural maps and atlases are different from the types of cultural maps advocated here, they do illustrate the powerful potential maps have in situating various types of cultural resources in the environment and orienting people to the different characteristics and locations of these resources.

12. See *Towards an Ontario Culturescape: A Probe into Cultural Development in the Province of Ontario* filed with the Ministry of Culture and Recreation, Government of Ontario, Toronto in 1976; see also *Four Community Cultural Probes* filed with the Ministry of Culture and Recreation, Government of Ontario the same year.

13. Biserka Cvjetičanin, 'Cultural Change', pp. 319–29; see also Michel Bassard, *Culture et régions d'Europe* (Lausanne: Presses Polytechniques et Universitaires Romandes, 1990).

14. D. Paul Schafer, *Municipalities and Regions: Powerful Forces in a Dynamic World* (Markham: World Culture Project, 1993).

Chapter 8

1. Wilfred, Felix, 'The Politics of Culture: Critical Reflections on Culture and Human Development from a Third World Perspective', *Jeevadhara.* 22(127) (Kerala: Jeevadhara Theological Society, 1992) p. 59.

2. D. Paul Schafer, 'The Age of Culture: Prospects and Implications', *Cultures* 2(4) (Paris: The Unesco Press and La Baconnière, 1975), pp. 13–34. This article is concerned primarily with alternative stereotypes of the state, such as the maximum growth state, the stationary state, the equilibrium state, and the cultural state.

3. John Stuart Mill, *Principles of Political Economy,* in *The Collected Works of John Stuart Mill,* edited by Vincent Bladen and J. M. Robson (Toronto: University of Toronto Press, 1965), p. 756.

4. World Commission on Environment and Development, *Our Common Future* (Oxford: Oxford University Press, 1987).

5. D. H. Meadows, D. L. Meadows, J. Randers and W. W. Behrens III, *The Limits to Growth* (New York: New American Library, 1972).

6. Wolfgang Sachs (ed.), *The Development Dictionary: A Guide to Knowledge as Power* (London: Zed Books, 1993).

7. Eliot, *Notes towards the Definition of Culture.*

8. Carlyle, *Home Book of Quotations*, p.348 (insert mine).

9. D. Paul Schafer and Salvatore A. Amenta, 'An Image of the Educated Person of the Future', paper prepared for the 43rd session of the International Bureau of Education's Conference on the Contribution of Education to Cultural Development, Geneva, September 14–19, 1992.

10. D. Paul Schafer, 'Cultures and economies: Irresistible forces encounter immovable objects', in *Futures: The Journal of Forecasting, Planning and Policy* 26(8) (Oxford: Butterworth Heinemann, 1994), pp. 830–45.

11. E. F. Schumacher, *Small is Beautiful: A Study of Economics as if People Mattered* (London: Sphere Books, 1979).

12. John Clauser, *Human Place: The Organizing Idea in Culture* (Chester Springs: The Yellow Springs Fellowship for the Arts, 1979), p. 11.

Chapter 9

1. Braisted, *Cultural Cooperation*, pp. 25, 28.

2. Unesco, *African oral traditions: Selection and formulation of some themes*, Cultural Development, Documentary Dossier 3 (Paris: Unesco, 1974).

3. Braisted, *Cultural Cooperation*, p. 13.

4. Weintraub, *Visions of Culture*, pp. 117–18.

5. Spengler, *The Decline of the West*, p. 18.

6. Toynbee, *A Study of History*.

7. Braisted, *Cultural Cooperation*, p. 7.

8. Paul J. Braisted, Soedjatmoko and Kenneth W. Thompson, *Reconstituting The Human Community* (New Haven: The Hazen Foundation, 1972), p. 14.

9. Ibid.; Paul J. Braisted, *Toward A New Humanism: Some Value Perspectives in Emerging Cultural Relations* (New Haven: The Hazen Foundation, 1975); Ali Mazrui, *A World Federation of Cultures* (Amsterdam: North Holland, 1975).

Chapter 10

1. Rajni Kothari (recorder), *The Scheveningen Report: Toward a New International Development Strategy*, Scheveningen Symposium 25–28 July, 1979, Ifda Dossier 13 (Nyon: International Foundation for Development Alternatives, 1979), p. 7.

2. D. Paul Schafer, *The Challenge of Cultural Development* (Markham: World Culture Project, 1994), pp. 19–38.

3. Wolfgang Sachs, *The Archaeology of the Development Idea* (Six Essays), *Interculture* 23(4) (Montreal: Intercultural Institute of Montreal, 1990), pp. 2–37.

4. Ibid., pp. 2–7.

5. United Nations/Unesco, *Rethinking Development: World Decade for Cultural Development 1988–1997* (Paris: Unesco, 1994), p. 7.

6. Unesco, *Cultural Policy: A Preliminary Study* (Paris: Unesco, 1969), p. 4.

7. Ibid., p. 8.

8. D. Paul Schafer, *Municipal Arts Policy: Vision to Reality* (Toronto: Co-operative Programme in Arts Administration, Scarborough Campus, University of Toronto, 1985), pp. 18–45.

9. Augustin Girard, *Cultural Development: Experience and Policies* (Paris: Unesco, 1972), p. 130.

10. See Some Readings for a list of some of the scholars who have made contributions to the intellectual and theoretical aspects of this tradition.

11. Hall, *Beyond Culture*, p. 14.

12. Rajni Kothari, 'The cultural roots of another development', *Development: Journal of the*

Society for International Development 3/4 (Rome: Society for International Development, 1981), p. 82.

13. See, for example, Herskovits, *Cultural Relativism.*

14. Alisjahbana, *Values as Integrating Forces,* p. 228.

15. Unesco, *Declaration of the Principles of International Cultural Co-operation* (Paris: Unesco, 1966).

16. United Nations, *Universal Declaration of Human Rights* (New York: United Nations, 1948).

17. Unesco, *Intergovernmental Conference on Institutional, Administrative and Financial Aspects of Cultural Policy, Venice. 1970: Final Report* (Paris: Unesco, 1970).

18. Member States and National Commissions of Unesco, *Studies and Documents on Cultural Policies for Member States* (Paris: Unesco, 1970–1996).

19. Unesco, *Intergovernmental Conference on Cultural Policies in Europe, Helsinki, 1972: Final Report* (Paris: Unesco, 1972); Unesco, *Intergovernmental Conference on Cultural Policies in Asia, Yogyakarta, 1973: Final Report* (Paris: Unesco, 1973); Unesco, *Intergovernmental Conference on Cultural Policies in Africa, Accra, 1975: Final Report* (Paris: Unesco, 1975); Unesco, *Intergovernmental Conference on Cultural Policies in Latin America, Bogota, 1978: Final Report* (Paris: Unesco, 1978). For an excellent summary and assessment of these conferences see Herbert Shore, *Cultural Policy: Unesco's First Cultural Development Decade* (Washington: U.S. National Commission for Unesco, 1981).

20. Unesco, *Intergovernmental Conference on Cultural Policies, Mexico City, 1982: Final Report* (Paris: Unesco, 1982).

21. Canadian Commission for Unesco, World Decade for Cultural Development (Ottawa: Canadian Commission for Unesco, 1988), p. 2.

22. Unesco, *General Conference: Twenty-Sixth Session: Commission IV.* Item 15.3 of the Agenda. No. 4. (Paris: Unesco, 1991); see also Javier Pérez de Cuéllar, *Address by Mr. Javier Pérez de Cuéllar at the Inaugural Meeting of the World Commission on Culture and Development: Presentation on the Work of the Commission,* Unesco, 19 March 1993 (Paris: Unesco, 1993); *Our Creative Diversity: Report of the World Commission on Culture and Development* (Paris: EGOPRIM, 1995).

Chapter 11

1. Masini, T*he Futures of Culture: Meeting of the Working Group on the Futures of Culture,* p. 6.

2. McHale, *The Future of the Future,* p.47.

3. D. Paul Schafer, 'Towards a New World Order: The Age of Culture', *Cultures* 2(3) (Paris: The Unesco Press and la Baconnière, 1975), pp. 13–29.

4. Meadows *et al., The Limits to Growth;* see also World Commission on Environment and Development, *Our Common Future.*

5. D. Paul Schafer, 'Towards a new world system: a cultural perspective', *Futures: The Journal of Forecasting, Planning and Policy* 28(3) (Exeter: Elsevier Science Ltd./Pergamon, 1996), pp. 285–99.

6. Sohail Inayatullah, 'Frames of Reference, The Breakdown of the Self, and the Search for Reintegration: Some Perspectives on the Futures of Asian Cultures', in Masini and Atal (eds.), *The Futures of Asian Cultures,* p. 95.

7. Peter Brook, 'The Three Cultures of Modern Man', *Cultures* 3(4) (Culture, society, and economics for a new world) (Paris: The Unesco Press and la Baconnière, 1976), p. 144 (insert mine).

8. Weintraub, *Visions of Culture*, p. 216.

Permissions and Acknowledgements

The author wishes to thank: McClelland & Stewart, Inc., Toronto, *The Canadian Publishers* for permission to use the quotation by Bernard Ostry from *The Cultural Connection* as the lead quotation for the book (Chapter 1); Gordon and Breach Publishers for permission to make extensive use of 'The Evolution and Character of the Concept of Culture', in *World Futures: The Journal of General Evolution* 38(4) (© Yverdon: Gordon and Breach Science Publishers, 1993), pp. 225–54 in the development of Chapter 2; Unesco for permission to make extensive use of 'The Culturescape: Self-Awareness of Communities, *Cultures* 5(1) (© Paris: Unesco, 1978), pp. 33–61 in the development of Chapter 7; and Dr. Prem Kirpal for permission to quote the poem in Chapter 6.

Appreciation is also expressed to the following institutions, publishers and journals for publishing or printing essays, papers and documents by the author relevant to the subject matter of this book:

Unesco:

The New World Order: A Contribution to the World Decade for Cultural Development. Major Programme I. Reflection on World Problems and Future-oriented Studies (Paris: Unesco Bureau of Studies and Programming, 1988).

'Towards a New World Order: The Age of Culture', *Cultures* 2(3) (Paris: The Unesco Press and La Baconnière, 1975), pp. 13–29.

'The Age of Culture: Prospects and Implications', Cultures 2(4) (Paris: The Unesco Press and la Baconnière, 1975), pp. 13–34.

'The Culturescape: Self-Awareness of Communities', *Cultures* 5(1) (Paris: The Unesco Press and la Baconnière, 1978), pp. 33–61.

'Culture and Cosmos: the Role of Culture in the World of the Future', *Cultures* 7(2) (Paris: The Unesco Press and la Baconnière, 1980), pp. 35–58.

Institute for Development and International Relations:

'Culture: Beacon of the Future', *Razvoj/Development International* 6(2–3) (Zagreb: Institute for Development and International Relations, 1991), pp. 283–95.

Talonbooks:

'The Cultural Interpretation of History: Beacon of the Future', in Robin Blazer and Robert Dunham (eds.), *Art and Reality: A Casebook of Concern* (Vancouver: Talonbooks, 1986), pp. 167–86.

Gordon and Breach Science Publishers:

'The Evolution and Character of the Concept of Culture', *World Futures: The Journal of General Evolution* 38(4) (Yverdon: Gordon and Breach Science Publishers, 1993), pp. 225–54.

Butterworth Heinemann:

'Cultures and economies: Irresistible forces encounter immovable objects', *Futures: The Journal of Forecasting, Planning and Policy* 26(8) (Oxford: Butterworth Heinemann, 1994), pp. 830–45.

Elsevier Science Ltd./Pergamon:

'Towards a new world system: a cultural perspective', *Futures: The Journal of Forecasting, Planning and Policy* 28(3) (Exeter: Elsevier Science Ltd./ Pergamon, 1996), pp. 285–99.

Some Readings

Abramms, Bob and Simons, George, *Cultural Diversity: Sourcebook* (Amherst: ODT, 1996).

Agnew, John A., Mercer, John and Sopher, David E. (eds.), *The City in Cultural Context* (Boston: Allen and Unwin, 1984).

Alisjahbana, S. Takdir, *Socio-Cultural Creativity in the Converging and Restructuring Process of the New Emerging World* (Jakarta: Penerbit Dian Rakyat, 1983).

—— *Values as Integrating Forces in Personality, Society and Culture* (Kuala Lumpur, University of Malaya Press, 1986).

Arensberg, Conrad M. and Kimball, Solon T., *Culture and Community* (New York: Harcourt, Brace and World, Inc., 1965).

Arnold, Matthew, *Culture and Anarchy* (Cambridge: Cambridge University Press, 1960).

Bagby, P., *Culture and History* (Berkeley: University of California Press, 1959).

Bauman, Zygmunt, *Culture as Praxis* (London: Routledge and Kegan Paul, 1973).

Ben-David, J. and Clark, T. N. (eds.), *Culture and its Creators: Essays in Honour of Edward Shils* (Chicago: University of Chicago Press, 1977).

Benedict, Ruth, *The Chrysanthemum and the Sword: Patterns of Japanese Culture* (Cleveland: Meridian Books, 1967).

—— *Patterns of Culture* (London: Routledge and Kegan Paul, 1963).

Bénéton, Philippe, *Histoire de Mots: Culture et Civilization* (Paris: Presses de la Foundation des Sciences Politiques, 1975).

Bernardi, Bernardo (ed.), *The Concept and Dynamics of Culture* (The Hague: Mouton Publishers, 1977).

Braisted, Paul J., *Cultural Cooperation: Keynote of the Coming Age* (New Haven: The Edward W. Hazen Foundation, 1945).

—— *Towards A New Humanism: Some Value Perspectives in Emerging Cultural Relations* (New Haven: The Hazen Foundation, 1975).

—— *Cultural Affairs and Foreign Relations* (Washington: Columbia Books, 1968).

——, Soedjatmoko and Thompson, Kenneth W. (eds.), *Reconstituting The Human Community* (New Haven: The Hazen Foundation, 1972).

Burckhardt, Jacob, *History of Greek Culture* (New York: Ungar Press, 1963).

—— *The Civilization of the Renaissance in Italy* (Washington: Washington Square Press, 1966).

Capra, Fritjof, *The Turning Point: Science, Society and the Rising Culture* (New York: Simon and Schuster, 1982).

Clark, Mary E., *Ariadne's Thread: The Search for New Modes of Thinking* (New York: St Martin's Press, 1989).

Desjeux, Dominique, *Le Sens de l'autre: Stratégies, réseaux et cultures en situation interculturelle* (Paris: Unesco/ICA, 1991).

Dixon, R. B., *The Building of Cultures* (New York: Charles Scribner's Sons, 1928).

Dorian, Frederick, *Commitment to Culture* (Pittsburgh: University of Pittsburgh Press, 1964).

Dupuis, Xavier, *Culture et Développement: De la reconnaissance à l'evaluation* (Paris: Unesco/ICA, 1991).

Eliot, Thomas S., *Notes towards the Definition of Culture* (London: Faber and Faber, 1963).

Emanuel, P., *Pour Une Politique de la Culture* (Paris: Le Seuil, 1971).

Feibleman, James, *The Theory of Human Culture* (New York: Humanities Press, 1968).

Freilich, Morris (ed.), *The Meaning of Culture* (Lexington: Xerox College Publisher, 1972).

—— *The Relevance of Culture* (New York: Bergin and Garvey, 1989).

Frobenius, Leo, *Voice of Africa* (London: Hutchinson, 1913).

—— *African Genesis* (New York: Arno Press, 1937).

Gamst, Frederick C., and Norbeck, Edward (eds.), *Ideas of Culture: Sources and Uses* (New York: Holt, Rinehart and Winston, 1976).

Geertz, Clifford, *The Interpretation of Cultures* (New York: Basic Books, 1973).

Girard, Augustin, *Cultural Development: Experience and Policies* (Paris: Unesco, 1972).

—— *Analyse et Prévision: Prospective du Développement Culturel* (Paris: Futuribles, 1973).

Gombrich, E. H., *Ideals and Idols: Essays on Values in History and in Art* (Oxford: Phaidon, 1979).

Haigh, Anthony, *Cultural Diplomacy in Europe* (Strasbourg: Council of Europe, 1974).

Hall, Edward, *Beyond Culture* (Garden City, NY: Anchor Press/Doubleday, 1976).

—— *The Hidden Dimension* (Garden City, NY: Doubleday and Co. Inc., 1966).

—— *The Silent Language* (Garden City, NY: Doubleday and Co. Ltd., 1959).

Hallowell, Irving A., *Culture and Experience* (Philadelphia: University of Pennsylvania Press, 1955).

Harding, Douglas (ed.), *Personal Character and Social Milieu* (Syracuse: Syracuse University Press, 1949).

Harris, Marvin, *The Nature of Cultural Things* (New York: Random House, 1964).

—— *The Rise of Anthropological Theory* (New York: Thomas Y. Crowell, 1968).

—— *Cannibals and Kings; The Origins of Cultures* (New York: Random House, 1977).

—— *Cultural Materialism: The Struggle for a Science of Culture* (New York: Random House, 1979).

Henry, Jules, *Culture Against Man* (New York: Random House, 1963).

Herskovits, Melville, *Cultural Anthropology* (New York: Alfred Knopf, 1963).

—— *Cultural Relativism: Perspectives in Cultural Pluralism*, edited by Frances Herskovits (New York: Random House, 1972).

Honigmann, John, *Culture and Personality* (New York: Harper and Row, 1954).

—— *Personality in Culture* (New York: Harper and Row, 1967).

Hsu, Francis (ed.), *Aspects of Culture and Personality* (New York: Abelard-Schuman, 1954).

Huizinga, Johan, *The Waning of the Middle Ages* (New York: Penguin Books, 1979).

Johnson, Lesley, *The Cultural Critics: From Matthew Arnold to Raymond Williams* (London: Routledge and Kegan Paul, 1979).

Jor, Finn, *The Demystification of Culture: Animation and Creativity* (Strasbourg: Council of Europe, 1976).

Kluckhohn, Clyde, *Culture and Behaviour* (New York: Free Press, 1962).

—— Murray, H. A. and Schnieder, D. M. (ed.), *Personality in Nature, Society and Culture* (New York: Alfred A. Knopf, 1953).

Kroeber, Alfred, *Configurations of Culture Growth* (Berkeley: University of California Press, 1969).

—— *The Nature of Culture* (Chicago: Chicago University Press, 1952).

—— and Kluckhohn, Clyde, *Culture: A Critical Review of Concepts and Defintions* (New York: Vintage Books, 1963).

Lévi-Strauss, Claude, *Structural Anthropology* (New York: Basic Books, 1963).

Linton, Ralph, *The Cultural Background of Personality* (New York: Appleton-Century-Crofts, 1945).

—— *The Tree of Culture* (New York: Alfred A. Knopf, 1955).

——(ed.), *The Science of Man in the World Crisis* (New York: Columbia University Press, 1964).

Lowie, Robert H., *Primitive Society* (New York: Boni and Liveright, 1925).

—— *The History of Ethnological Theory* (London: George G. Harrap and Co., 1937).

MacLachlan, Colin M. and Rodríguez, O., Jamie, E., *The Forging of the Cosmic Race: A Reinterpretation of Colonial Mexico* (Berkeley: University of California Press, 1980).

Malinowski, Bronislaw, *A Scientific Theory of Culture* (Chapell Hill: University of North Carolina Press, 1965).

Mannheim, Karl, *Essays on the Sociology of Knowledge* (London: Routledge and Keegan Paul, 1964).

Masini, Eleonora Barbieri (ed.), *Visions of Desirable Societies* (Oxford: Pergamon Press, 1983).

—— (coordinator), *The Futures of Culture*, Vol. I: *Meeting of the Working Group on the Futures of Culture* (Paris, 9–10, January 1990) (Paris: Unesco, 1991).

—— (coordinator), *The Futures of Culture*, Vol. II: *The Prospects for Africa and Latin America* (Paris: Unesco, 1992).

—— (ed.), *The Futures of Cultures* (Paris: Unesco Publishing, 1994).

—— and Atal, Yogesh (eds.), *The Futures of Asian Cultures* (Bangkok: Unesco Principal Regional Office for Asia and the Pacific, 1993).

Mazrui, Ali, *A World Federation of Cultures: an African Perspective* (N Y: Free Press, 1976).

McMurtry, Ruth Emily, *The Cultural Approach: Another Way to International Relations* (Chapell Hill: University of North Carolina Press, 1947).

Mead, Margaret (ed.), *Cultural Patterns and Technical Change* (New York: Mentor Books, 1954).

—— *Culture and Commitment: A Study of the Generation Gap* (Garden City, NewYork: Natural History Press/Doubleday, 1970).

—— and Métraux, Rhoda, *The Study of Culture at a Distance* (Chicago: University of Chicago Press, 1962).

Mennell, Stephen, *Cultural Policy in Towns* (Strasbourg: Council of Europe, 1976).

Mesnard, André-Hubert, *La Politique Culturelle de l'État* (Paris: Presses Universaires de France, 1974).

Minnihan, J., *Nationalization of Culture* (New York: New York Press, 1977).

Mitchell, J. M., *International Cultural Relations* (London: Allen and Unwin, 1986).

Montague, Ashley (ed.), *Culture and the Evolution of Man* (New York: Oxford University Press, 1962).

—— *Culture, Man's Adaptive Dimension* (London: Oxford University Press, 1968).

Mooney, Michael M., *The Ministry of Culture* (New York: Wyndham Books, 1980).

Mumford, Lewis, *The Culture of Cities* (New York: Harcourt, Brace and World, 1938).

Nieburg, H. L., *Culture Storm* (New York: St Martin's Press, 1973).

Nettleford, Rex M., *Cultural Action and Social Change: The Case of Jamaica: An Essay in Caribbean Cultural Identity* (Ottawa and Kingston: International Development Research Centre and Institute of Jamaica, 1979).

Northrop, F. S. C., *The Meeting of East and West: An Enquiry Concerning World Understanding* (New York: The Macmillan Company, 1946).

Petrie, W. M. F., *The Revolutions of Civilisation* (New York: Haskell House Publishing, 1911).

Powys, John C., *The Meaning of Culture* (New York: W. W. Norton and Company, 1929).

Redfield, Robert, *The Little Community: Viewpoints for the Study of a Human Whole* (Chicago: University of Chicago Press, 1973).

Rigaud, Jacques, *La Culture Pour Vivre* (Paris: Gallimard, 1975).

Róheim, Géza, *The Origin and Function of Culture* (New York: Johnson Reprint Corporation, 1968).

Salins, Marshall, *Culture and Practical Reason* (Chicago: University of Chicago Press, 1976).

—— and Elman, R., *Evolution and Culture* (Ann Arbor: University of Michigan Press, 1961).

Sapir, Edward, *Selected Writings of Edward Sapir on Language, Culture and Personality* (Berkeley: University of California Press, 1963).

Sargent, Stansfield and Smith, Marian, *Culture and Personality* (New York: Viking Fund, 1949).

Schweder, Richard A. and Levine, R. (eds.), *Culture Theory* (Cambridge: Cambridge University Press, 1984).

Sennett, Richard (ed.), *Classic Essays on the Culture of Cities* (Englewoods Cliffs: Prentice-Hall, 1969).

Shore, Herbert, *Cultural Policy: Unesco's First Cultural Development Decade* (Washington: U.S. National Commission for Unesco, 1981).

Simons, G., Abramms, B., Hopkins, A., with Johnson, D., *Cultural Diversity: Fieldbook* (Princeton, NJ: Peterson's/Pacesetter Books, 1996).

Smith, Anthony, *The Geopolitics of Information: How Western Culture Dominates the World* (New York: Oxford University Press, 1981).

Smith, G. Elliot, *The Diffusion of Culture* (London: Watts, 1933).

Smuts, Jan Christiaan, *Holism and Evolution* (New York: The Viking Press, 1961).

Snow, Charles Percy, *The Two Cultures and the Scientific Revolution* (Cambridge: Cambridge University Press, 1959).

—— *The Two Cultures: and a Second Look* (Cambridge: Cambridge University Press, 1963).

Sorokin, Pitirim A., *Social and Cultural Dynamics* (New York: American Book Company, 1957).

—— *Modern Historical and Social Philosophies* (New York: Dove Publications, 1963).

Spengler, Oswald, *The Decline of the West* (New York: Alfred A. Knopf, 1962).

Tax, Sol (ed.), *Anthropology Today: Selections* (Chicago: The University of Chicago Press, 1962).

Thompson, William Irwin, *At the Edge of History: Speculations on the Transformation of Culture* (New York: Harper and Row, 1971).

Toynbee, Arnold, *A Study of History* (London: Oxford University Press, 1972).

Turner, Ralph E., *The Great Cultural Traditions* (New York: McGraw-Hill, 1941).

Tylor, Sir Edward Burnett, *The Origins of Culture* (New York: Harper Torch Books: Harper and Row, 1958).

Unesco, *Cultural Policy: A Preliminary Study* (Paris: Unesco, 1969).

Unesco, *Cultural Rights as Human Rights* (Paris: Unesco, 1970).

Unesco, *Cultural Development: Some Regional Experiences* (Paris: Unesco, 1981).

Vachon, Robert, *Alternatives au Développement: Approches interculturelles du développement et de la coopération* (Montreal: Centre Interculturel Monchanin, 1988).

Verhelst, Thierry G., *No Life Without Roots: Culture and Development* (London: Zed Books, 1990).

Wagar, W. Warren, *The Next Three Futures: Paradigms of Things to Come* (New York: Praeger, 1991).

Wagner, Roy, *The Invention of Culture* (Chicago: University of Chicago Press, 1981).

Wallace, Anthony, *Culture and Personality* (New York: Random House, 1970).

Weintraub, Karl J., *Visions of Culture* (Chicago: University of Chicago Press, 1966).

White, Leslie, *The Science of Culture* (New York: Farrar, Strauss and Cudahy, 1949).

—— *The Evolution of Culture* (New York: McGraw-Hill, 1959).

—— *The Concept of Culture* (Minneapolis: Burgess Publishing Company, 1973).

Williams, Raymond, *Culture and Society 1780–1950* (London: Penguin Books, 1966).

—— *The Long Revolution* (New York: Columbia University Press, 1961).

—— *Keywords: A Vocabulary of Culture and Society* (New York: Oxford University Press, 1976).

—— *Culture* (London: Fontana, 1981).

Wissler, Clark, *Man and Culture* (New York: Thomas Y Crowell Company, 1923).

Worsley, Peter, *The Three Worlds: Culture and World Development* (Chicago: University of Chicago Press, 1984).

World Commission on Culture and Development, *Our Creative Diversity: Report of the World Commission on Culture and Development* (Paris: EGOPRIM, 1995).

Zajaczkowski, Andrzej, Piganiol, Pierre, and Richeri, Guiseppe, *Essais sur le Développement Culturel* (Dakar: Institut Culturel Africain, 1985).

Index

Note that a chapter reference, e.g. *Ch 6*, is given where a whole chapter, or a large part of it, is devoted to the relevant subject. However, for most items, references are given to specific pages or page sequences. The page numbers of especially important citations are often given in italics.

About the Author

D. PAUL SCHAFER is Director of the World Culture Project, based in Markham, Canada. He has taught Cultural Policy at York University and Arts Administration and Policy at the University of Toronto.

ISBN 0-275-96499-X

9 780275 964993

HARDCOVER BAR CODE